The Wisest T
Said About C

Andrew Soltis

D0916483

First published in the United Kingdom in 2008 by

B T Batsford
10 Southcombe Street
London
W10 0RA

An imprint of Anova Books Company Ltd

ISBN 978 19063 8800 3

A CIP catalogue record for this book is available from
the British Library.

10 9 8 7 6 5 4 3 2 1

Reproduction by Spectrum Colour Ltd, UK
Printed and bound by Creative Print and Design Ltd, Wales

This book can be ordered direct from the publisher at the website
www.anovabooks.com. Or try your local bookshop.

CONTENTS

INTRODUCTION

Each new generation of chessplayers discovers ways to play the game better. What we don't appreciate is how much of this is rediscovery. We rediscover what was simply forgotten. When Vladimir Kramnik said calculation is "far more important in defense than in attack" it was a profound insight. Kramnik indicated it was also original. It wasn't. Rudolf Spielmann – and, most likely, others before him – expressed the same idea in similar words (as in # 39).

This is a book about ideas like that. Some are well remembered, others have been forgotten. These thoughts are expressed in maxims, aphorisms, wisecracks, kibitzes and proverbs that have been passed down to us. Some can be called "rules." That's a word that divides players. Amateurs love rules. Masters love to ridicule them. "A chessplayer's talent is measured not by his knowledge of the rules but his ability to find exceptions to them," wrote Viktor Korchnoi. "Only the exceptions matter," said Alexei Shirov. But GMs follow rules like everyone else. The occasions when they do so vastly outnumber the times that they break rules, as a look at any grandmaster game plainly shows.

Rules and maxims should not be used as a substitute for thinking. But they are wonderful as prompters *to* thinking. Good rules point in the right direction. They "should be used only as mnemonics, reminders of what to think about," as Kenneth Mark Colby, an avid amateur player and respected psychiatrist, wrote. One of the great chess teachers, Cecil Purdy, got it right. "The true art of the teacher lies in stating rules in memorable form," he wrote.

I've tried to collect the wisest of sayings expressed in the most memorable forms. That doesn't mean the earliest form, and this is not a book of forensic etymology. In many cases the collective wisdom of chess has come to us as folk wisdom, of unknown origin. In many other cases, the first way a thought was expressed was improved by others. Wilhelm Steinitz wrote in *The Modern Chess Instructor*, "In the ending...it is generally best to place the rook behind the pawns in order to not obstruct their advance. But when fighting against hostile pawns, it is most advisable to attack them in the rear or to stop the one furthest advanced in the same manner." This is an extremely useful thought, and may very well have passed through other minds before Steinitz's. But the version we remember is Siegbert Tarrasch's succinct "A rook belongs behind a passed pawn."

Many if not most of the great sayings like that are sweeping generalizations. That's part of the reason we remember them. When Tarrasch wrote, "There is no move that does not weaken some part of the position," what was remarkable is that he could preface it with a single exception – "Except for the mating move..." He admitted he was joking, several pages later in *The Game of Chess*, when he offered another rule without an exception: "Never move a pawn and you will never lose a game."

Wit, like exaggeration, is a common feature of great sayings. But there are many familiar witticisms that you won't find in these pages because they have little application that will help you improve your game. As much as I enjoy sayings like "A draw, like love, requires two participants" (Georg Marco) or "Every chess master was once a beginner" (Irving Chernev), to name a few, I didn't feel they belonged in a book devoted primarily to advice.

The wise sayings I chose, and in some cases paraphrased, vary widely in form and content. Some just give you something to think about ("A castled rook is already developed," #178 and "A knight endgame is a pawn endgame," #68). Others provide a plan of action ("With a pawn on e5 White must attack the king," #4 and "You're never mated with a knight on f8," #36).

Others tell us what not to do ("Never look for other possibilities when you have one satisfactory winning line," #271). Still others try to puncture your prejudices ("There is no such thing as a winning move," #97 and "A passed a-pawn looks more dangerous on the second rank than on the seventh," #91).

One can only marvel at the richness of wisdom that has been handed down to us. Our task is to build on it. But first we have to remember it. Lev Polugayevsky said the benefit of "book" knowledge in the opening is to enable players to explore at move 15 without having to rediscover what to do at move two. "Most of all, it's necessary to use book to avoid inventing the bicycle," he wrote, according in *64* magazine, July 2001. That's true of all aspects of chess skill. Remembering will save us from having to invent a lot of bicycles.

CHAPTER ONE: **ATTACK**

1

Modern chess is much too concerned with things like pawn structure. Forget it. Checkmate ends the game.

Many wise sayings by masters apply only to master chess. But with these words Nigel Short was reminding players of all strengths of the object of the game. You don't need to find 50 moves of finesse if you can end the game by the caveman method at move 25.

When mate is possible in the near future, it takes precedence over everything else. Both players follow that simple priority in the following game.

Anand – Ftacnik
Biel 1993

Black to play

You could spend hours trying to find the best move in such a chaotic position if you consider criteria such as strategic goals, pawn structure and the esoteric stuff. But mate simplifies the move-selection process enormously. Natural moves that have nothing to do with delivering mate, such as 1...e5, must

be viewed suspiciously – or not at all. (In this case 1...e5? 2 ♘xd5! exd4 3 ♗xd4 is needlessly dangerous.)

Black correctly played **1...♘xb2!**. He would be the one with better mating chances after 2 ♔xb2 ♘a4+ 3 ♔c1 ♘c3 and 4 ♕d3 e5!.

White hardly looked at 2 ♔xb2 because he, too, understood that in this position only one thing mattered. "White should just ignore everything except mate itself and just hack away," he wrote in his best-game collection. He won brilliantly after **2 fxe6!**.

He spent only 30-35 minutes for the entire game. His task was aided by looking mainly at lines such as 2...♘xd1 and finding the way to mate after 3 exf7+ ♔xf7 4 ♖xd1, e.g. 4...♘e4 5 ♗xe4 dxe4 6 ♕c4+.

2

The first essential for an attack is – the will to attack!

So said Savielly Tartakower in *500 Master Games of Chess*. Let's face it, attacking is more fun than defending. But some players are reluctant to attack if it means burning bridges. At certain moments, bridges must be put to the flame or else the flame goes out.

Gongora – Perea
Las Tunas 2003

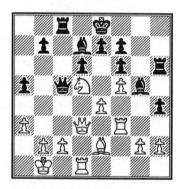

White to play

White has a clear positional advantage. But the center is blocked, his best piece is about to be kicked back with ...e6 and the kingside, while porous, is not easily penetrated.

But White had the will to attack. He knew he had to search for a target. He found **1 b4! axb4**

2 axb4. This may seem bizarre because he is ruining his own king's pawn protection. Yet it is the only good plan because the queenside is the only area White can open quickly. He would be much better in the endgame that follows 2...♕c6 3 ♕b3 – threatening ♖c3 – 3...♕a4 4 ♘b6.

Black tried to launch his own attack, **2...♕a7?**. It can't succeed because of White's space edge – **3 ♔b2! ♗c6 4 ♖a1 ♕b8 5 ♘b6 ♖d8 6 b5 ♗d7 7 ♕d4.**

The threats include ♖3a3-a8. Black tried the desperate **7...d5!? 8 ♕xd5 ♕e5+ 9 c3 e6** and **resigned** after **10 ♕xb7! ♕xh2 11 ♖d3**.

White's use-it-or-lose-it decision follows another of chess' fundamental rules:

3
The player with advantage must attack.

Wilhelm Steinitz was famous for making rules. Some became the foundation of how we play the game. Others couldn't even be followed successfully by Steinitz himself.

One of his most famous rules – what we can call Steinitz's Law – is based on the premise that sound attacks stem from positional advantages. Your attack cannot succeed if you don't have an edge to justify it, he said.

This was brilliant and original. It replaced the older view that attacks succeeded or failed because of the attacker's genius or lack of it. Steinitz could have stopped there. But he added a guide to action: The player who obtains that edge not only has the right but the obligation to attack. If he doesn't, his advantage is bound to evaporate.

van Wely – Ki. Georgiev
Groningen 1997

Black to play

Black has just opened the c-file with ...dxc4? and that made White's pieces much better than Black's. On 1...♛b8 he obtains a powerful passed d-pawn with 2 d5! ♖xc4 3 bxc4.

But what happens if Black plays 2...exd5 instead? Logic indicates White should still be better but there is no purely positional way to prove it. Steinitz's answer is White must attack – 3 ♘g4!.

Then 3...dxc4 4 ♘xf6+ is deadly (4...gxf6 5 ♗xf6 and ♛g5+ or ♛h6, and 4...♔h8 5 ♛c2).

In the game, Black avoided all this with **1...♛e7** instead of 1...♛b8. But **2 d5!** again converts White's advantage into an attack. For instance, 2...♘xd5 3 ♘g4 with ideas of ♗xg7 or ♘h6+, e.g. 3...h5 4 ♗xg7 ♔xg7 5 ♛h6+ ♔g8 6 ♗xd5 and ♘f6+.

Vladimir Kramnik said the only one who managed to violate Steinitz's Law successfully was Anatoly Karpov. Karpov didn't always attack when his position improved; he found other ways to enhance his chances, Kramnik said on *e3e5.com*. "In my opinion, there were no players before or after him who were able to do this," he added.

4

With a pawn on e5
White must attack the king.

The Russians credit Alexander Alekhine with this rule: a pawn on e5 gives White not only an incentive but a duty to go for the king. The pawn denies Black the f6 square for a knight. Often that means f7 can be attacked by a knight on g5 and rook on the f-file or that h7 can come under fire from a bishop at d3 and a queen at h5. Most successful ♗xh7+ sacrifices occurred with a White pawn on e5.

A pawn at e5 protected by another pawn also provides strategic benefits. Early writers used to advise White, when he has pushed his pawn to e5 in a French Defense, to maintain it there at all cost because of its positional plusses. Alexander Petroff – of the Petroff Defense – wrote in 1824, "When several pawns form a diagonal chain one must maintain the one that stands at the head."

Alekhine – Euwe
Amsterdam 1936

White to play

Alekhine found himself forced to attack: Black has taken aim at his only targets, e4 and d4, and is threatening ...dxe4. White defended with **1 e5** and that convinced him to go after the Black king.

Play went **1...♘h7 2 ♘f5 f6 3 g4! fxe5 4 ♗xe5 ♘f6 5 ♕d3** followed by ♖g1 and f3-f4. Of course, the pawn on e5 didn't guarantee the attack's success. In fact, White lost. But 1 e5 made kingside attack the best plan.

5
The king makes his neighborhood vulnerable.

This may sound obvious today. But Evgeny Znosko-Borovsky was contradicting Steinitz when he wrote in *The Middle Game in Chess*:

"Wherever the king is placed, the position in his vicinity becomes automatically weaker, for his presence attracts enemy attacks."

In contrast, Steinitz believed a king was capable of defending itself and needed no security blanket. Castling makes that wing *stronger*, not weaker, because the king is there, he wrote.

There are plenty of Steinitz losses to show that he really believed this nonsense. But on other occasions, Steinitz violated his own rules and won.

Steinitz – Tchigorin
World Championship 1892

White to play

Steinitz the theorist would say to himself, "White can't attack because he has no advantage and because Black's king makes the kingside stronger."

Yet Steinitz the player chose **1 h4!**, launching an attack that succeeded in spectacular fashion, after **1...♘e7 2 h5 d5 3 hxg6 fxg6 4 exd5 ♘xd5 5 ♘xd5 ♕xd5 6 ♗b3!**.

The end was dramatic, **6...♕c6 7 ♕e2 ♗d7 8 ♗e3 ♔h8 9 0-0-0 ♖ae8 10 ♕f1 a5? 11 d4! exd4 12 ♘xd4 ♗xd4 13 ♖xd4! ♘xd4 14 ♖xh7+! ♔xh7 15 ♕h1+** and mates (**15...♔g7 16 ♗h6+ ♔f6 17 ♕h4+**).

In reality, the presence of the Black king on the kingside, plus the ...g6 weakening justified 1 h4!, as Znosko-Borovsky would have said. Z-B's principle can also be illustrated by the following game:

Svidler – Kramnik
World Championship 2007

White to play

White chose a natural plan, directed at h7 and f7 – **1 h4! ♕d7**

2 ♕d5 ♕c6 3 ♕f5, with the idea of ♘g5. Black in turn went after the queenside, (3...♕c4), and a sharp middlegame followed.

But let's imagine that the king positions are reversed. We'll replace 0-0-0 by White with 0-0. For Black, we'll suppose he castled queenside (K on c8, Q on d7, QR on d8).

Then White would ignore the kingside and prefer the queenside attack with ♕d5 and ♗xa7 or ♕a5. Black would not have attacking chances of his own and would have to find counterplay elsewhere.

Of course, pawn structure also plays a role in determining how successful an attack will be. But Philidor was overstating the case when he wrote, "Pawns alone form the basis of attack and defense" (#155). Pawns delineate the avenues and supply lines of attack. But the king's location provides the incentive for attack.

Even if the king's neighborhood seems rock solid, his presence makes it less so. Compare it with banks. They have more security than candy stores. But for some reason robbers target banks more often than candy stores.

6

True attacks are realized only with many coordinated pieces and rarely with one or two.

This should be apparent to anyone who has played chess for more than a few months. Yet it was considered a remarkable insight when Francois-Andre Philidor wrote it in *L'analyse du jeu des Echecs* in 1749.

His successors offered rules to ensure coordination of the attacker's pieces. "Never commence your final attack until the queen's rook is in play," Joseph Blackburne wrote in his game collection. An illustration of complete coordination is:

Karpov – Polugayevsky
Candidates match 1974

White to play

The pressroom grandmasters were going into rapture over 1 ♖xf6 gxf6 2 ♗h6 and 3 ♕e3, with the threat of ♕g3+-g7 mate.

But White preferred to attack only after he trained all five of his pieces on the kingside, 1 ♗f4! ♖a8 2 ♕f2 ♖ad8 3 ♕g3 ♕c3 4 ♖f3 ♕c2 5 ♖df1 ♗d4 6 ♗h6 ♘c6 7 ♘f5!.

By then Black was doomed, e.g. 7...♗e5 8 ♗xg7! ♗xg3 9 ♖xg3 and mates.

This doesn't mean you cannot attack unless you coordinate all of your pieces against the king, as Anatoly Karpov did here. His longtime rival Garry Kasparov attacked brilliantly when he could employ most, but not all, of his pieces. What both Karpov and Kasparov agreed on was that an attack was doomed to failure if only one or two pieces were enlisted in it.

7

When you have opposite attacks going, the quantity of pieces is often more important than their quality.

One of the apparent contradictions in chess is this: A successful attack means applying superior force at a target. But an attack may need to be launched by a sacrifice. By definition, a sacrifice reduces the size of the attacker's force. How then can a smaller army defeat a greater army?

Garry Kasparov helped clear up the matter, at least in regard to Exchange sacrifices, with #7, which he said about this position.

Movsesian – Kasparov
Sarajevo 2000

Black to play

Black is several moves away from castling, connecting rooks and coordinating all of his forces. Yet he played **1...♖xc3! 2 bxc3 ♕c7**.

The fact that the "quality" of his remaining pieces was less than White's, to the tune of the Exchange, didn't matter because Black soon had more in quantity in the target area: **3 ♘e2 ♗e7 4 g5 0-0 5 h4 ♘a4 6 ♗c1 ♘e5 7 h5 d5**.

White's rooks would be bystanders to the winning Black attack after 8 exd5 ♗xd5. Instead, White tried to use his heavy pieces with **8 ♕h2 ♗d6 9 ♕h3**.

But he lacked an open line there, **9...♘xd3 10 cxd3 b4! 11 cxb4 ♖c8 12 ♔a1 dxe4** and Black was winning. A cute finish would have been 13 fxe4 ♗xe4! 14 dxe4? ♗e5+ 15 ♘d4 ♗xd4+ 16 ♖xd4 ♕xc1+! and mates.

8
Three pieces is a mate.

This adage, which has been attributed to several authors, tries to quantify Philidor's "true attacks" rule, #6. Three attacking pieces working in tandem usually succeed against a castled king.

Yes, it's an exaggeration. Castled kings defended by three pieces can withstand a lengthy assault by three attackers. It's a mismatch – more attackers than defenders – that makes an attack succeed. The greater the mismatch, the better the chance of success.

In the following position all but one of the heavy pieces are engaged on the queenside, where Black threatens to liquidate into a won endgame after ...罩xc6. Yet White won in five moves by exploiting his opponent's inability to shift pieces to the other wing:

Adams – Morozevich
Sarajevo 2000

White to play

When White pushed his pawn to c6 earlier, he foresaw that it would be lost. But he figured that when Black encircled it, his kingside would be ripe.

He looked at 1 豐g3 罩xc6. But he concluded that 2 ♘xf7, with its threat of 豐xg7 mate, wouldn't be clear at all after 2...g5!.

Instead he chose **1 ♔h1! 罩xc6 2 罩xc6 罩xc6 3 罩g1!** and it all became simple. With four attacking pieces, the kingside mismatch is bound to make an attack on g7 or f7 work.

The rest was **3...豐xb2 4 ♘xg7! 豐c3 5 ♘xe8 Resigns**. (No better was 4...♔xg7 5 ♘xe6+ or 3...g6 4 ♘e4! dxe4 5 豐h6.)

9

With bishops of opposite color, the player with the attack has an extra piece.

This maxim of the Soviet school makes two points. First, the presence of the bishops rewards the player who seizes the initiative. "Some like to attack, others to defend and there are some worshippers of maneuvering strategy," Vladimir Simagin wrote in *Shakhmaty v SSSR* in 1967. "However, to achieve success in play with bishops of opposite color, a player is obligated to fight for the initiative."

The second point is that such an initiative will be directed at squares that your bishop can attack and which the enemy bishop cannot defend. This is illustrated by the following game, which Russian annotators dubbed "The White Square Symphony." White had a positional edge earlier and realized it could be exploited only by attack. He began with 17 consecutive moves on light squares. Then:

Karpov – Kasparov
World Championship 1985

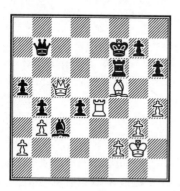

White to play

As Gerald Abrahams said of opposite-colored Bs, "They operate each in a different diocese, and ignore each other." Here White ignored Black's bishop and began the final assault with more light-square moves, **1 ♕c4+ ♔f8 2 ♗h7!**.

To meet the threat of 3 ♕g8 mate, Black played 2...♖f7. Then 3 ♕e6! set up another light-square threat, ♕e8 mate.

Black resigned after **3...♕d7 4 ♕e5!** because he couldn't cover b8 as well as the light squares (4...♖e7 5 ♖f4+ ♖f7 6 ♕b8+ ♕e8 7 ♕d6+ ♕e7 8 ♖xf7+ ♔xf7 9 ♗g6+ and mates).

10

A 'bad' bishop is much better in attack than in defense.

Philidor was the first to write about the significance of good and bad bishops. He appreciated that good bishops were excellent for attack. But "he held the incorrect opinion that from a purely defensive point of view the bad bishop could render better service than the good," wrote Max Euwe.

Euwe took a more modern view that the real difference between good and bad bishops lay in attack. "A good bishop is one which is the same color as the squares on which the enemy pawns are placed," wrote Ludek Pachman in *The Middle Game in Chess*, "whilst a 'bad' bishop is one which is restricted by its own pawns."

This view assumes a bad B will be a bad attacker. But that's not necessarily true if there are bishops of opposite color. When Boris Gulko wrote #10, in *American Chess Journal* (issue 2, 1993), he cited this case:

Kamsky – Kasparov
Manila 1992

Black to play

Both sides have a slightly bad bishop. Black's is limited by the pawn at d6 but otherwise enjoys great firepower. White is worse because his own bishop can't attack anything, thanks to that pawn on d5.

If those pawns were moved back a rank, to d4 and d5, "Black's bishop would become 'good' but useless," Gulko said. White's bishop would have something to attack but remains hopeless in defense.

But as it stands, Black's bishop confirms #9. After **1...♕a7** and **...♖a8**, White's bishop and heavy pieces cannot defend the key squares, a1 and b2.

White tried to create a light-square fortress with **2 ♖c1 ♖a8 3 b3**. But Black shifted the assault to other dark squares, **3...♗f4 4 ♔c2 ♖e7! 5 ♕d3 ♕c5 6 ♖b1 ♖e3 7 ♕d4 ♖a2+ 8 ♔d1 ♖xf3!** and won.

11

When the opponent has no counterplay, patience is the attacker's greatest asset.

This comment, from John Nunn in *Secrets of Grandmaster Chess*, underlines the difference between quick and slow-developing attacks. Quick attacks are more like combinations. They achieve a knockout in a few moves and can often be calculated in advance. Slow-developing attacks occur when you can pin the enemy down but can't break through immediately. Victory usually comes from shifting the attack from one point to another, while denying counterplay. That requires patience.

Svidler – Sakaev
St. Petersburg 1996

White to play

White is playing "with an extra piece" thanks to the opposite-colored bishops. But his natural target, g7, is well defended. White must rely on other winning ideas, such as getting the queen to g6 and perhaps h7.

At same time he should try to watch out for ...e5! when it means that ♗xe5 will permit ...♕xc5+ and when fxe5 allows Black counterplay on the f-file.

White took simple precautions – 1 h3 ♗d7 2 ♔h2! ♗e8 and then 3 ♕e2! ♔g8 4 ♕g4 ♕d7 5 ♗e5!. Threats such as ♕g6xh6 couldn't be averted for long – 5...♖e7 6 ♗f6 ♖f7 7 ♕g6 ♔f8 8 ♗e5.

The threat is ♕h7 followed by ♗d6+ or ♕h8+. The rest was 8...♔g8 9 ♕xh6 ♕e7 10 ♖g4 ♗b5 11 ♕g6 ♗e8 12 ♖g5! (idea: ♖h5/♕h7+) ♖xf4 12 ♕xg7+ ♕xg7 14 ♖xg7+ ♔f8 15 ♖xb7 ♖a4 and **Black resigned**.

12

Too many checks means there's something wrong with the attack.

This comment from Viktor Korchnoi seems odd to young attackers. They love to check because the consequences are easier to foresee. They know the old chestnut – "Always check. It may be mate" – isn't quite true. But they enjoy making forcing moves anyway.

However, there are natural limits to the number of desirable checks. "The king should not be checked to death or it may escape alive," as W.H.K. Pollock said. Restricting the king serves better than chasing it.

Gelfand – Kramnik
Candidates match 1994

White to play

White sacrificed a bishop on h7 and Black managed to create an escape route for his king with his last move, ...♖fe8. White responded with the obvious checks and added a pawn to his compensation, **1 ♕h7+? ♔f8 2 ♕h8+ ♔e7 3 ♕xg7**.

But something was clearly wrong with the attack because Black's queen could have defended with **3...♕f4!**, based on **4 ♖f3 ♕xf3! 5 gxf3 ♖g8**.

The correct way to finish off was **1 ♕h5!**, threatening mate on h8, and then **1...♔f8 2 ♕g5! ♔g8 3 ♖g3!**. Now none of Black's pieces are allowed to defend the king. After **3...g6 4 ♖h3** there is no way to stop mate on h8.

In that example White violated another cardinal rule of attack. He missed the knockout. As Leonid Stein put it:

13

The most important thing in our business is an ability to deliver the final blow.

It's not enough to correctly identify when to attack, to choose the right target, to act with speed and accuracy and to limit the number of checks. You also have to finish your opponent off when you get the chance.

Anand – Kamsky
Dortmund 1992

Black to play

Black had already missed three wins as he drove the king from g1 to c5.

Here he has another chance to put White away, **1...♗d7!** and ...♖c8+ since 2 ♗xd7 ♕xd7 is easy. But Black chose **1...♕d5+?** and after **2 ♔b4! a5+ 3 ♔a3 ♕d3 4 ♔b2 b4 5 ♔a1!** White's king is safe.

In fact, White even had winning chances after **5...a4 6 ♗e2 ♕e4 7 ♕d1 bxc3? 8 ♗xc4+!** with the idea of ♕g4+ before a draw was agreed. As Gerald Abrahams had said, "Good positions don't win games. Good moves do."

CHAPTER TWO: CALCULATION

14

The essence of chess is seeing the move after.

Good players are good predictors. They can often see the move after — that is, foretell how their opponent will respond to the move they are considering playing.

During Boris Spassky's first World Championship match, former champion Mikhail Botvinnik asked him, "Do you always guess Petrosian's moves?" "Not always," Spassky conceded. He lost that match and realized one reason why was he was often surprised by Tigran Petrosian's moves. In their second match, three years later, he said, "I guessed everything," and won the match.

van der Wiel – Karpov
Amsterdam 1988

White to play

Black's last move (...♗d7) made a threat of ...♗a4, skewering queen and rook. But it also cut off a key escape route for Black's queen.

White felt confident when he chose **1 ♗d3** because it attacks the queen and gains time for the 2 ♕c2 defense.

But he didn't see that the obvious reply, **1...♕a5**, would prevent 2 ♕c2 because 2...♗a4 3 b3 ♕xc3! leads to a won endgame for Black.

Instead, White settled for **2 ♕b4 ♕xb4 3 cxb4**. But his weakened queenside, **3...♖fd8 4 ♖b1 ♘a4** (5 ♗f4 ♘xb2 or 5 b3 ♘c3), eventually cost him the game.

It was Gerald Abrahams, in *Technique in Chess*, who said #14. But good calculation requires efficiency, not just foresight:

15

Masters don't calculate more.
They calculate better.

"If anything, grandmasters often consider fewer alternatives" than non-grandmasters, said British GM David Norwood. Extensive research on how masters choose moves, by master/psychologist Adrianus de Groot and others, tends to support this.

The alternative moves we consider playing are called candidate moves. Grandmasters are more efficient calculators because they intuitively ignore candidates that lesser players agonize over. "Weak players spend more time considering weak moves, while strong players spend more time considering strong moves," said Jonathan Levitt in *Genius in Chess*.

Topalov – Aronian
Wijk aan Zee 2006

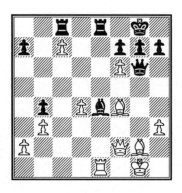

White to play

Black would love to trade bishops and rooks after ...♗xg2. A master sitting in White's chair wouldn't take long to consider any line that allows that. Instead he'd be attracted to 1 ♖xe4.

Of course, to play that with confidence requires quite a bit of variation-crunching. But by spending "more time considering strong moves" White was able to see that the pawns cannot be stopped after **1 ♖xe4!! ♖xe4 2 d5**.

The game ended with **2...♖ce8 3 d6 ♖e1+ 4 ♔h2 ♕f5 5 ♕g3 g6 6 ♕g5! ♕xg5 7 ♗xg5 ♖d1 8 ♗c6 ♖e2+ 9 ♔g3 Resigns**.

In the dark ages before chess clocks, masters routinely took hours over a single move. They justified this by exaggerating the number of candidates they needed to consider. "A fine player examines occasionally from five to twenty or more moves on each side," William Lewis, one of the strongest masters of his era, declared, according to Howard Staunton's *Handbook*. "Can this be done in a moment?"

The answer is "No – and it's not necessary." Masters calculate more efficiently today.

16
You'll never become Alekhine if variations rule you, rather than the other way around.

This was Mikhail Botvinnik's warning to a youngster named Garry Kasparov who very much wanted to be an Alekhine. "This pained me," Kasparov recalled in the Russian magazine *64*. "But the wise Botvinnik was right."

What he meant is that if you seek complications because you are good at calculating them, you lose control of the move selection process. You are seeking complexity for the sake of complexity, not because it is right in this position.

"Do not calculate complicated lines before you are absolutely sure it is necessary" was the sound advice of another great teacher, Mark Dvoretsky. Another former Botvinnik student, Vladimir Kramnik, could have taken that to heart.

Karpov – Kramnik
Monaco 1997

Black to play

Black's pieces are much more aggressively placed and he got his internal calculating machine running at high speed when he considered **1...♘e4!?!**.

He easily saw five moves ahead, **2 fxe4! ♖xf2 3 ♔xf2 ♕xh2+ 4 ♔e1 ♕xg3+ 5 ♔d2 d4**. That's impressive. But the variations had taken control of him. After **6 ♔c2!** his very strong position had become very difficult.

This wasn't at all necessary. With the simple **1...♖f6!** and **...♖df8** or **...♖g6** Black has a brutal attack which would likely have won faster and without risk.

There are also natural limits to how much you can calculate:

17
You can't see 64 squares at the same time.

When psychologist Alfred Binet studied blindfold chess he conducted a survey of leading players. He asked whether they could mentally see the entire board at the same time. "Of course," Siegbert Tarrasch responded. "But it is difficult."

In truth, it is virtually impossible even with eyes wide open.

A player typically examines sectors of the board, perhaps as few as 12 or 16 squares at a time, while considering a tactic. After he's seen what he wants to see, his eyes quickly shift to another sector.

But unless you're looking at an endgame with only a few pieces, you can't take in everything at once. That's why even world-class players miss tactics that are staring them in the face in a distant sector.

Kasimdzhanov – Topalov
Leon 2007

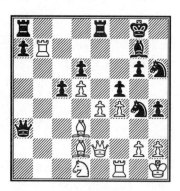

White to play

Black's queen had been shifting between a5, a2 and a3 when he found himself in trouble after **1 e5!** and then **1...dxe5 2 d6** and **3 d7**.

Annotator Maxim Notkin blamed Black's problems on his inability to look at both the queenside and kingside at the same time. That's why he missed **1...②xh2!** which would have given him good chances (2 ♔xh2 c4! 3 ♗xc4? ②g4+ 4 ♔g1 ♕g3).

"If our eyes had the capability of taking in various sectors, probably we'd play stronger chess," Notkin wrote on *e3e5.com*. "However, an argument with the Creator is beyond the scope of this article."

18

The hardest moves to see are very long moves backwards, and knight moves.

This is one of many perceptive observations from Cecil Purdy. We often overlook long retreats because we typically look for our opponents to make forcing moves, usually advances. We have a problem with knights because they don't move in straight lines. Even masters overlook strong knight moves in time pressure.

If it's a knight that is retreating, it can be doubly easy to miss. In the diagram below White appears to enjoy some superiority because of his better pawns and minor piece. It seems that Black's knight would only be dangerous if it lands on d4 or f4 in some tactically dangerous way. However, the knight won the game in one move – by going backward:

Morozevich – Movsesian
Sarajevo 2007

White to play

White jumped at the chance to activate his queen, **1 ♕e3**, with a threat of 2 ♕xa7.

However, 1 ♕e3?? lost to the unlikely **1...♘g7!**. There is nothing to be done about 2...♘f5 or 2...♘h5, followed by a killing check on g3.

The game ended with **2 ♖g1 ♘f5 3 ♕e1 ♖xg1+ 4 ♔xg1 ♖g8+ 5 ♔h1 ♘g3+ 6 ♔g1 ♘f1+ 7 ♔h1 ♘xh2! Resigns**.

No better is 4 ♕xg1 ♖g8 5 ♖g2 ♖xg2 6 ♕xg2 ♕xg2+ 7 ♔xg2 ♘e3+ and ...♘xc4.

19
Knowing when to calculate is just as important as knowing how to calculate.

Masters streamline their thought processes by choosing some moves based on general principles, intuition, positional understanding or some other criterion. They don't spend time on calculating those moves, except for a "blunder check" – making sure they didn't allow a simple enemy tactic.

How do you know when you need to calculate more? A good tipoff is when the first candidate you are attracted to doesn't meet your expectations.

Gerard – Glek
Clermont-Ferrand 2003

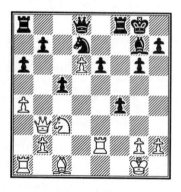

White to play

White naturally looks at the forcing 1 ♕xe6+. But after seeing how good 1...♔h8 and 2...f3! is for Black he turns to 1 ♖xe6, which threatens a deadly discovered check.

This meant he has to calculate beyond two moves into the future. He sees that after 1...♔h8 2 ♖e7! Black's pieces would be severely restricted, e.g. 2...♗d4+ 3 ♔h1 ♖f6? 4 ♘e4 and ♕xb7.

He played **1 ♖xe6!**. Black also saw 1...♔h8 2 ♖e7!. Like White he turned to a second candidate, even though it meant he, too, would have to calculate several moves ahead.

He checked out 1...♕h4 and found that the most dangerous-looking tactic, 2 ♖e7+ and 3 ♖xd7, would walk into 3...♕e1 mate.

There were more difficult lines to calculate but they all turned out well for him (2 ♗xf4 ♕xf4! 3 ♖f6+ c4! and 2 ♖e7+ ♔h8 3 ♕xb7 ♘e5!).

So Black played **1...♕h4!** and White found nothing better than **2 g3 ♕h3! 3 ♗xf4 ♔h8**, with advantage to Black.

"Knowing when..." has been attributed to several masters and appears in several forms. Garry Kasparov wrote in *How Life Imitates Chess*, "You have to realize when you are leaving the realm of what can be confirmed beyond a reasonable doubt."

20
Long variation, wrong variation.

Bent Larsen said his aphorism applies to both long variations of published analysis, which he instinctively distrusted, and to over-the-board calculation. The further you try to see with certainty, the more likely you're missing something.

David Bronstein agreed. "At first you see the position clearly," he said in one of his last interviews. "Within three moves it becomes somewhat like in a fog. And within five moves you only see the contours of the position."

The other problem with calculating a long variation is that you spend so much time on it that you tend to forget about the other alternatives at move two. "The things you overlook in your long calculation will seldom be as important as the move you overlooked at the start," as Jacob Aagaard said in *Excelling at Chess Calculation*.

Fischer – Petrosian
Bled 1961

Black to play

Black saw that 1...♘xe4 would likely draw but recognized that White could press him for some time because of his better rooks and passed c-pawn after 2 ♖xe4.

He also noticed **1...♖d6**. It seems to just lose a pawn after 2 ♖xd6 ♚xd6 3 ♖xe6+ and 4 ♗xa8.

However, he correctly carried his analysis further and realized **3...fxe6! 4 ♗xa8 ♚c5 5 b3 ♘d7** followed by ...♚d4 and ...♘c5 creates an absolute blockade.

Black rechecked this seven-move variation, found no flaw and played **1...♖d6?**. He was "shattered," according to White, by the reply **2 ♗xa8!**.

Normally, Black would have recognized that this should favor White on general principles, because of his passed pawn and better minor piece. But Black hardly looked at **2...♖xd1+ 3 ♚c2 ♖f1**, apparently because he was wrapped up in his seven-move fantasy.

He lost soon after **4 ♖xa5 ♖xf2+ 5 ♚b3 ♖h2 6 c5** and that emphasizes the role of evaluation:

21
Calculation without evaluation is possible only in the endgame or studies.

Veteran trainer Adrian Mikhalchishin made this point in *64* (July 2005) when he advised his colleagues about how to teach young players:

A youngster should learn to evaluate the position after each half move. That is, when considering a candidate, he should determine who is better after each reasonable response by his opponent. Then he should look for his best reply to each enemy response and again evaluate the position. And so on.

Skipping the evaluation step is as bad as not looking for a tactical shot in response to it:

Yusupov – Speelman
Linares 1991

Black to play

Black seems in trouble in view of ♖h6 and ♖ah1. That's why he

calculated **1...♖xf3** in considerable detail, e.g. **2 ♔xf3 ♘d4+** or 2...♕f5+ followed by ...♕xe4+ or ...♕xg4(+).

But it didn't matter which player had calculated 1...♖xf3 2 ♔xf3 better. White won because only he correctly evaluated **2 ♕h6+!** and saw it leads to a winning endgame, **2...♕xh6 3 ♖xh6** and **4 ♖ah1**.

Had Black seen how bad that was he would have pushed 1...♖xf3? out of his head. Then he might have found the best try, **1...h5!** with the idea of **2 ♘gf2 d5!**.

22

As a rule, an experienced master never calculates all the variations of a combination.

After saying this in his best-game collection, Yuri Averbakh added, "Relying on his intuition, he works out only the necessary minimum."

This may sound like a recipe for blunder. After all, not calculating every variation should increase the possibility of an oversight. But a master knows that you are *more likely to err* when relying on calculation than when relying on intuition.

Timman – Short
Candidates match 1993

Black to play

White played the opening quickly and Black assumed he couldn't play 1...♕xa1 because of a prepared refutation.

He chose **1...f3**.

In fact, White didn't have an answer prepared for 1...♕xa1. "I had intuitively relied on it that White, with three pawns for a rook and his good piece coordination, should be able to launch an assault on the unprotected enemy king," he wrote in *New In Chess*.

In other words, White trusted his intuition about the position – and Black trusted White. Neither tried to determine the absolute "truth" by calculation. (Later analysis indicated that **1...♕xa1 2 ♕e6 ♖f8 3 ♖e1 ♖f5 4 ♘c3** is far from certain.)

23

I don't think like a tree?
Do you think like a tree?

What tree are we talking about? The one Alexander Kotov made his trademark in *Think Like a Grandmaster*.

Kotov endorsed a rigorous, if not rigid, procedure which called for analyzing each candidate move as if it were a tree branch, with subvariations sprouting from it. Analyze each branch and sub-branch once and only once, Kotov said, and when you're done, play the candidate that results in the best position when met by the best defense.

But few people actually think this way. The most famous put-down of Kotov is #23, from another Soviet-trained GM, Anatoly Lein, (as quoted in *Improve Your Chess Now*). In practice, masters employ a much more chaotic method, as Veselin Topalov explained when annotating the game that made him famous.

Topalov – Kasparov
Moscow 1994

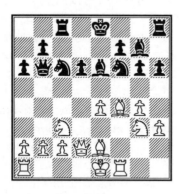

White to play

White felt he had to stop Black from castling or he would get the worst of it. He looked at **1 &xd6** and concluded that only **1...&xg4**, threatening 2...♕xb2!, would be dangerous.

Then he found 2 ♘a4 and concluded 2...♕e3 3 hxg4 was best and would favor him. So far, so good. He played 1 &xd6.

But as Black was thinking, he suddenly remembered that during his tree-climbing he had found a flaw on the 2 ♘a4 ♕e3 limb – 3 hxg4? allows 3...♕xd2+ 4 ♔xd2 ♖d8!, which favors Black. But he forgot about that line when he took the d-pawn.

Fortunately by the time Black played 1...♘xg4, he had found an apparent refutation, 2 &xg4 ♕xb2 3 e5.

This is based on 3...♕xa1+ 4 ♔f2 ♕b2 5 ♖b1, trapping the queen. Black jumped at the opportunity to play the 3...♘xe5 4 ♖b1 ♕xc3 endgame and eventually lost.

But it needn't have lasted that long. Only after the game did White realize he had botched his analysis not once, but twice. After **2 ♗xg4! ♛xb2**:

Instead of 3 e5?, he could simply play **3 ♘ge2!**. Black, a piece down, can resign because **3...♛xa1+** loses to the same idea White had seen in the 3 e5 branch, **4 ♔f2 ♛b2 5 ♖b1**,

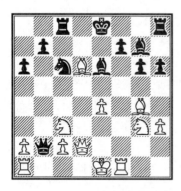

White to play

— again winning the queen.

The truth is each player finds the method of move selection that is most comfortable to him. Psychologist Alexey Bartashnikov of the Lvov State Institute of Physical Culture reported in *64* (12/1997), "Research shows that masters calculate variations on an average of five-to-six moves deep." But great calculators often reject a candidate move without looking one move deep. During his 2003 match with X3D Fritz, Garry Kasparov passed up the chance for a kingside pawn storm in one game. He said he relied on intuition rather than calculation. "Without a light-squared bishop, such attacks never work," he explained.

And after Alexander Alekhine won a game with a rook sacrifice at Margate 1938, Miguel Najdorf expressed doubt that anyone could see all the head-spinning complications. Najdorf told the world champion he didn't believe "you saw the entire combination." Alekhine replied, "I also didn't see it. I felt it."

24

More often than not it's difficult to calculate the consequences of the strongest move. It's easier to convince yourself that all the others are worse.

Mark Dvoretsky was making two points with this comment in *64* (March 1998). First, in most cases you can't easily prove a particular candidate works better than all the others. Many candidates result in fuzzy conclusions. But, second, you may be able to prove that all the alternatives are worse in some way or another.

The process of elimination works well when your opponent's intentions are clear, such as when he is making threats. One by one, you can eliminate the candidate moves that fail to blunt those threats.

Svidler – Hansen
Groningen 1995

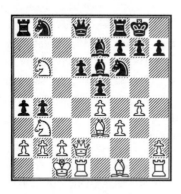

White to play

White didn't like the messy 1 ♘xa8 axb3, followed by ...bxa2, ...♛a5, or ...♘bd7 and ...♛xa8. He found 1 ♘c5!.

Black shot back **1...b3!** quickly. That surprised White. But it shouldn't have if he had realized

that Black was using the process of elimination. All the other candidates would have allowed White a powerful knight move, such as ♘xa8, ♘xe6 or ♘cxa4.

For example, 1...dxc5? 2 ♛xd8 ♝xd8 3 ♘xa8 and the knight is not trapped (3...♘bd7 4 g5 ♘h5 5 ♝b5!).

White replied quickly to 1...b3! even though the position was highly complex. He said later that it wasn't difficult to determine **2 axb3!** was the best move – because everything else would lose, e.g. 2 cxb3 ♛xb6! 3 ♘xe6 ♛c6+! costs a piece, or 2 ♘xe6 bxa2!.

After 2 axb3! play went **2...♛xb6 3 ♘xe6 axb3! 4 ♛c3!**. White had the upper hand and won.

25
Chess isn't checkers.

Benjamin Blumenfeld was a celebrated teacher of the early Soviet era, best known for the Blumenfeld Counter Gambit and for his advice on calculation. With #25 he was trying to correct a bad habit of young players, who assumed that if their opponent could capture a piece or pawn he would do so.

Nothing is automatic, Blumenfeld told them: "When you combine and give up a piece, look carefully then to see if your opponent is obligated to take it or not." The opponent might be able to make a stronger move than the capture. Or he might play a zwischenzug, a forcing in-between-move that allows him to capture more favorably on the next move.

Kramnik – Ki. Georgiev
Moscow 1994

White to play

Black had just retreated the knight from a6 and threatens the queen. But White saw a mating pattern: If the knight is out of the picture and the a-file is open,

White mates with ♖a1.

With that in mind he looked at 1 ♖a1. It is based on 1...♘xe6?? 2 ♘b6+! axb6 3 axb6 mate.

But chess isn't checkers, he added, and Black could reply 1...♖e8!. Then White has to force a draw with knight checks.

Instead, White found a more forcing order – **1 ♘b6+! axb6 2 axb6** so that 2...♘xe6?? 3 ♖a1 mate.

Black defended with **2...♘a6** but White continued **3 ♖a1 ♖d8 4 ♕e7**, threatening 5 ♖xa6+ bxa6 6 ♕a7 mate. This was decisive after **4...♕d6 5 ♖xa6+! ♔b8 6 ♕xd6+.**

26
Chess isn't Tennis.

This old Marshall Chess Club kibitz points out the deceptive nature of the back and forth, serve and volley rhythm of a middlegame: White makes a threat. Black parries. White makes another threat. Black parries, and so on. In that way White always controls the cadence of play.

But the rhythm is broken if Black can reply with a move that both defends and attacks. Then he controls the rhythm. If his opponent can do the same – defending against the Black threat and making one of his own – he can regain control. But often a good calculator makes a gross error by losing control, as in the following example:

Gelfand – Anand
Biel 1993

Black to play

Black, two pawns down and with a bad king, allowed this position to come about because he thought he could play **1...♖xd2**.

He had seen **2 ♖a4!**, with its threat of ♖h4+. But Black based his survival on **2...♕g5**, which covers h4 and gains time by threatening his own mate on g2.

Some strong GM-spectators thought Black had turned the tables – until they saw the "only" move, **3 g3**. This, too, defends against a threat and makes one of its own.

The volleying is over. Black has no adequate answer and he resigned soon after **3...e5 4 ♖h4+ ♕xh4 5 gxh4**.

27

Wing attacks can be estimated before they're calculated.

This is the essence of what Eduard Gufeld said in *Chess Strategy*: You can get a quick estimate of the chances for success of a wing attack before you decide whether it's worth time calculating.

Imagine a position in which White is attacking on the kingside while Black is going for mate or material on the queenside. Who will succeed? A speedy way to guess is to count up how many moves it would take White to deliver mate, assuming Black passes on the kingside. Then do the same for Black's version of success on the queenside.

If the difference is 2-3 moves in White's favor, he can assume that his attack will win, Gufeld wrote. If the difference is only one tempo, he may still have a good chance of success. But he needs to calculate because the margin of error is small, Gufeld added. For example:

White to play

White is pursuing a familiar plan of pushing his pawn to h5, exchanging on g6 and then crashing through with g2-g4-g5 and ♗xg7 (or with the immediate ♗xf6/ ...♗xf6?/♕h6 and mates).

But Black has counterplay, particularly from pushing his

a-pawn to a4 and eliminating the b3-bishop. Black needs to clear a path for the pawn, and he must protect it first, say with ...♖c7, because without it, ...♕b5? will allow ♗xa7!.

Let's count up: It will take White one move to get his pawn to h5 and two to get the g-pawn to the fifth rank. That's a total of three. (We won't count hxg6 or ♗xg7 because Black has to spend tempi to recapture.)

Black meanwhile will spend four tempi to create counterplay – ...♖c7, ...♕b5, ...a5 and then ...a4. Since White moves first, his attack will arrive two moves ahead of Black's.

The bottom line is White doesn't have to calculate deeply here. He can estimate and conclude **1 h5!** is strong. In contrast, here is what happened in real life.

Fischer – Larsen
Portoroz 1958

White to play

White is a tempo behind the previous diagram because his pawn is at h2. Also his bishop is on d5 so he has to decide whether to spend another tempo on 1 ♗b3 to avoid ...♘xd5.

That means he has to invest two extra tempi and cannot rely on an estimate. He won't know if his attack stands a chance unless he calculates **1 ♗b3** and then **1...♖c7 2 h4 ♛b5 3 h5**.

In fact, he would be winning after all, following 3...a5 4 hxg6 hxg6 5 ♗xf6! ♗xf6? 6 ♛h6 or 5...exf6 6 ♛xd6.

Instead, Black played **3...♖fc8 4 hxg6 hxg6 5 g4! a5 6 g5 ♘h5** and was lost after **7 ♖xh5! gxh5 8 g6** and gxf7+. In both diagrams, White was winning but in only the latter did he have to calculate.

This calculation-saving technique can also be applied to other kinds of positions, including promotion races in pawn endgames, as we'll see later in #65. Gufeld, assisted by collaborator Nikolai Kalinichenko, said in those races you should count how many moves White needs to promote his pawn, and how many Black needs. If White queens two moves ahead of Black, you can safely conclude he is winning. No calculation is necessary. But "if both sides queen at the same time, the newly arisen queen ending has to be assessed," they wrote.

28
When calculation of a move and its follow-up fails, reverse the order.

In analyzing a complex position you typically look at several forcing or semi-forcing moves. One of them may stand out as the best candidate while another move may appeal to you as the follow-up.

But if this one-two punch fails to work, it often pays to try two-one. "When your intuition tells you that there should be a forcing combination in the position, but your concrete analysis can't make it work, try the brainstorming technique of reversing the move order," Lev Alburt said in *Chess Rules of Thumb*.

Anand – Gelfand
Wijk aan Zee 1996

White to play

Black allowed this position even though he saw 1 ♕xg6+ ♕g7 and

the clever followup, 2 ♖xe6 ♗xe6 3 ♗xe6+ ♔h8 4 ♖h5+ and mates.

He felt safe because the combination has a big hole. On 2 ♖xe6? Black has 2...♕xg6! 3 ♖exf6+ ♔h7 and wins.

But there's another hole and it lies in the move order. White won with **1 ♖xe6!** because then 1...♗xe6 2 ♕xg6+! reverses the sequence and transposes into the mating line.

Black replied **1...♔g7** instead and resigned after **2 ♖xe7+ ♗xe7 3 ♖xf8 ♗xf8 4 h4**.

29
Calculate one move more
than you have done.

The great Hungarian tactician Laszlo Szabo lamented in his game collection that he often let a win slip away by stopping his calculations too early. He would look at a candidate move and examine it three moves into the future. Three moves ahead is a lot for average positions. It made sense to Szabo that if a candidate didn't prove itself worthy after three moves, it was time to drop it and consider another candidate.

But too often he discovered after the game that his first candidate was the best move after all – and that this would have been obvious if he had looked four moves into the future, not three. Szabo concluded that the remedy was to continue calculating as he had in the past but whenever he thought he was done, he had to look one move further. It's a formula that avoids accidents like:

Rowson – Yermolinsky
Philadelphia 2002

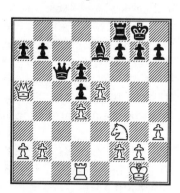

White to play

Black could have defended his a-pawn on the last move. But he concluded he didn't have to because **1 ♕xa7** would be met by **1...♕c2 2 ♖d2 ♕c1+ 3 ♔h2 ♗g5**.

Then White's pieces are overloaded and their mutual defense cracks, e.g. **4 ♖d3 ♗f4+ 5 g3 ♕f1!** followed by ...♕xd3 or ...♕xf2+.

He also calculated **4 ♖e2 ♗f4+ 5 g3 ♕d1**, which seems to win for Black in the same manner.

But after **6 ♘g1!** in that line it was suddenly clear he was lost. He had calculated one move short.

30

Half the variations calculated in a game turn out to be superfluous. Unfortunately, no one knows in advance which half.

Jan Timman's quip recalls one attributed to various business magnates, including department store founder John Wanamaker: "Half the money I spend on advertising is wasted. The trouble is I don't know which half."

In chess, saying that "half" of what you see is wasted is too conservative. It's usually much more. Only one line of play will actually occur on the board, and this is a fraction of the variations you invested your time examining at the board. Only after the game do you know which lines are superfluous.

Kramnik – Anand
Dortmund 2001

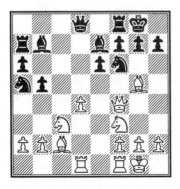

White to play

White played **1 d5!** with two ideas, bringing his rook to the kingside via d4 and sacrificing on d5 depending on how Black captures the pawn.

Yet neither idea occurred in the game, which went **1...♗xd5**

2 ♘xd5 exd5 3 ♕h4, with a strong attack.

There were several lines that had to be calculated in advance. In some cases the tree branches were short (1...exd5 2 ♕h4 threatens ♗xf6/♕xh7 mate and 2...g6 3 ♘e4! or 2...h6 3 ♗xh6!).

There was also 1...♘xd5 2 ♘xd5 exd5? 3 ♕h4! and 2...♗xd5 3 ♖xd5!, which was analyzed out to mate seven moves later – but only occurred in the notes.

The great moves of the 19th century occurred on the board. Many of the great moves of the 20th century appeared only in annotations. What will the 21st century bring?

CHAPTER THREE: DEFENSE

31

To defend it's necessary, most of all, to know that you need to defend.

If Steinitz's Law, #3, tells us when to attack, shouldn't it tell us when to defend? Logic says "Yes" but experience hands us a resounding "No!".

Just because your opponent has an advantage doesn't mean you should swap queens or batten down the hatches. You would be minimizing your winning chances out of fear of an offensive your opponent may have no intention of launching.

What Alexander Kotov meant by #31 was that good defense begins with knowing when it is truly necessary to defend. He conceded, in *The Chess Legacy of A.A.Alekhine*, that this isn't easy. If it were, there would be many great defenders, not just the few. "To develop a 'feeling of danger' is very difficult, perhaps significantly harder than other qualities of a chessplayer," he said.

I. Sokolov – J. Polgar
Hoogoveen 2006

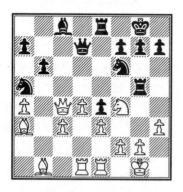

White to play

White's queen is attacked – and that's good for him because he has to choose between retreating to the kingside or queenside. If he reads the signs, such as Black's rook maneuver to g5, he knows an attack is coming and he should begin to defend with 1 ♕e2!. Then 1...♕xa4 2 ♗b4 is roughly balanced.

But he chose to keep his extra pawn with **1 ♕b4?**. He was soon lost because **1...♘d5! 2 ♘xd5 ♕xd5** stripped him of his only kingside defender, e.g. 3 ♔h2 ♗xh3! 4 gxh3 ♕f5 and ...♕xf2+ or ...♖h5 and wins.

White offered the pawn with **3 h4 ♖g4 4 ♕b5**, hoping for 4...♕xb5 5 axb5 ♖xh4. But it was too late. The train had already left – **4...♕d8! 5 g3 a6 6 ♕b4 ♕xh4 7 ♗xe4 ♖xg3+! 8 fxg3 ♕xe4** and the attack won.

32
The stronger the piece,
the weaker the defender.

The defensive food chain starts with a pawn. It's the best protector on the board precisely because it is the weakest unit. If a pawn defends a piece and is in turn protected, it doesn't mind being threatened by an enemy piece. If it is captured, then so will the enemy piece, with a resulting loss of material.

This had been known at least since Howard Staunton's day, and the true origin of #32 must predate his comment, "The pawn being less important than a piece, it is usually better to defend with it than with a piece."

Minor pieces are good defenders (but not as good as pawns). If attacked by a rook or queen, they need only be protected by another piece. Heavy pieces are more easily driven off. If attacked, they have to give up their defensive duties or risk a net loss of material:

Razuvaev – Middelburg
Porto San Giorgio 2000

White to play

Black is worse but his queen is holding things together. However, it can't remain at e7 after **1 ♗g5!**.

There followed **1...♛xg5 2 e6!** and the queen was again attacked. It tried to defend f7 with **2...♛f6** but then came **3 exf7+ ♛xf7 4 ♖xd7!**.

For the third time the queen is attacked by a weaker piece and this led to **4...♖xe2 5 ♖xf7 ♖c2 6 ♖f4+ ♔h8? 7 ♖h4 mate**.

This "stronger/weaker" principle also applies to blockade duty. The best blockaders are pawns and knights. Then come bishops, followed by rooks and worst of all, the queen and king, which must give way when attacked.

33

The general principles of defense are simply the general principles of attack in reverse.

This is how Reuben Fine, in his *The Middle Game in Chess*, said the defender's priorities are the mirror image of the attacker's. While the attacker seeks to open files and diagonals leading to a target, the defender wants to close them. When the attacker wants to keep pieces on the board, the defender seeks trades.

When both players are attacking and defending you see situations like this:

Rublevsky – Ivanchuk
Aerosvit 2007

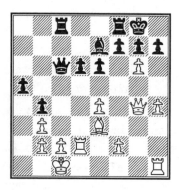

Black to play

White has just pushed his pawn to g6, correctly judging that the opened lines after 1...hxg6? 2 h5! should win. Black closed the kingside line that he wanted to be closed, **1...f5 2 gxh7+ ♔h8**.

This slowed the White attack, and it's axiomatic that when an attack on one wing brakes, the counter-attack speeds up. It did here with **3 ♕g3 a4! 4 ♖g1 ♗f6.**

Now it was White's turn to defend by avoiding open lines (5 bxa4? ♕xa4). He tried to defend the attack on b2 with **5 ♗g5**, intending ♗xf6.

But **5...f4!** was strong, based on 6 ♕xf4?? ♗xb2+ or 6 ♗xf4? a3! with a big edge. After **6 ♕d3**:

Black to play

Black has the initiative and therefore should avoid trades, with 6...♗e5!. But he misjudged **6...axb3?**. White was able to survive by exchanging pieces and keeping the right lines closed, **7 ♗xf6! ♖xf6 8 ♔b1!.**

34

If a defender finds the best possible moves he can put up virtually infinite resistance.

Kotov said the key to good defense is the "principle of maximum difficulty." That is, the defender should put as many obstacles in the attacker's way as possible. Aron Nimzovich called this the American approach: "Not to despair, to find the relatively best chance in the worst circumstances! To make the win as difficult as possible" (*Chess Praxis*). Or as Paul Keres said, "Play the move that you would least like to see if you were your opponent!" (*The Art of the Middle Game*).

These great defenders indicated that defeat could be delayed for quite a while. But an even more optimistic view holds that it can be postponed indefinitely. Larry Evans endorsed a "Theory of the Second Resource." Unless your position is hopeless, you will have an opportunity to draw or even win at some later point, if you avoid additional errors, he said. An Australian, Bill Jordan, carried this further with the "Theory of Infinite Resistance," expressed in #34. An illustration is:

Alekhine – Blackburne
St. Petersburg 1914

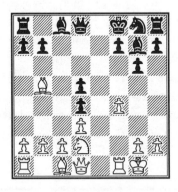

Black to play

This position is often cited as the result of a classic blunder (1 ♘d2??) which allowed **1...♕a5!** and **2 a4 a6**. "I simply forgot about the bishop," White said. Some sources, including several databases

and a book co-authored by Anatoly Karpov, claim he resigned here.

In reality he put up infinite resistance, beginning with **3 ♘b3 ♕d8 4 ♗d2 axb5 5 axb5 ♖xa1 6 ♗b4+ ♘e7 7 ♕xa1 ♗f6 8 ♕a7!**.

Is White still lost? Good defenders would say he isn't lost until you find a forced win for Black. There wasn't one in what followed, **8...b6 9 ♖e1 ♗e6 10 ♔h1 h5 11 ♗xe7+! ♕xe7 12 ♕xb6 ♕b4 13 ♕c5+! ♕xc5 14 ♘xc5**. In fact, no improvements were found for Black until the very end of the game when White had already secured a draw by trading off the queenside pawns.

One of the reasons he survived was he followed another principle:

35
Never make a purely defensive move.

Edward Lasker said this motto was passed on to him by his distant relative, Emanuel Lasker. Even under a ferocious attack, a player should look for a move that keeps alive his chances of winning, not just drawing.

This is important for the morale of the defender because it gives him more to look forward to than "If I survive the next few moves, I may get a draw." It also has an effect on the morale of the attacker:

Sutovsky – Andriasian
Aeroflot 2007

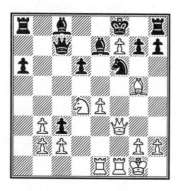

Black to play

Black's position certainly looks dicey. But he saw that even if it were White's move, 1 e5 dxe5! 2 ♕xa8 exd4 is harmless.

Moreover, traditional defensive policies, such as trading pieces or getting his king to a safer square, don't seem appropriate.

Instead, he found **1...cxb2!**. This makes sure White won't have enough pawns as compensation (as he might after bxc3) if his initiative fails. It also means Black can divert a White rook in emergencies with ...b1(♕). And it reminds White how lost he will be in an endgame.

White needed a sharp reply and chose **2 ♔h1 ♖b8 3 ♗h6!?**. There was nothing good in any event but this lost quickly – **3...gxh6! 4 ♕f4 ♘g4 5 ♘f5 ♗xf5 6 exf5 ♘f6 7 ♖e6 ♖b5** and so on.

36
You're never mated with a knight on f8.

Bent Larsen was annotating a win over Anatoly Karpov, in the August 1979 *Chess Life*, when he made this sweeping assertion. It's a general reminder of the terrific defensive resources of certain piece-and-pawn formations, as well as specific advice about how well ...♘f8 defends a castled king. The knight safeguards h7 and can jump to g6 to blunt an attack on g7. It is a well-protected defender because on f8 it cannot be driven away by a pawn, exchanged off by a minor piece or removed by an Exchange sacrifice, as it would be on f6.

Even when a mismatch looms on the kingside ("Three pieces is a mate") a knight at f8 may defend virtually single-handedly. But as with any defensive task, the first step is realizing that it's necessary to defend. Black failed to do that in the following example:

Carlsen – Aronian
Candidates match 2007

Black to play

White's last move was 1 e5, an Alekhine-like declaration of intent.

Once Black recognizes that ♕e4, ♘g5 and ♗g5 are coming, he is faced with two basic choices: He can try to break through on the queenside before White arrives on the other wing. Or he can secure the kingside first, 1...♖fb8! and ...♘f8!.

Black chose the former, offering a pawn sacrifice with **1...b4?! 2 axb4 axb4**. But White just ignored it, **3 ♗g5!**. It was too late to defend the kingside with pieces and after **3...♘b6 4 ♕e4! g6 5 ♕h4** Black was on the way to a loss.

37
The defender should make the least concession that suffices.

In the last diagram Black could have anticipated the ♕e4/♗g5/♘g5 ideas with 1...g6 or 1...h6. But both are bad because they make greater concessions than are necessary. For instance, 1...h6 keeps pieces off g5 but makes it harder to play ...g6 (after 2 ♕e4) since the h-pawn will be hanging.

#37 is the principle of economy that Emanuel Lasker attributed to Steinitz in his *Manual of Chess*. Steinitz hated to move pawns around his castled king when a piece move would defend just as well:

Lasker – Steinitz
World Championship 1894

Black to play

White eyes e4-e5 and ♕xh7+. Black can defend with 1...g6 but that weakens f6 and h6. Or he can blockade the e-pawn with 1...♘e5, with the possibility of hopping to c4. But after 2 b3 White's attack will accelerate when he plays f2-f4.

Steinitz chose the third option, **1...♘f8!?**. This forced White to come up with a new plan because a kingside attack is more or less ruled out. It freed Black to begin counterplay (**2 ♗e3 ♕a5 3 a3 ♕b5 4 ♗c1** when **4...♕c5!** and **5...b5** should have been fine for him).

A more modern version of the principle of economy was offered by Ludek Pachman in *Play on the Wings*. "Prophylactic measures are always correct and effective when they use less force and time than would be necessary to counter a direct attack," he wrote.

38
Play for surprise, not according to the rules.

This comes from Domenico Ercole del Rio in the 18th century and shows a very modern appreciation of psychology. When your position is distinctly worsening, he wrote, feel free to forget book principles and try to derail your opponent's train of thought instead.

Del Rio made the distinction between putting up the longest resistance – the one that takes the largest number of moves to crack – and the most perplexing defense – the one that might lose faster against best play but makes it harder to find "best play" moves. The latter, he said, is better.

This used to be disparaged as a rationale for swindles. The "surprise" defense was brought to legitimacy by Mikhail Tal among others.

F.Olafsson – Tal
Portoroz 1958

Black to play

White threatens ♖a8 mate. Analysis showed that even with best play, 1...f6, Black is lost. White would only have "to demonstrate elementary technical knowledge," Tal wrote. For example, 2 ♔e6! ♖e3+ 3 ♔xf6 ♖xf3+ 4 ♔xg5 wins eventually.

Instead, he played the surprising **1...♔f8!** and followed with...♔g7, seemingly going in the wrong direction.

But this defense set traps and forced White out of his train of

thought. At first, he avoided the traps, **2 ♔d7 a4 3 d6 ♔g7 4 ♔e8! ♖xf3 5 ♖xa4 ♖e3+ 6 ♔d8**.

Black set the final trap with **6...f5!?**.

Black to play

Then 7 ♖a5! would win – and it would likely win faster than if Black had adopted the "best" defense, 1...f6.

But by giving White difficult choices he was rewarded by **7 gxf5?**. The win was gone after **7...♔f6!**, e.g. **8 ♖a5 g4 9 d7 ♖c3!**, which stops 10 ♔c7/11 d8(♛) and prepares ...g3-g2.

39

Exact calculation is, generally speaking, needed more in defensive positions than in attack.

This counter-intuitive truth comes from Rudolf Spielmann in *The Art of Sacrifice in Chess*. A modern version, from Vladimir Kramnik on *e3e5.com*, is that calculation is "far more important in defense than in attack." He added:

"In order to succeed in defense one must be a brilliant tactician and see all the possibilities and all the tactical points of the opponent. I'd even suggest such a 'seditious' idea that the attack is a more positional technique than the defense. The attack can be based on general considerations while the defense must be specific."

Avrukh – Rublevsky
Rethymnon 2003

White to play

White can launch an attack with **1 ♘g5!** based largely on maxims, such as "With a pawn on e5, White must attack." He can visualize how to attack h7 with ♕c2 or g7 with a rook shift to g3. But he didn't calculate Black replies yet.

But Black had to calculate lines such as 1...♕b6, in view of 2 ♕c2 g6 3 b3 because he's the defender. It takes quite a lot of tree climbing to find the best move, 3...f6!, which keeps things double-edged.

Instead, Black played **1...h6?** and was hanging by a thread after **2 ♘ge4**. Black replied **2...♕b6** and once again White had an easy move, **3 ♖g3**. But once again Black's reply was hard because he had to calculate.

The best is 3...♔h7!, which violates general principles by putting the king on an open diagonal. Yet analysis indicates it might hold (4 b3 ♖d4). Instead Black played **3...♔h8??** and lost after **4 ♘f6!**, e.g. 4...♖xb2 5 ♕xh6+! gxh6 6 ♘xf7+ and mates, or 4...♘f4 5 ♘d7 ♖d4 6 ♕xf4!.

Miguel Najdorf won the brilliancy prize at the 1953 Candidates tournament with an attack based on general principles. "I never looked further than two moves ahead," he said. His opponent, Mark Taimanov failed to calculate deeply and was crushed.

There's some consolation for the defender who calculates more than his opponent and survives. If the game ends in a draw, he is pleased. But the attacker feels he must have missed something, Wolfgang Heidenfeld wrote in his game collection.

40
A wing attack is best met by a counterattack in the center.

This theme appeared in Philidor's games in the 18th century and a case can be made that it was understood by Greco more than a century before: If the defender opens the center he can distract the attacker or bring in reinforcements from the other wing.

One of the corollaries to this rule is – If you can keep the center closed, your wing attack stands a better chance of success. Another is – A center attack is best met by a wing counterattack.

Bareev – Topalov

Monte Carlo 2003

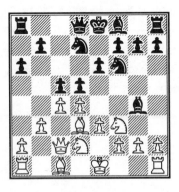

White to play

Black has just attacked the center by pushing a pawn from c6 to c5. White replied **1 h3 ♗h5 2 g4!**, citing what he called "the rule" that if your opponent strikes at your center when your king is there, you should initiate play on the wing.

Black's grip on the center was loosened after **2...♗g6 3 ♗xg6 hxg6 4 g5! ♘h5 5 dxc5 ♗xc5 6 cxd5 exd5 7 ♕d3**. He tried to catch up with a pawn sacrifice but it failed and he lost the endgame.

41
Flee before a pawn-based attack arrives.

There are two basic ways to attack an enemy king. One is using pieces, such as shifting a knight and rook to the area. The best defenses to that are bringing in defensive pieces or trading off the attackers.

But if the attack is led by pawns, sound defense calls for getting out of their way. "As soon as a pawn-attack can be foreseen, that part of the front should, as far as possible, be denuded of pieces. Then the pawns will only have the opposing pawns as the object of attack," Znosko-Borovsky wrote in *The Middle Game in Chess*. We often see this when White launches a kingside pawn storm like:

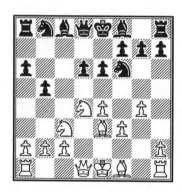

Black to play

If Black heeds #40, by playing 1...d5?, his backward development is exposed by 2 g5! ♞h5 3 exd5 exd5 4 f4.

If he tries to slow the attack by 1...h6, it may make matters worse because White can force open a line with g4-g5 or prepare it with h2-h4/♖g1.

A modern approach is **1...♞fd7!**. White lacks a kingside target then, while Black can mount a queenside counterattack, **2 ♕d2 ♞b6!**. A typical continuation is **3 0-0-0 ♞8d7 4 ♕f2 ♝b7 5 ♝d3 ♖c8**. Black may threaten a ...♖xc3!? sacrifice and after **6 ♞3c2 ♞c5 7 ♚b1 ♞ca4** it is White's king that has more to fear.

42

In bad positions, don't create new weaknesses.

In beginners' books you find such evergreen tips as "Don't make weaknesses." More honest authors amend it: "Don't make weaknesses without a good reason." But there's often a good reason to incur a weakness, so the hedged version is nearly as useless as the original.

What is useful is #42, a warning from Tigran Petrosian and others, against accepting additional weakness when you're busy trying to defend older ones. When a master ignores this warning, the usual reason is that it never occurred to him that he had a bad position. Here's a case of a merely dubious one.

Morozevich – Shipov
Krasnoyarsk 2003

Black to play

Black has lost time with his risky queen maneuver. But he could minimize the danger by developing, 1...♘bc6 and 2...♘ge7 or 1...b6 and 2...♗a6.

Instead, he tried for counterplay where he was weakest, **1...f6?**. He was unaware of the thin ice on which he was treading until 2 ♕g4! ♔f7 3 ♖h3!.

Black tried to shift pieces to the kingside and close the center, 3...h5 4 ♕f4 ♘c6 5 ♖g3 ♘ce7 6 ♘f3 c4.

But it was too late and 7 exf6 gxf6 8 ♘e5+ ♔e8 9 ♘g6 ♘xg6 10 ♖xg6 ♕xc2 11 ♕g3 gave White an overwhelming attack.

The warning about a new weakness in bad positions has been tweaked by this paradoxical thought:

43
In a really difficult position, create *more* weaknesses.

When normal defensive moves are not enough to safeguard your most vulnerable points, Lev Psakhis said, you may do better by giving your opponent more targets – and consequently more to think about.

The reason this might work is that a player who has a significant edge or strong initiative wants to finish the game off simply. He is looking for the obvious candidate that he can analyze two moves into the future and mentally conclude "and wins." He doesn't want to be confronted with choices.

Tal – Bronstein
Kiev 1964-65

Black to play

White's earlier piece sacrifice is difficult to refute over the board in view of Black's vulnerable first rank. A queen move may allow a strong ♖a8+ and a knight move invites ♕h8+.

Black created a new weakness with the bizarre 1...♔e7! 2 ♖a7+

♔f6, walking into a pin on the dark diagonal.

White said he was "simply staggered" by this. If he had more time he would have calmly activated his bishop at d2 or e3 and the outcome would be unclear, he felt. But he tried to win quickly and miscalculated 3 ♖e4? ♕d1+ 4 ♔h2 ♖xe4! 5 ♕xc3+ ♖e5.

He counted on 6 ♖a5 ♕d6 7 ♗f4, missing 6...♕e2!, which defends e5 and threatens mate. He resigned shortly.

After the game Tal's fans felt he had been beaten by unworthy fakery. But Tal himself had benefited by fakery before. And there's nothing unworthy about it because:

44

Good defensive play often involves an element of bluff.

The attacker is supposed to be the one who can afford to make dangerous-looking but not quite sound moves. He often gets away with them because the defender errs on the side of super-caution. But as Colin Crouch pointed out in *How to Defend in Chess*, the attacker can also be knocked off stride by a not-quite sound defense that includes "an element of bluff."

If he is given a choice between a distinct advantage in a secure position and a greater advantage in a risky-looking one, he will be strongly tempted to choose the former. Crouch was victimized by such a bluff in this example, which he gave in *British Chess Magazine*.

Crouch – Rendle
Hastings 2003-4

Black to play

White's positional superiority is considerable and he is ready to enlarge it with ♗xg7 followed by ♖he1-e5. Black bluffed with

1...♕a4??!, with the threat of ...♕xa2-b1 mate.

This forced White to make a choice he'd rather avoid: He could calculate 2 ♗xg7 ♕xa2 or go into the better endgame, 2 b3 ♕a3+ 3 ♕b2 ♕xb2+ 4 ♔xb2.

He chose the safe, second way and saw his edge disappear after 4...♗xd4 5 ♖xd4 ♖he8! in view of 6 ♗xd5 c6 7 ♗f3 ♖xd4 and 8...♖e3.

He should have called Black's bluff with **2 ♗xg7!**. Then **2...♕xa2** can be handled by **3 ♕e2!** ♖he8 4 ♗e5 and wins.

45

There is no such thing as a premature counterattack.

A counterattack is nothing more than a defender's attempt to mount an initiative, typically in a second area of the board, away from the attack that is threatening him. It can be and frequently is launched too late, with fatal results. But as Savielly Tartakower claimed with #45, it cannot come too early.

Here's a counter attack that was launched at the right time and in the same vicinity as the attack.

Adams – Anand
FIDE World Championship 2005

Black to play

White has an edge in queenside space and that creates a plan, ♖ec1 and c2-c3 followed by cxb4 (or ...bxc3/♖xc3!) with pressure against c7.

Black didn't wait until his c-pawn became a target. He anticipated the danger with **1...♗b5!**. The first point is that 2 ♗xb5 axb5 traps the c4-knight.

But the main point is Black can now try for ...c6xd5! without fear of ♘b6. There followed **2 b3 ♗e7 3 ♖ec1 c6!**. The counterattack would win after 4 c3? bxc3 5 ♖xc3 cxd5!.

Instead, White adopted another safety policy: There is no such thing as a premature draw offer in a good but worsening position. He made it after **4 ♗xb5 ♖xb5 5 ♘b6 ♕b7 6 dxc6 ♕xc6 7 ♕c4** and it was accepted.

46

After an attack has been repulsed, the counterattack is generally decisive.

We use the terms "attack" and an "initiative" interchangeably. If there is a real difference, it's a matter of degree of commitment.

The player with an initiative commits some of his energy, both materially and emotionally. But if the initiative runs cold, he is able to regroup and defend against his opponent's counter-initiative. The game may peter out into a draw.

But when an attack runs out of steam, the consequences are usually worse. The attacker may have committed too much. He can't regroup and the counterattack usually wins, according to Richard Reti, who called #46 an "old aphorism."

Lie – Avrukh
Heraklion 2007

White to play

White's **1 ♘f5?!** looked impressive in view of 1...gxf5

2 ♕h6 followed by 3 g5 or 3 gxf5/♖g1+.

However after **1...♕c5! 2 ♘h6+ ♔g7** Black began the counterattack with **3 ♕d2 ♖d4! 4 f4 ♗e4!**.

Now we see how useless White's pieces are when needed for defense, e.g. 5 g5 ♖xd3! 6 gxf6+ ♔xf6 and Black wins.

The game ended with **5 ♖e3 ♗xd3 6 cxd3** and now **6...♘e4! 7 ♕e2 ♖c8! 8 ♕d1 ♘f2 9 ♕d2 ♖xd3 10 ♖xd3 ♘xd3 White resigns**.

47

If you seek, you will find, no matter how dangerous the attack may look.

"In bad positions, all moves are bad," Siegbert Tarrasch said of a position he reached in a 1904 consultation game. Emanuel Lasker took the opposite, optimistic view of #47 in *Common Sense in Chess*. Lasker believed that any position that isn't a forced loss contains hidden defenses that are revealed only if you search for them.

True, the search may be in vain. You may discover in the post-mortem that you were completely lost. But Lasker's point was you won't find what you don't look for.

Bologan – Bacrot
Enghien-les-Bains 2001

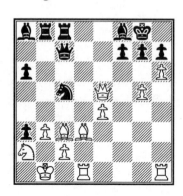

Black to play

Black would have a far superior endgame after 1...♕xe5 2 ♗xe5 ♘xd3, since 3 ♗xb8 is met by 3...♘f2, regaining the Exchange.

But Black saw that by altering the move order, **1...♘xd3** and 2...♕xe5, he would avoid even that complication. He won after 2 ♕xc7?? ♖xc7.

But 1...♘xd3? gave White a reprieve. If he had sought, he might have found **2 ♕f5!!**. It has a spectacular threat of 3 ♕xh7+! ♔xh7 4 hxg7+ and mates.

White wins after 2...g6 3 ♕f6 and would have a clear edge after 2...♘e5 3 hxg7! ♗xg7 4 ♖xh7!, threatening ♖xg7+ (4...♖e8 5 ♖dh1).

Tartakower underlined the difference between attackers and defenders when he imagined a conversation between his great predecessors: "He who attacks, seeks," said Tchigorin. "He who defends, finds," replied Steinitz.

48

In lost positions,
use the process of elimination.

This follows Simon Webb's recommended policy, in *Chess for Tigers*, of "controlled desperation." When all the candidates before you look bad, reject the ones that allow your opponent a simple way to win. If that leaves you with one move that doesn't seem to lose by force, play it. You have nothing to lose.

As we'll see in #123, the hardest decisions are those that have to be made when confronted with several candidate moves that appear equally good. On the other hand, when you have a terrible position it will be easier to find the best move – because it will likely be an "only" move. Black escaped in the following example because it was much easier to find his moves than White's.

Topalov – I. Sokolov
Wijk aan Zee 2004

White to play

Black's position looks hopeless after 1 ♕b6!. His queenside pawns fall after 1...♖a8 2 ♕xb7. Also lost is the 1...♕xb6 2 cxb6 ♖a8 endgame in view of 3 ♗xg7!.

That might be depressing for Black. But it actually eases his task considerably. It means he must play the only alternative, **1...♕a8!**. As awful as it looks, it doesn't lead to a "matter of technique" loss.

White was able to make some progress with **2 ♗c7 ♗f6 3 ♗d6 ♖d8 4 ♘a4 ♘h6 5 ♕a5** and the threat of ♘b6.

But after Black played another "only" move, **5...♕c8!**, White began to lose the thread, **6 h3 ♕f5 7 ♖ae1 ♕d3 8 ♖e8+? ♖xe8 9 ♖xe8+ ♔h7 10 ♗e5? ♗xe5 11 dxe5**. After **11...♕b1+ 12 ♔h2 ♕e4!** a miracle had happened. Black drew.

49

Once you understand that you are lost you can do anything.

Experienced players know that wonderful feeling when you realize your position is dead won. You don't have to find any hard moves to win. You can relax. Your shoulders sag. You may even slump in your chair.

A parallel but opposite situation occurs when you're sitting on the other side of the board. You realize that no matter what you do, you're going to lose if your opponent finds the best – or even good-enough – moves. That moment is liberating. You no longer have the burden of feeling that you absolutely must find the right move. The game is lost anyway. You are free to play anything that comes into your head.

Karpov – Anand
Dos Hermanas 1997

Black to play

Black, who had been hanging on for several moves by finding "only" replies, recalled how he suddenly felt calm when he played **1...♞e3!?**. "Once you understand you are lost, it is easy," he wrote. "You can do anything."

The knight move worked magic. White didn't appreciate how easily winning 2 fxe3! and 2...♛g6 3 ♖ad1! would be.

Instead, after he played **2 ♞ce5?!** ♞c2! 3 ♞c6? ♞xa1 his winning chances had evaporated. A draw was agreed ten moves later.

"Once you've accepted that your position is lost, you should be in a position of psychological strength," Webb observed. "Don't worry if you can't see a good continuation. You know in your heart there isn't one," he added. Your only hope is that your opponent will make a mistake, so give him a chance to do so.

50
It is easier to defend *successfully*
than to attack *successfully*.

What Larry Evans meant by this is that the defender's basic task is to meet threats. If he can succeed in that, the inherent balance in most chess positions may be enough for him to draw.

Success in attack requires more effort, C.H. O'D. Alexander said. The attacker is under greater strain because "he is taking the positive step of creating tension" and trying to overcome the balance. This is why the attacker often gets rewarded with more exclamation points than his opponent – and loses.

Kasimdzhanov – Morozevich
FIDE World Championship
2005

White to play

White took the normal Sicilianista attitude that if he didn't do something with such a nice position, Black will be at least equal following ...♕e5/...♖ac8/...b5-b4.

He found a nice idea – **1 ♘d5! ♗xd5 2 exd5**, based on 2...♖xc2 3 ♗d3 ♖-moves 4 ♖xf6! and 5 ♖f1 with a terrific attack.

He needed more good moves after **2...♖cc8** and found them in **3 ♖xf6! gxf6 4 ♗d3 ♖e8 5 ♕h4! ♔f8 6 ♖f1**.

But that wasn't enough. After **6...♕xd5 7 ♕h6+?** – instead of 7 ♕xf6! with good chances – White's attack was dying (**7...♔e7 8 ♕xf6+ ♔d7**). He eventually lost when he overreached. And finally...

51
Resignation never saved a single game.

Another Tartakowerism, also rendered as "Nobody ever won a game by resigning." How to win a won game is an art but how to lose a drawable game is simple: Give up.

Carlsen – Topalov
Morelia 2007

Black to play

Black felt he couldn't stop the threat of ♕h7+ followed by ♕h8+ and ♕xg7+ so he stopped the clocks.

However, **1...♕d5+!** would have made the queen available for defense – **2...e5 3 ♕h7+ ♔f8 4 ♕h8+ ♕g8 5 ♘h7+ ♔f7**.

The good defender plays out his lost positions until he is certain they are beyond redemption. Giving up before that point is worse than the loss of a half point. It's embarrassing.

CHAPTER FOUR: ENDGAME

52

It is a well-known phenomenon that the same amateur who can conduct the middlegame quite credibly is usually perfectly helpless in the endgame.

Every aspiring youngster learns the sad truth of Aron Nimzovich's statement when he starts getting into favorable endings that don't win themselves. Before then, which is usually before the youngster reaches about 1600 strength, he can get by with rudimentary endgame knowledge, such as how to win with an extra piece or what the opposition is. He doesn't need to know the other 99 percent of endgame lore – such as how to win with an extra pawn or how to draw a pawn down – because the vast majority of his games are decided in the middlegame. But once he gets stronger, the holes in his knowledge begin to gape.

Sveshnikov – Keres
Moscow 1973

Black to play

Black is a pawn down and both of his bishops are attacked. He might have tried 1...♗xb2 and then 2 ♘xg4 ♗xa1 3 ♖xa1, leaving an imbalance of rook versus bishop and knight.

Computers estimate White's advantage then is about +2. He would have excellent attacking chances after 3...♖a6 4 c3 followed by ♗d4 and f4-f5-f6.

White, a future GM, was hardly a "perfectly helpless" amateur. But Black counted on his not being able to win what he called an "easily won" ending after **1...♛xe5!** and then **2 fxe5 ♖xf2 3 ♗xf2 ♗xb2 4 ♖ae1 ♗f5 5 ♗c5 g6**.

It's another +2 advantage for White. But he lacks the kind of obvious plan he would have had in the 1...♗xb2 middlegame.

It takes quite a different set of skills to win this kind of position and this was evident after **6 e6?** (instead of 6 h3 ♗xe5 7 g4 ♗d7 8 ♖xe4). After other minor White errors, Black drew.

White to play

Students are always being told that the endgame should take primacy over all the other aspects of the game. "If you want to win at chess, begin with the endings," wrote Irving Chernev. After all, what good does it do to amass a winning advantage as White did in the last example if you can't convert it to victory?

But the question can be turned around. What good does it do to be a competent endgame player if you can't get past move 25 because your opening knowledge is poor or your middlegame skills are woeful? The endgame is important but certainly not more important than the other phases of a game.

53

The endgame arrives when you can forget about king safety.

Experience teaches us that endgame thinking is different from middlegame thinking. How? The most important change is we can stop thinking about mate and perpetual check and think about matters like pawn promotion and zugzwang. The precise moment when that happens has never been clear. Cecil Purdy's formula – when neither side has the equivalent of queen plus pawn – is too conservative. Queen-plus-minor piece is more accurate. Anything more is a late middlegame:

Karpov – Yusupov
Candidates match 1989

White to play

They call this a "heavy piece endgame." But that's misleading. If it were truly an ending, Black would be winning because the b4-pawn can't be held. But this remains a middlegame because king safety is a major issue, as **1 ♖c1!** showed.

White prepares to attack the b-pawn with ♖c6. But his main threats are directed at the Black king. They include ♖c8 and ♕f8+, as well as ♖c6 and h4-h5. The position is remarkably tactical because White's first rank also becomes vulnerable to a mating attack once his rook advances on the c-file

After **1...♖xb4 2 ♖c6** White threatened ♕f6+ and mate. Black did have a defense after **2...♔h7 3 h5!** but it had nothing to do with the usual endgame skills. He drew by perpetual check, **3...♖b1+ 4 ♔h2 ♖h1+!** (5 ♔xh1 ♕f1+ 6 ♔h2 ♕xf2+).

54

Some endings are played with calculation, some with logic and some are just played.

Dimitry Jakovenko, the rare young grandmaster who *likes* to play endgames, divided them into these categories. Knowing which type of endgame you've landed in will help organize your thoughts:

First, there are "calculable" endgames, such as queen endings or minor piece endings with few pawns. Many, if not most, candidate moves in them can be calculated to a definite result. You can expect that a move leads to a forced win or draw, not merely to "good chances."

In "logical" endings, there are more pieces to contend with. You cannot calculate more than a few moves into the future, Jakovenko said. What counts more is finding the best placement for your pieces and, hopefully, a plan. The example illustrating #55 fits this category.

In the third category, "playing" endings, errors are the main feature. These endings are so complex that the game's outcome depends on who is most successful in avoiding mistakes, Jakovenko wrote in *64* (January 2005). For example:

Short – I.Sokolov
Sarajevo 2007

Black to play

Black began a queening race with **1...b5?** but White's pawns are already several steps ahead. Analysis showed that 1...♘e3+! and

2 ♗xe3 ♖xe3 would reach a drawn rook ending.

White stopped that idea with the natural **2 ♔f2?**. But 2 ♗g7+! is right since 2...♔f7 3 ♗b2+ ♔g8 4 ♖h8+ gets to a won minor piece ending. And 2...♔g5 3 h3 and 4 ♖h5+/5 f6 would lose faster.

After Black played **2...a4** White missed an easier win when he replied **3 bxa4?** (3 ♗g7+!) and then **3...bxa4 4 h4?** (4 ♗g7+!). Black missed drawing chances with **4...♔e5?** (4...♖g8 5 ♔f3 a3!).

In the end White won with **5 ♔f3! ♔d4 6 f6! ♘xf6 7 ♗g7 ♖f8!? 8 g5 a3 9 ♖h8! Resigns**.

55
The basic rule of endings is not to hurry.

Masters praise speed in endgames. But they hate haste. And they leave it to non-masters to figure out the difference.

Jose Capablanca's first rule of endings was "Time increases in importance in endings." He cited pawn promotion races as examples. The first player to queen almost always has an advantage, often a decisive one.

But one of the tenets of the Soviet school was #55, from master Sergei Belavenets. Soviet teachers took it very seriously. They advised their students to repeat the position when possible. If a student could advance a pawn two squares, he should consider pushing it one square now and then going further later on, they said. *64* magazine called the following "a textbook example of 'Don't hurry!'"

P. Nikolic – Short
Moscow 1994

White to play

White might be tempted to go after the kingside pawns with 1 ♖g3?! g5 2 h4? so that 2...gxh4 3 ♖xg7+. But instead 2...♖h8! 3 hxg5? ♖xb3! 4 axb3 ♖h1+ would turn the tables.

Or he could try a forcing line to liquidate the queenside, 1 ♘c5+ ♔d8 2 ♘a4 ♖b4 3 ♖xc6. But he'd end up in a doubtful rook ending after 3...♖xa4 4 ♖xc7 ♖xa2 5 ♖c8+ ♔d7 6 ♖1c7+ ♔d6 7 ♖xe8 ♔xc7 8 ♖e7+ ♔d6 9 ♖xg7 g5.

Instead, White took his time. He got his house in order first, **1 h4! ♖h8 2 g3** and then **2...♘d5 3 ♖3c2 ♖e8 4 ♘c5+ ♔d8 5 a3!**.

Nothing seems to have changed. But it has. Black now lacks access to b4 and White's kingside is secure. White was able to liquidate into a better rook endgame: **5...a5 6 ♘a4! ♖b3 7 ♖xc6 ♖xa3 8 ♖6c5 ♔e7 9 ♖xd5 ♖xa4 10 ♖c7+ ♔e6 11 ♖dd7 ♔f5 12 ♖c5+ ♔e4 13 ♖xg7 ♔xd4 14 ♖c1 ♖f8 15 ♖xg6** and wins.

56
Imagination is of little value in an endgame.

As much as we talk of endgame artistry, Evgeny Znosko-Borovsky was accurate when he wrote #56 in *How to Play the Chess Endings*. In the endgame, "the artist must give way to the artisan, who is sure of his craft," he said. Great endgame play is not the result of inspiration and strokes of genius. Rather it is applying learned technique and methodically calculating somewhat obvious candidates. And yes, it can be boring.

Fischer – Spassky
Match 1992

White to play

White found the right idea with **1 d4!** since 1...exd4+ 2 ♕xd4+ forces a won pawn ending. Black replied **1...♔h7** to get his king away from fatal cross-checks like that.

White followed with a move of inspiration and intuition, 2 d5 –

which any computer will tell you is a blunder. After the greedy 2 dxc5! White would have won without much difficulty.

He had a chance to redeem himself after **2 d5?? ♕f6+ 3 ♔c2 ♕d6 4 ♕g5 ♔h8 5 ♔d2 ♕b6** – if he tried 6 ♕f4! and advanced his king even at the cost of the c-pawn. But that's less a matter of imagination than of applying a principle that the player with the extra pawn in a queen endgame usually has to activate his king. Instead White played **6 ♕e5+?** and his king was still sitting uselessly on the third rank when a draw was agreed.

Extra material (2 dxc5!) decides almost all endgames. But there is an important caveat:

57

An extra pawn wins only if there are pawns on both wings.

The vast majority of endgames are won because of a pawn's promotion or its threat to promote. Grandmasters seem to win extra-pawn endings on a regular basis. But this is usually because their opponent has to divide his forces and defend on two wings. When all the pawns are on one side of the board, winning chances plummet.

Grischuk – Carlsen
Biel 2007

White to play

White forced the win of a pawn with **1 a4**. But that wasn't enough because of **1...b6!**.

For example, 2 ♖xa7 ♖b2 3 ♖b7 ♖xb3 4 a5 looks logical. But after 4...b5 5 a6 ♖a3 6 a7 f6 Black will push his b-pawn until White has to exchange it for the a-pawn. The result would be a dead draw.

Better is **2 ♖xf7! ♖b2 3 ♖xa7 ♖xb3 4 ♔h2**. But **4...b5! 5 axb5 ♖xb5** again liquidates the queenside. This time White has a 3-2 pawn edge on the kingside. But with just minor care Black can prevent him from creating a significant passed pawn.

The best known version of this rule comes from Reuben Fine in *Basic Chess Endings*, "If you are one pawn ahead, in 99 cases out of 100 the game is drawn if there are pawns on only one side of the board."

This doesn't mean it's a dead draw, of course. The example that accompanies #277 shows how even Garry Kasparov could lose the inferior side of such an ending. But it's a draw with best play.

58

Before even beginning to think of making a passed pawn, get all your pieces into as good positions as possible.

This was one of Cecil Purdy's endgame rules, from *Guide to Good Chess*, and it follows the common sense of maximizing the power of your pieces before taking decisive action.

The decisive action of endings is promotion of a pawn. But inexperienced players mistakenly think this means they should start creating a passed pawn as soon as the queens are traded. Only after they've lost a few of those pawns – by pushing them too far – do they learn to take their time.

Rukavina – Karpov
Leningrad 1973

Black to play

Queens have just been exchanged and Black enjoys a healthy extra pawn. But he didn't try to use it for more than 20 moves. First, he got all of his pieces to optimal squares: **1...♘c4 2 ♗c1 ♖ac8 3 ♖ab1 ♖c5 4 ♔f1 ♔f8 5 ♔e2 ♔e7 6 ♖5b3 ♔d7 7 a4 ♔c7 8 ♗f4 ♔b7**.

The tournament book explained that Black is following the sacred

rule of "not to hurry and to force events only when everything is arranged in the best manner."

Once Black's king protected his b-pawn, his pieces were freed for **9 ♗e3 ♖5c6 10 ♗d4 f6 11 ♖d1 ♖d8 12 f4 d5**. "It's time!" said the tournament book.

Black's king and rooks were repositioned in the next phase, **13 ♗f2 ♖cd6 14 ♗c5 ♖c6 15 ♗f2 ♖dd6 16 exd5 ♖xd5!**.

Black wanted to trade a pair of rooks because his remaining rook will be the more active one. The rest was: **17 ♖xd5 exd5 18 ♖b5 ♖e6+ 19 ♔d3 ♔c6 20 g3 ♖e7! 21 ♖b1 ♖b7 22 ♖b5 ♘d6 23 ♖b2**.

Only now did Black use his material advantage, **23...b5! 24 axb5+ ♖xb5**. But thanks to the preparation the a-pawn can't be stopped. White played **25 ♖e2** and **resigned**.

59
Strongest first.

In the opening, pieces are typically introduced in reverse order of strength. A pawn usually moves first, then another pawn or a knight. A bishop comes out, and is joined some time later by the heavy pieces.

Heavy pieces are not developed earlier because they have no files to control and would become targets of minor pieces. But in the ending, these factors don't apply. The order is usually reversed: Strongest first. Rooks should seize open files. Then come the minor pieces.

Seirawan – Korchnoi
Monaco 1993

White to play

A novice whose head has been filled with scary Nimzovich stories about bad bishops and centralized knights might think Black is better. In fact he is much worse after **1 ♖fb1!**.

He must choose between allowing 2 ♖b7 or 1...♖ab8 2 ♘e5.

He decided that he could neutralize a rook on the seventh by offering trades, so there followed **1...f6 2 ♖b7! ♗d8 3 ♖e1 ♖c7! 4 ♖xc7 ♘xc7 5 ♗f4!**.

Black missed his chance to sacrifice a pawn to activate his pieces with 5...♖b8 6 ♗xc7 ♗xc7 7 ♖xe6 ♔f7 or 6 ♖xe6 ♔f7 7 ♖e1 ♖b4.

After **5...♔f7?** Black was squeezed, 6 ♖b1 ♔e8 7 ♘d2! ♘d5 8 ♗d6 ♗a5 9 ♘c4 ♗b4 10 a5 ♖d8 11 a6. He cannot block the b-file forever because of ♘e3xd5. Black tried **11...♗c3** and **resigned** after **12 ♖b7! ♗xd4 13 ♖xa7 f5 14 ♖b7**.

Note that there was one White piece that didn't take part in the final stage. It doesn't have a specific place in the "strongest first" hierarchy, but:

60
The king is a strong piece. Use it!

These are Reuben Fine's words but the thought is much older. "Your king is a most useful piece, and should actively be brought into play" towards the end of the game, J. H. Sarratt wrote two centuries ago. Useful indeed, strong yes. But how strong?

Von der Lasa estimated that a king was stronger than a minor piece in the endgame. Steinitz said this was also true in the middlegame. "The action of a king and one defended pawn is about equal to a rook," he wrote in *The Modern Chess Instructor*. Alexey Suetin, in *Chessplayer's Laboratory*, said the king was worth "five units," the same as a rook.

We usually talk of "units" in terms of a piece's exchange value. A king cannot be exchanged, of course. But what Suetin et al were emphasizing was its under-appreciated power.

Kik – Kaidanov
Norilsk 1987

Black to play

White might appear to be better because he can attack the b4 and a6

pawns. But what decides the game – in fact, what created a mating attack – is the Black king: **1...♔e7 2 ♖a4 ♖hb8 3 ♗c4 ♔f6 4 ♔f1 ♖a7 5 ♖e1 ♗h6 6 ♔e2 ♔e5!**.

White had few useful moves and passed, **7 ♔f1 ♔f4 8 ♔e2**. But Black made progress with **8...♖e7!**, threatening ...d5 and ...f5.

Then came **9 ♔f1 ♔xf3 10 ♗xa6 d5 11 exd5 ♖xe1+ 12 ♔xe1 ♖e8+ 13 ♔f1 ♖e2!**. **White resigned** after **14 ♖a1 ♖xf2+ 15 ♔g1 ♖g2+ 16 ♔h1 ♗e3** in view of ...♔g3 and ...♖h2 mate.

61

Pawn endings are to chess what putting is to golf.

The value of Cecil Purdy's parallel lies in reminding us of the finality of pawn endings. It's too late then to make up for previous sins.

Earlier, you can. You can remedy your opening mistakes in the middlegame. You can make up for middlegame errors in the endgame. But as Pal Benko said, "In the endgame, there is no later." And since there are no later endgames than pawn endings – barring a promotion – it is essential to understand the principles that govern them. That means triangulation, opposition and the infamous "square."

Kasparov – Anand
Amsterdam 1996

White to play

Knowing about the square saved White from a potentially difficult technical task.

He played **1 ♖xe7+!**.

Black resigned because he could see that White's king is within range of his pawns after **1...♖xe7 2 ♛xe7+ ♛xe7 3 ♗xe7 ♚xe7 4 ♔f1!**. But his king can't stop White's pawns (**4...♚f7 5 h5 ♚g7 6 g4 ♚h6 7 f4** and Black soon runs out of moves).

62

Kings fight kings with their shoulders.

Yuri Averbakh described what he called the king "shoulder-block" in *Shakhmaty v SSSR*: "The maneuver of a king who advances to his goal while simultaneously stopping the king of the opponent...is universal. It is used in attack and in defense." He was talking, of course, about the closest form of opposition. Kings are the only pieces that cannot come into direct contact with one another and, like hockey players, they can use their shoulders to keep the adversary at a safe distance.

The shoulder-block is most evident in pawn endings. Here's a case of hockey chess:

Sigfusson – J. Polgar
Reykjavik 1988

Black to play

Black is the favorite in a queening race but after 1...♔c4 2 ♔xg4 d5

3 ♔f3! and 3...♔c3 4 ♔e2 d4? 5 ♔d1! the win is gone.

Instead, Black must shoulder the enemy king to a square that either blocks its own pawn or allows promotion with check. Black did that with 1...♔d4! 2 ♔xg4 ♔e4! and 3 ♔h3 ♔f3! 4 g4 ♔f4 5 ♔h4 d5 6 g5.

White's fate was sealed by 6...♔f5! and then 7 ♔h5 d4 8 g6 d3 9 g7 d2 10 g8(♕) d1(♕)+ 11 ♔h6 ♕h1+ 12 ♔g7 ♕g2+ 13 ♔f8 ♕xg8+ 14 ♔xg8 ♔e6 15 ♔f8 ♔d5.

63

Geometrical theorems are not valid on the chessboard.

Evgeny Znosko-Borovsky was referring in #63 to what Pythagoras had to say about right triangles. We see those triangles on the board, such as the one bordered by a1, a4 and d4. Our eyes tell us the hypotenuse (a1-d4) is longer than the other sides. But the way the chess pieces see it, all three sides have the same length, four squares.

What this means in practice is: "A diagonal movement is equivalent to the same number of moves horizontally or vertically" (Eduard Gufeld). The most famous illustration of this is the K+P-vs.-K+P study composed by Richard Reti. Its theme occurs regularly in real life.

In the following diagram, our eyes tell us Black's king can easily stop and capture the White pawn. They also tell us White's king cannot capture the Black pawn. And they add that if White manages to take the knight, he is too far away to stop the h-pawn's advance. But our eyes are deceiving us:

Lugovoi – Skachkov
St. Petersburg 1997

White to play

White doesn't seem capable of defending his pawn or of capturing Black's. However, 1 ♔g6 ♔c4 2 ♔xf7! performs geometric magic.

Black can't keep his pawn after 2...♔xd4 3 ♔g6. Nor can he win after 2...h5 3 ♔e6!. White will either promote after 4 d5 or catch the Black pawn with 4 ♔f5.

64

It is always advantageous to have the opposition in pawn endings.

The right to move is always a good thing – except in endings. Then a player can lose because of zugzwang, or as some linguistically-challenged players call it, "Volkswagen."

The simplest form of imposing zugzwang is having the opposition in pawn endings. With #64, Edmar Mednis was advising readers (in *Practical Endgame Lessons*) to grab the opposition when it's available.

Chiburdanidze – W.Watson
Brussels 1987

White to play

Defining the opposition in simple terms is impossible. Composer Andre Cheron's version is as good as it gets: "The kings are in opposition only when the rectangle formed by the files and the ranks that they occupy has all its corners of the same color."

If you can visualize the rectangle here (f2-f6-d6-d2) you'll realize that whoever has to move has lost the opposition. But White can regain it with a non-king move, 1 g4!.

Then after 1...♔e6 2 ♔e2! ♔e5 3 ♔e3! Black must lose due to Volkswagen (3...♔d5 4 ♔f4 ♔e6 5 ♔e4! ♔f6 6 ♔d5 ♔e7 7 ♔e5! ♔f7 8 ♔f5 ♔g7 9 ♔e6 ♔g6 10 h5+! ♔g5 11 ♔f7 ♔xg4 12 ♔g6).

But this didn't happen. White allowed Black to keep the opposition with **1 ♔f3??** and then **1...♔e7! 2 ♔f4 ♔e6! 3 g4 ♔f6!**.

White to play

White set a trap with **4 ♔f3!?**. According to #64 Black should maintain the opposition – 4...♔f7! would draw.

But he played **4...♔e7??** after which **5 ♔e3 ♔f7 6 ♔d4!** transposed into the lost zugzwang line (**6...♔f6 7 ♔d5 ♔e7 8 ♔e5!** and so on).

65
Pawn queening races can be counted, not calculated.

Remember the warning against "calculation without evaluation" back in #21? That came with the exception of endgames. You don't have to evaluate the result of a promotion race. If one player queens and the other doesn't, the first player usually wins.

Cecil Purdy reduced it to arithmetic: "Never calculate from move to move in the ordinary way. Simply count up the moves the first queener will queen in, and then see how far the opponent's queening pawn will get in the same number of moves."

Fritz 3/Pentium – Hertneck
Munich 1994

White to play

We can see that it will take Black four pawn moves to promote on c1. That means White, who moves first, can save the game if he can promote in no more than five moves.

However, the computer inexplicably played 1 fxg6??. That costs a sixth move and lost following 1...c4 2 h4 c3 3 h5 c2 4 h6 c1(♕).

The arithmetic method would show that **1 h4! c4 2 h5!** draws (2...gxh5 3 g5! or 2...c3 3 h6!). And you thought computers are good at arithmetic.

66
The simplest and safest rule is always advance the first unopposed pawn.

Every "healthy" pawn majority must be able to create a passed pawn, Aron Nimzovich said in *My System*. One pawn will stand out as the nominee for promotion and the others will serve as supporters.

The nominee, according to Jose Capablanca's #66, is the pawn free of enemy obstruction. Here is his rule in action.

Tal – Djurasevic
Varna 1958

White to play

Since it's White turn it seems he should rush to get his king to the fourth rank and use its shoulders to block Black's king. But White's real advantage lies in his ability to create a passed pawn well before his opponent.

To make something of his majority White advanced his unopposed c-pawn, **1 ♔d3 ♔d6 2 c4!** and then **2...bxc4+ 3 ♔xc4**.

Black's only defense was to do the same with his unopposed e-pawn, **3...e5! 4 fxe5+ ♔xe5**.

This created two new unopposed pawns, at b2 and f7. Play went **5 b4! f5! 6 b5 axb5+ 7 ♔xb5 f4.**

Who is winning then? Black's pawn is advanced. But he is lost. The reason is:

67

A pawn majority is like a passed pawn that has to start right back from the table – from two ranks *behind* its home rank.

This insight from Purdy is worth remembering, even if the wording is a bit confusing. It points out that an advanced pawn in a majority usually needs two extra moves to become passed. This becomes clearer when we go back to where we left off:

Tal – Djurasevic
Varna 1958

White to play

White's a-pawn is only on the third rank while Black's f-pawn is on the fifth. But White's pawn is passed. Black will need to spend two tempi to create a passer. It's as if his f-pawn were "two ranks behind its home rank," per Purdy —that is, on the third rank.

There followed **1 a4 g5 2 a5 g4**. The nominees for queening are now equally advanced (3 a6? f3 4 gxf3 gxf3 and Black promotes with check).

The reason White sought this position was **3 ♔c4!**. Then on **3...f3**, his king is in the square and can stop promotion. Black's only try is 3...♔e4, seizing the opposition. But then White queens with check and wins.

68
A knight endgame is a pawn endgame.

Endgames with one pair of identical pieces have their own rules of conduct. For example, putting pawns on the right color squares is crucial to many bishop endings but doesn't mean much in any other endings. In queen endings – unlike other endings – having an extra pawn is often much less important than how far a passed pawn has advanced.

With #68 Mikhail Botvinnik pointed out the two endings that have the most in common. An outside passed pawn, zugzwang and the opposition are vital in both pawn endings and knight endings. Not only should you use the same techniques in both but you should realize that a trade of pieces in a knight ending almost always produces an equally favorable pawn ending.

Rogers – Saltaev
Hamburg 1999

White to play

For example, after **1 ♘e4! ♘xe4?** White must win because he has the outside passed pawn (**2 ♔xe4 ♔d7 3 ♔d5 f6 4 a4** etc.).

Black kept knights on but the opposition dooms him – **1...♘g4 2 h3 ♘h6 3 ♘d6 ♔d7 4 ♔d5! f6 5 a4 ♘g8 6 b5 ♘e7+ 7 ♔c5 f5** (or **7...g5 8 ♘e4 ♔e6 9 a5**).

Then **8 h4!** leads to zugzwang. For example, **8...♘g8 9 a5 ♘f6 10 b6 axb6+ 11 axb6 ♘g4 12 ♘f7**, e.g. **12...♘f2 13 ♘e5+ ♔c8 14 ♔c6!** and **15 b7+.**

69
You can't dance at two weddings at the same time.

This is one of the oldest Manhattan and Marshall Chess Club kibitzes and it explains why a piece can be fatally overworked. The piece tries to stop two passed pawns but fails because they are too far apart.

Knights and kings are frequently victimized this way. Bishops, however, can attend two weddings if they can do it on the same diagonal. This was formulated in Mark Dvoretsky's rule: "For both the stronger and the weaker side it is very important that the bishop should defend its own pawns and stop the enemy pawns 'without tearing' – that is, on one diagonal."

Black failed to appreciate Dvoretsky's rule in this notorious case:

Kramnik – Svidler
Wijk aan Zee 2004

Black to play

He resigned because he saw his bishop can't dance on both wings and therefore he must lose the a-pawn or h-pawn. For example, **1...♔c7 2 ♗e4 ♗e1 3 ♔c5! ♗b4+ 4 ♔d5 ♗e1 5 c5 ♗b4 6 c6 ♗e1 7 ♔e6 ♗d2 8 ♔f6 ♗e1 9 ♔g6 ♗h4 10 ♔xh6**.

White's king gets back to other wing, **10...♔c8 11 ♔g6 ♔c7 12 ♔f5 ♔d6 13 ♔f6!** (zugzwang) **♔c7 14 ♔e6 ♗e1 15 ♔d5 ♗d2 16 ♔c5 ♗e1 17 ♔b5** (ditto).

Then after Black protects the a-pawn with **17...♗d2**, White creates a winning g-pawn (**18 h4!**) that his king will shepherd to victory after the return trip, **18...gxh4 19 ♔c5** and so on. There's no counterplay because White's bishop can protect the c-pawn and prevent ...h1(♕) on the same diagonal, as per Dvoretsky.

All true. But resignation was a blunder. Black can draw even after he loses the a-pawn, **1...♔c7 2 ♗e4 ♔d6! 3 ♔xa5**, as long as he heeds Dvoretsky.

Black to play

He keeps his bishop on the g1-a7 diagonal, **3...♗g1 4 ♔a6 ♔c7 5 a5 ♗f2 6 ♔b5 ♔d6**. The pawns can't reach c5 or a7 safely because both squares are controlled by the dancing bishop. Draw!

The more mobile the piece, the less likely it will be embarrassed by #69. Queens and rooks rarely have a two-wedding problem. On the other hand, we saw in the example that accompanied #61 how a king can be victimized. White's king only had to deal with two connected pawns but Black's king was overburdened trying to handle four White pawns.

70

In endings with bishops of opposite color, material means nothing, position everything.

Well, maybe not "everything" and "nothing." But this overview, credited to the British/Australian player Maurice Goldstein, is one of the key principles of "B's of opps."

We saw how control of the key g1-a7 diagonal was more important than an extra pawn in the last example. With opposite colored bishops, controlling the right diagonals or even a single square can be worth two or more pawns.

Skachkov – Shcherbakov
Ekaterinburg 1997

White to play

White is a pawn down but saw that he could maintain a kingside blockade. What he didn't see is that his bishop cannot defend both the b-pawn and f-pawn forever. He found that out after **1 ♔h3?? ♗e7!** because Black threatens 2...♔c5 and 3...a4! 4 bxa4 ♔xc4.

White defended with **2 ♗d3 ♔c5 3 ♗e4 ♔b5 4 ♔g2 ♔b4 5 ♗d5** but Black penetrated with his king, **5...♔c3 6 ♔h3 ♔d4 7 ♗c6 ♔e3.**

Then **8 ♔g2** lost to **8...h3+! 9 ♔xh3 ♔f2!** and queens, or **9 ♔g1 h2+ 10 ♔g2 h1(♕)+! 11 ♔xh1 ♔f2.**

A few moves before the end White realized what he missed. "Oh, why didn't I play e7?" he said to himself. What he meant was that back at the diagram he could have drawn with **1 e7!**.

White didn't need the e-pawn. But his bishop needed the light square that the pawn occupied, e.g. **1...♗xe7 2 ♗g8** (pass) **♔e5 3 ♗f7 ♔d4 4 ♗g8 ♔e3 5 ♗e6!** with a cold draw.

71

A rook on the seventh is worth a pawn.

This maxim applies best to the early endgame, typically around moves 30 to 45, when the kings are still sitting on their first rank. Max Euwe said a player with a rook on the seventh enjoyed good drawing chances because the enemy king is confined and there are opportunities for perpetual check.

But #71 is Reuben Fine's maxim and he didn't limit it to situations when the enemy king is confined. It is the location of enemy pawns, on their original squares, that makes the maxim work.

Tzerimiadanos – Kuzmin
Rethymnon 2003

White to play

Here 1 ♖d1 ♖hc8 allows a Black rook to reach the seventh or eighth rank (2 ♔f1 ♖c1 3 ♖ed2? ♖xd1+ 4 ♖xd1 ♖c2).

The right way is **1 ♖ae1!** so that 1...♖xd4 2 ♖e7+ ♔d6 3 ♖xb7 wins a second pawn.

The game went **1...♖f8 2 g3 ♖xd4 3 ♖e7+ ♔c8**. Black has regained his pawn. But White doubled on the seventh and that's worth much more than a pawn: **4 ♖c1+ ♔b8 5 ♖cc7 ♖b4 6 b3 a5 7 h4**.

Seeing that White could liquidate with ♖xf7 whenever he wanted,

Black also tried to use Fine's maxim with **7...♖d8!**. The idea is 8 ♖xf7? ♖d2! and ...♖xa2/...♖xb3.

But **8 ♖c5! b6 9 ♖cc7!** gave White's doubled rooks complete control of the seventh.

Black to play

Getting his own rook to the seventh, **9...♖d2**, is not enough and **Black resigned** after **10 ♖b7+ ♔c8 11 ♖ec7+! ♔d8 12 ♖xf7 ♔c8 13 ♖fc7+**.

Note the breakdown of White moves since the first diagram: three by pawns, ten by rooks. All the rook moves, save 1 ♖ae1, were attacking moves. This follows another maxim:

72

Nothing is more disastrous in a rook endgame than a passive attitude.

This was Rudolf Spielmann's warning in his book on rook endings. "The spirit of attack dominates in these endings," he added.

This code of conduct is exclusive to rook endings. In bishop endgames, maneuvering and quiet play is often best. In knight endgames finding the right square, particularly one that blockades pawns, is crucial. But rooks are built to attack enemy pawns and push friendly ones.

Vitiugov – Dreev
Moscow 2007

Black to play

This bears a resemblance to a textbook endgame in which White,

Salo Flohr, punished passive defense. But here Black activated his rook, **1...c5! 2 ♖xa6 ♖b7!**.

The threat of 3...♖xb2 led to **3 b3 c4! 4 bxc4 dxc4** and a new threat, ...♖c7 and ...c3-c2.

White had to acquiesce to a trade of passed pawns, **5 g4 ♖c7 6 ♖d6 c3 7 ♖d1 ♖a7!** (active rook!) **8 ♖c1 ♖xa2 9 ♖xc3 ♖a5**, to trade pawns with 10...h5 11 gxh5 ♖xh5!. He conceded a draw soon after **10 f4 ♖a2!**. As Reti wrote, "In the rook endgame one should always prefer attack than to play defense."

Whenever you find yourself considering a "pass" move in a rook endgame you should ask yourself why. Flohr found himself making a purely defensive move in a rook ending in the 1951 Soviet Championship and later wrote in the tournament book, "It's hard to believe that the man who made such a weak move has played chess for 30 years. Beginners learn that a rook is never placed in a passive position."

73

A rook belongs behind a passed pawn.

Siegbert Tarrasch's best-known endgame rule applies to both a player's own passed pawn and to his opponent's. When a pawn is far advanced both players may try to get behind it.

Afek – Timman
Amsterdam 2002

White to play

White's only hope is to keep his rook on the a-file until he needs to check the king away from promoting it. It's fatal to allow Black to get his rook behind the pawn, as in 1 ♔xg4? ♖d4+! and 2...♖a4.

There followed **1 ♖b8+! ♔c2 2 ♖a8! ♔b3 3 ♖b8+ ♔c4! 4 ♖c8+**

♔b5!. Black threatens to get behind the pawn (5 ♖b8+ ♔a6 6 ♖a8+ ♖a7! and wins).

But even getting behind the pawn again, **5 ♖a8!**, isn't enough. Black used his rook as a shield in another way, **5...♖d2 6 f4 gxf3 7 ♔xf3 ♔c4 8 ♔e3 ♖h2 9 ♖a7 ♔c3** (elbow!). **White resigned** because the enemy king can reach b1 where it can meet ♖b8+ with ...♖b2.

Tarrasch joked about the way his rule was taken so religiously. When an amateur complained that he followed it to his regret, Tarrasch ran his letter in his newspaper column and said he wanted to "amplify it."

"Always put the rook behind the pawn," he wrote, "except when it is incorrect to do so."

74
Repetition rules endgames.

This follows another recommendation of Sergei Belavenets and is consistent with his #55. Among the virtues of repeating a position, when you have the advantage, is it gains clock time and plays mind games. The opponent is bound to wonder if he should break the repetition by playing something different. Usually, he does so at peril.

Masters repeat positions even when they seem to be reaching the decisive stage. In the following example Black set a repetition trap just as he was about to make a new queen. White knew enough to suspect that there was more to the repeating of moves than appeared:

Ponomariev – Kramnik
Linares 2003

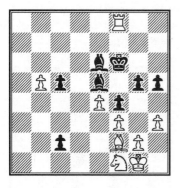

Black to play

Why is this game still going on? All Black has to do is get out of check and promote on c1, right?

Well, yes, but the Q-vs.-R ending can take quite a while to win. That's why Black tried the coy **1...♔g7 2 ♖e8 ♔f7!?.**

He wanted to see if White would fall for 3 ♖e7+? ♔xe7 4 ♗xc5+ ♔-moves 5 ♗a3, which stops promotion. But this would lose outright to 4...♗d6!.

White saw it and played **3 ♖f8+!.** But the repetition didn't cost Black anything and he proceeded to win the long way – **3...♔g6 4 ♖e8 ♗c4! 5 ♖xe5 c1(♕)** etc.

75

All endings are drawn but some of them are more drawn than others.

There are some endings that are drawable, provided the defender finds "only" moves. There are others that "more drawn" because they require only routine defense.

In addition, there are some drawable endgames that allow the player with an edge various ways to try to win. There are others that are "more drawn" because there is only one winning idea and once it is thwarted, the handshake comes swiftly.

Jonathan Speelman's ironic #75, in *New In Chess* (3/1995), recalls Tarrasch's more sweeping claim that "rook and pawn endings are never won." (A minority credits a version of this to Tartakower.) Case in point:

Kasparov – Kramnik
New York 1994

Black to play

After **1...f6** White had to decide whether to go into a rook ending. His pawns would advance faster that way.

But keeping minor pieces on enables White to combat Black's queenside pawns better. After 2 ♗e3! ♖xe7 3 h4 he would have won slowly but surely.

Instead, play went **2 ♗xf6?** and then **2...♔c7! 3 ♖e6 ♘xf6 4 ♖xf6 ♖xe7 5 ♔f1**. White still seems to be

winning in view of 5...c3 6 bxc3 bxc3 and now 7 ♖f3 c2 8 ♖c3.

But **5...♖e4!** is the kind of annoying move that occurs so often in rook endings.

White to play

Black threatens to win (6 h4?? c3! 7 bxc3 bxc3 8 ♖f3 ♖c4 and 9...c2).

White took refuge in the pawn endgame, **6 ♖f4 ♖xf4 7 gxf4**. But **7...♔d6 8 ♔e2 a5** allowed Black to draw by creating a passed pawn (**9 a4 c3 10 bxc3 b3!**). Let's say it one more time: Don't hurry.

CHAPTER FIVE: **EVALUATION**

76

A master's strength is in the evaluation of a position.

Accurate evaluation leads to good decisions, said the early chess writers. But they allowed that other skills such as tactical sight were more important. Mikhail Botvinnik indicated otherwise with #76 (*International Computer Chess Association Journal*, August 1983 and elsewhere).

Botvinnik often blamed a bad move, made by him or an opponent, on a misreading of who had the advantage. Nothing seems to ruin a good position faster than thinking it was better than it is:

Kamsky – Karpov
FIDE World Championship 1996

White to play

Black lost time in the opening (...♚d8 and later ...♚e8) and that convinced White he had a significant edge. He doesn't. But he tried to seek candidates that would prove he did. He chose **1 ♗c2?!** because an advantage might be evident after ♕d3-h7.

But after **1...♕c3** his best option was the equal ending of 2 ♕d3 ♕xd3. Still hopeful of advantage he lost remarkably quickly: **2 ♗b3?! ♚f8 3 ♖c1 ♕f6 4 ♗c2 ♖ae8 5 ♕d3? ♗g4 6 ♗d2? ♖e2! 7 ♖xe2 ♖xe2 8 ♖f1 ♖xd2! White resigns** (10 ♕xd2 ♕f3+ 11 ♔g1 ♗h3 and mates).

77
First, look at the kings.

The No. 1 criterion is king vulnerability, David Bronstein said. "When evaluating a chess position, the first thing we shall look at is the position of the kings," he wrote in *Sorcerer's Apprentice*. That tells us whether aggressive measures have a chance against either king.

Leko – Piket
Tilburg 1996

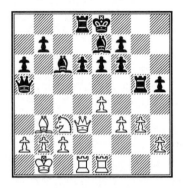

White to play

Black would be justified in wondering why he wasn't better. After all, he has the two bishops, more pawns in the center and queenside play brewing from ...b5-b4.

The reason he's worse is simple. His king is in the center and that's significant after **1 f4 ♖c5 2 ♘d5!** (or 2 ♕d4! and ♘d5, which may be better).

Had Black accepted the knight he'd be losing (2...exd5? 3 exd5 and ♕h7 or ♕f5). Black managed to draw after **2...f5! 3 exf5 ♖xd5 4 ♗xd5 ♗xd5 5 c4 ♗xc4 6 ♕xc4 ♕xf5+** because his king was no longer Topic A.

Does everyone agree with Bronstein? No. "First we count material," Kasparov wrote in *How Life Imitates Chess*. "The first thing to look at is material," Jose Capablanca said in his *Primer*. But Bronstein tends to have more supporters.

After king vulnerability and material, the next most important evaluation factors are: Piece activity (or development) followed by space, and then pawn structure. There is no consensus on their proper order. A Karpov will stress lasting features such as pawn structure while a Kasparov will focus more on the dynamic elements.

78
Evaluate without calculating.

Soviet trainers urged students to size up a position without considering whose turn it is to move. They felt that if students were told it's White's move they will look for tactics as if it were a "play and win" exercise. As a result, they'll be biased in White's favor and overvalue dynamic features at the expense of the static ones.

By appraising the position first, a player is freed of the tyranny of "play and win" thinking. "Suspending the game in time is a useful way to teach students how to evaluate qualitative factors such as (pawn) structure and space," Kasparov wrote in *How Life Imitates Chess*. "We do this by showing a chess position without revealing whose move it is."

Topalov – Yusupov
Novgorod 1995

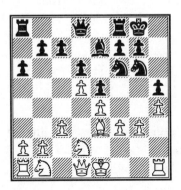

A novice might like Black's superior development and try to prove he's better by analyzing 1...c6. But this is an illusion. White is distinctly superior regardless of whose move it is, thanks to the pawn structure, his ability to expand on either wing and the absence of light squared bishops.

It was actually White's move and **1 c4** prepared a strong plan of ♘c3, b2-b4, ♘b3 and c4-c5. Black thwarted that with **1...c5** but his inferiority was clear after **2 ♘c3 ♕d7 3 a4 a5 4 ♕e2 ♔h7 5 0-0-0**

Black had no counterplay and White was able to slowly prepare a kingside breakthrough following 5...♖h8 6 ♘f1 ♔g8 7 ♗d2 ♘e8 8 ♘e3 ♘f8 9 b3 g6 10 f4 ♗f6 11 ♖df1 ♕e7 12 f5. Black resigned eight moves later.

79

Space is the most difficult element of chess strategy to understand.

Evaluation would be easy if we could reduce each of the components to mathematical equations. We try to do this with material in sayings like "A knight is worth three pawns." We attempt to quantify time with "Three tempi are worth a pawn." We guess at the value of king safety when we sacrifice a pawn to wreck an enemy castled position.

But Michael Stean's #79, in *Simple Chess*, tells us we can't properly assess a middlegame based on how many squares one player controls or how far advanced his pieces lie.

Saeed – Salov
Belfort 1983

Black to play

Siegbert Tarrasch, who wrote, "Cramped positions carry within them the germ of defeat," would have hated to play Black here. Jose Capablanca, who wrote, "A cramped position is a bad position," might have been a little kinder to Black's chances because he considered piece coordination a worthwhile criterion.

The modern view is quite different: "White's position is difficult, although he controls significantly more space," Black wrote in *Shakhmaty v SSSR*. He thought he'd have good chances if he released his pent-up energy, 1...d5!? 2 cxd5 ♗xf4. But he preferred **1...♖cd8!**, to make ...d5 stronger.

White was in trouble after **2 f5 ♘e5 3 fxe6?! fxe6 4 ♗g5 ♖f8 5 ♘d4 ♖de8 6 h3 ♘h5!** and was in a tailspin following **7 ♗e2 ♘g3+ 8 ♔g1 ♗d8! 9 ♗xd8 ♕xd8** and ...♕f6.

Another explanation of #79 is that a spatial edge diminishes as pieces are traded. In the Belgrade Gambit (**1 e4 e5 2 ♘f3 ♘c6 3 ♘c3 ♘f6 4 d4 exd4 5 ♘d5**), for example, White controls much more terrain in a main line, **5...♗e7 6 ♘xd4 ♘xd5 7 exd5 ♘xd4 8 ♕xd4 0-0**.

White to play

But without a knight to plant on d4, it means little. Many players would prefer to be Black after 9...♗f6, 10...d6 and 11...♗f5 because White can become over-extended.

80

A weakness is a weakness if and when it can be attacked.

R.N. Coles credited the post-World War II generation for coming to this realization. In *Dynamic Chess* he wrote:

"What had for generations been accepted as a weakness, such as a hole or an isolated pawn, was not weak unless the opponent began to attack it. A much smaller hostile weakness which could be attacked first was in fact a greater weakness."

For example, a hole isn't a hole if it cannot be exploited.

Portisch – Kasparov
Skelleftea 1989

Black to play

There are two holes, an obvious one at h6 and a more subtle one at c4. White can occupy the first with ♗h6 or perhaps ♘e5-g4-h6+ but that won't mean much without help from other pieces.

The other hole can, however, be exploited and that's why after 1...♘xc3 the natural 2 ♕xc3? was a positional blunder. The position would have been dead even after 2 ♗xc7!. There would still be a hole at c4 but there would be no Black knight to occupy it.

The difference appeared as a tiny edge following **2 ♕xc3? ♗d6! 3 ♗xd6 ♘b5 4 ♕b3 ♘xd6 5 a4 a6 6 ♘e5 ♖e8 7 ♖fe1 ♕g5 8 h3 ♔g7 9 ♕c2 ♖e6 10 ♖ac1 ♖ae8 11 ♕b1 ♕h5 12 ♕b3 f6 13 ♘d3**.

Black's last move created another hole, at e6. But it isn't a weakness because White can't occupy it. By the time Black exploited c4 it decided the game: **13...g5 14 ♕d1 ♕g6 15 ♕c2 ♖6e7 16 ♖ed1 h5 17 ♕b1 h4 18 ♕c2 g4 19 ♘f4 ♕xc2 20 ♖xc2 g3! 21 ♖d3 ♔h6 22 ♔f1 ♔g5 23 ♘e2 ♘c4!** and wins.

#80 helps explain why backward pawns are often considered worse than doubled pawns:

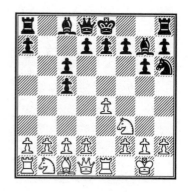

White to play

White can't attack the doubled c-pawns so it seems logical to put his pawns at d3 and c4 to make up for his lack of a light-square bishop.

But experience shows that **1 c3!** and **2 d4** is best. After 2 d4 cxd4 3 cxd4 one of the doubled pawns is gone. But after the inevitable ...d6, the remaining c6-pawn will be exposed to pressure on the half-open file.

81
Two weaknesses are more than twice as bad as one.

This is the foundation of the Principle of the Second Weakness. As Saviolly Tartakower wrote in *500 Master Games of Chess*: "Although the force of resistance, inherent in any inert mass, may make it possible to hold a slightly weakened king's field, such is not the case when two or more weaknesses occur in the position."

Tartakower was thinking about two or more open lines leading to the king. But the principle is more familiar when applied to positional weaknesses. Unless a defender's position is very bad, he can safeguard one weakness by throwing his pieces around it. But if there are two weaknesses, simultaneously under pressure, the defense can be stretched beyond its limits.

Bu Xiangzhi – J. Polgar
Biel 2007

Black to play

Black's weak d-pawn isn't enough to lose. Neither is the b-pawn. But together they make it likely that routine defense will fail.

That was a warning to Black to look for a tactical escape. There is one – **1...♗xf2+!** so that 2 ♔xf2 ♕c5+ 3 ♔f1? ♘xd2+ or 3 e3 ♘xd2!.

Instead, Black tried to cover both weaknesses at once, **1...♗e6?** **2 ♗e1! b5**. But after **3 axb6 ♘xb6 4 ♕a2!** at least one pawn had to fall. Defending the a-pawn, like 4...♖a8 or 4...♗c8, would lose the d-pawn.

The game went **4...♗b4 5 ♗xb4 ♕xb4 6 ♕xa6** – and to make matters worse, Black's defense had been stretched so thin that the second pawn fell soon after, **6...♘c4 7 ♘xd5**.

82
Tempi should not be counted but weighed.

Developing moves are not of equal value. Some are lightweight while others are worth their weight in gold. Therefore, Tartakower concluded in # 82, merely counting up the extra moves one player has gained is bound to skew the evaluation.

White viewed the next diagram as very good for him because he considered himself two tempi ahead of a normal position in the same opening. But it wasn't the number that was significant. It was that these extra moves were highly useful here.

Gelfand – Shirov
Istanbul 2000

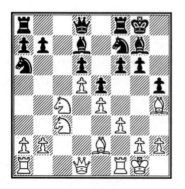

White to play

Where are the extra tempi? They're hard to see unless you know that this King's Indian pawn structure usually comes about after

White invests a tempo in pushing the c-pawn to c5 and then exchanges on d6.

Here it was Black who spent a tempo on ...c6 and then exchanged on d5. That's a net gain of two tempi for White. It meant he could carry out a very good maneuver (♘f3-d2-c4) for free.

He can't pick off the d-pawn yet. But he can put the entire queenside under pressure after **1 a4** followed by ♘b5, ♗f2 and ♕b3-a3. He was winning soon after **1...♕b8 2 ♘b5! ♖c8 3 ♗f2 ♗h6 4 ♕b3 ♘c5 5 ♕a3**, intending 6 b4 or 6 ♘bxd6.

83

Great positional advantages such as structural ones increase in significance as the game goes on.

We know material appreciates in value as the endgame approaches. But so do other tangible assets, Alex Yermolinsky concluded in *The Road to Chess Improvement*. Their value may be masked during the middlegame by the large number of pieces. Textbooks often illustrate the two bishops advantage by giving a middlegame example in which the bishops deliver mate or win a decisive amount of material. But more often, they decide games by picking off distant pawns in the endgame when the pawns' defenders have been traded off.

The practical application of #83 is that a player with the worst of it must act aggressively to break a downward spiral before it starts.

Mieses – Wolf
Karlsbad 1907

Black to play

Black's best bet was **1...♛xc4!** despite the appearance of 2 ♖c1

♛xa2 3 ♖xc7. White's rook and passed d-pawn look dangerous but Black can defend after 3...♖ad8 4 d6 ♛e6!.

Instead, he played **1...♛xd1? 2 ♖fxd1 ♗g4** in order to trade one of the White bishops. There is some logic to that. But the other White asset, his superior pawns, grew in significance after **3 c5! ♗xf3 4 gxf3 ♖ad8 5 ♖ab1**.

He created a winning outside passer with **5...b6 6 d6! cxd6 7 cxb6 axb6 8 ♗xb6**.

84

All chess units have, in the language of the stock market, two prices – the par value and the quoted one.

This is Rudolf Spielmann's often-quoted explanation, in *The Art of Sacrifice in Chess*, of what justifies giving up material. "The par value represents the absolute" worth of a piece, regardless of other factors, he said. He contrasted this with the "day to day" value, which depends on fluctuations in the position in the same way that stock shares rise and fall.

A sacrifice exploits the difference between the two. You give up par value in order to get better "day to day" value out of your remaining pieces. This will cost you dearly if you reach an endgame, where piece values tend to be absolute. But in the middlegame you profit from the soaring market.

Svidler – Ponomariev
FIDE World Championship 2001

Black to play

White is hoping to trade rooks, after say 1...♗c6 2 h3 and ♖xe8/♖e1, to reach a superior endgame. He allowed 1...♗xh2+ because after 2 ♔h1 the threat of 3 g3, trapping the bishop, would allow him to regain the pawn favorably with ♕xd5+ or ♗b3xd5+.

But Black offered an Exchange, **1...♖e4!**. It makes sense because 2 ♗xe4 fxe4 would sharply change the "day-to-day" values:

Black's "bad" light-squared bishop would become strong. White's dark-squared bishop becomes very bad once White's other B is gone. Also, White's rooks depreciate because they lack the open e-file. The clincher is that Black can safely grab the h-pawn once the attacked queen retreats and he would be much better after 3 ♕e2 ♗xh2+ 4 ♔h1 ♖f5 and ...♖h5.

White didn't take the rook immediately. But **2 g3 ♗b5! 3 ♗f4 ♗xf4 4 gxf4 ♕d6** was difficult for him and he eventually lost after **5 ♗xe4 fxe4 6 ♕g3 ♖xf4**.

Note that if a pair of rooks had previously been traded off – that is, no rooks at a1 and f8 in the diagram – then 1...♖e4 would have much less effect. Why? As Spielmann said, "The simpler the position, the more the absolute value carries weight."

85

One piece stands badly, the whole game stands badly.

This is one of Tarrasch's most famous observations. Capablanca turned it from a tool of evaluation to a guideline for action: If you can make one enemy piece bad, you make the enemy position bad.

And if you can make more than one piece bad:

Aronian – Anand
World Championship 2007

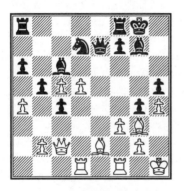

Black to play

Black can't keep his extra piece (1...♗b7 2 c6). But **1...♗e5!** is powerful in view of 2 ♗e1 g3! and ...♕xh4+ or 2 ♗xe5 ♕xh4+.

White replied 2 f4 and Black retreated 2...♗g7. Didn't Black just lose two tempi? No, he improved his game considerably by making both White bishops horrible.

White tried to free them after **3 dxc6 ♘xc5 4 ♖d5 ♘e4 5 ♗e1 ♕e6 6 ♖xh5**, with the idea of 6...♕g6? 7 f5! ♕xh5 8 ♕xe4 with survival chances.

But Black shot back **6...f5!** and the rook had joined the bishops in captivity. He picked off the rook and won easily.

The Tarrasch-Capa recipe is so appealing that it's easy to take it too far. A piece's "badness" may be irrelevant in the overall evaluation if other pieces pick up its share of the workload. Garry Kasparov cited one of his own World Championship middlegames: His White QN was stuck on a3 and doomed to capture whenever Black wanted to take it. But all the other White pieces were trained at Anatoly Karpov's kingside and they forced resignation at move 41.

86

To evaluate material imbalances, you have to cut a pawn in half.

This follows from what Tarrasch said about certain piece equations. "The difference between a rook and a minor piece is, according to my reckoning, equal to one and a half pawns," he wrote in *The Game of Chess*. "The difference between two minor pieces and a rook is exactly the same."

Other writers included fractional pawns when estimating how much material a queen is worth. But what in the world is a "half pawn"? And how do you apply this in a game?

Tarrasch's point is that two pawns would be too much compensation in his examples. If a player has two pawns and a bishop in return for a rook, he would have the advantage. If he had two pawns and a rook in return for two minor pieces he again would have the edge.

On the other hand, Tarrasch said, one pawn would be too little and would turn the advantage over to the other player. The proper balance lies somewhere in the middle – at one and a half pawns.

A good way to apply this is: Look for positional compensation worth a half pawn whenever you are considering creating an imbalance.

For example, suppose you want to sacrifice the Exchange but would only get one pawn as compensation. If you'd also receive the two bishops in the process, that might be worth the extra half pawn that makes it an equitable transaction. Here's a more subtle version:

Sutovsky – McShane
Hastings 2000

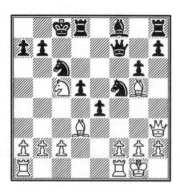

White to play

With two pieces hanging White played **1 ♘xb7 ♕xb7 2 ♗xd8**

♔xd8 **3 ♗e2**. That looks good for Black because he got two minor pieces in return for a rook and only one pawn.

But as Black evaluated the position he realized White has additional positional compensation – superior development and safer king – that might be worth at least an extra half pawn.

So, based on the evaluation that he wasn't better, he went into the complications of **3...♕xb2!? 4 ♖ab1 ♕e5** and **5...♗c5**. It was a wise decision and gave him enough play to draw.

87
The older I grow, the more I value pawns.

A player's way of evaluating a position tends to change with age. Typically, he begins to view material as more solid, while the initiative becomes more ephemeral. The initiative may evaporate after a few moves, he says to himself. But an extra pawn is an extra pawn.

Paul Keres was in his 50s when he said #87. Bobby Fischer aged even faster. By the time he was 21 he had already played the vast majority of his great sacrificial games and was becoming more of a materialist. During a game at Siegen 1970, an opponent said, "I don't know who is better Bobby but I offer a draw." Fischer refused, saying "I don't know who is better either – but I have an extra pawn."

But, as Keres and Fischer found, the inclination to value material more highly can get you into difficulties you rarely faced before:

Keres – Portisch
Bled 1961

White to play

White had cashed in a positional advantage to grab a pawn on e5. Rather than consolidate (1 ♘e3 and 2 ♘d4) he took another risk with **1 ♘cxa5!?**.

After **1...♗b8!**, however, it was time to acknowledge he had no more than equality. Instead, he tried to make certain that all endgames would be limited to two results and played **2 ♘xc6?**, based on 2...♗xc6 3 ♕e6+ and ♕xc6.

But this was too much. The third result, a loss, would have been the most likely one after **2...♗xe5 3 ♘xd8** and then 3...♗xb2! 4 ♖c2 ♖xb3 5 axb3 ♗d4+ and 6...♖xd8.

White's faith in extra pawns was justified when Black mixed up the move order with **3...♖xb3?**, expecting to transpose after 4 axb3 ♗xb2. He lost after **4 ♖xe5! ♖xb2 5 c6 ♗xc6? 6 ♘xc6 ♖8xa2 7 ♘e7+ ♔f7 8 ♖f1+ ♔e8 9 ♘xd5+ ♔d7 10 ♖h5!**.

88

Positions with a material imbalance tend to depend heavily on the initiative.

We know the initiative is a key to evaluating sacrifices. John Nunn took that further, with #88 in *Secrets of Grandmaster Chess*, to encompass all imbalances.

The initiative is the missing part of the equation in many "half-pawn" imbalances. Whether two minor pieces outplay a rook and pawn (or two pawns) usually depends on whether the rook has the initiative when the dust settles.

Here's an example of how two elite grandmasters badly misjudged who stood better after an imbalance arose. They underestimated the energy of White's rooks once the dust had settled:

Anand – Belyavsky
Groningen 1993

White to play

White fled here from a toxic middlegame. He believed 1 ♘g5!

would eliminate the last kingside pawn as well as Black's winning chances (1...♘xg5?? 2 ♗b6+ and 3 ♖e8 mate).

But White vastly underestimated how important his initiative is. Black would be distinctly worse after 1...♔c8 2 ♘xf7, despite his half-pawn edge.

He, too, misjudged how badly he stood and lost soon after **1...♔e8? 2 ♘xf7! ♘e5? 3 ♘d6+ ♘xd6 4 ♖xd6 ♔f8 5 ♗h6 ♗xh6 6 ♖xh6 ♘f7 7 ♖b6.**

89

Endgame assets are often middlegame liabilities.

Early chess thinkers formulated separate rules for the opening, middle and endgame, stressing that what governed one phase had little application in another.

They were followed by a new school, lasting from Steinitz to the Soviet era, that stressed the connections between the phases, not the boundaries: By the 10th move or so, White should have a pretty good idea of the kind of middlegame he wants to play. If he launches a minority attack he should visualize in general terms what the endgame will look like.

Today there's a trend to emphasize the boundaries again. When Mihai Suba wrote, "in most cases the endgame principles are reversed" in the middlegame (in *Dynamic Chess Strategy*) he gave the example of a passed queenside pawn. "The outside passed pawn is more of a weakness in the middlegame, when the fight is concentrated on the center and kingside," he wrote.

Think of the Benko Gambit. Black grants White a passed a-pawn and a potentially passed b-pawn. But until the endgame these pawns are often more of a target than a benefit. Another case:

D. Gurevich – Shabalov
Stillwater 2007

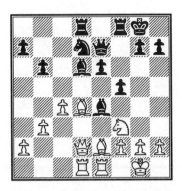

Black to play

Steinitz called a queenside majority a distinct advantage. Hans Kmoch elaborated on that in *Pawn Power in Chess* by saying it was "an advantage in time" because it can create a quicker passed pawn.

Eduard Gufeld, reflecting a Soviet point of view, said in a knight or same-colored bishop or pure pawn ending, "the queenside majority usually wins the game."

But in the middlegame, a kingside majority can be the more immediate weapon, as in this case: **1...e5! 2 ♗c3 ♘c5 3 ♕b2 ♗xf3! 4 ♗xf3 e4**.

Black's looming kingside attack was so dangerous after **5 g3 ♕g5!** that White became desperate with **6 h4? ♕g6 7 h5 ♕g5 8 ♗g2 f4**. He lost following **9 ♖d5 ♕g4 10 ♗xe4 ♘xe4 11 ♖xe4 ♗c5!**, threatening ...♕xg3+.

As Tarrasch might have said, between the opening and the ending, the Gods have placed the muddlegame.

90

What matters is not the breadth of the center but its solidity.

This was how Max Euwe explained the great contribution of the Hypermoderns, in *The Development of Chess Style*. Even the broadest of pawn centers, such as the one White builds in the Four Pawns Variation of the King's Indian Defense, can be exposed as fragile.

Euwe helped push the Four Pawns out of fashion for more than three decades thanks to a game against Fritz Sämisch at Wiesbaden 1925 that began **1 d4 ♘f6 2 c4 g6 3 ♘c3 ♗g7 4 e4 d6 5 f4 0-0 6 ♘f3 c5!**.

After **7 d5** he introduced a new move, **7...e6!**. It's standard today but some 80 years ago it was a revelation in the way it exposed how flimsy White's center was. Play went **8 ♗d3 exd5 9 cxd5 ♕b6 10 ♘d2 ♘g4 11 ♘c4 ♕d8 12 ♗e2 h5 13 ♘b5**.

Black to play

This is refuted by **13...a6! 14 ♘bxd6 b5 15 ♘xc8 bxc4,**

winning a piece because the knight is trapped.

White sought compensation in **16 e5 ♕xc8 17 h3 ♘h6 18 g4**.

But Black was able to prove – for the second time in the game – that a broad pawn center can be weak. He had a winning attack after **18...♘d7! 19 gxh5 ♕d8 20 0-0 ♕h4 21 ♖f3 gxh5 22 ♖c3 ♖ae8 23 ♗d2**

23...♘xe5!.

White resigned after **24 fxe5 ♖xe5 25 ♗e1 ♕e7 26 d6 ♕e6 27 ♗f1 ♖g5+ 28 ♖g3 ♕e3+ 29 ♔g2 ♗d4! 30 ♖xg5+ ♕xg5+**

91

A passed a-pawn looks more dangerous on the second rank than on the seventh.

Steinitz claimed that the a-pawn was the strongest pawn on the board because it was the one most likely to become an outside passer. Savielly Tartakower answered him with the smart-alecky twist, #91.

It's a case of a threat (of promotion) being stronger than the execution. A player who is obsessed by a distant enemy passed pawn early in a game will make bad decisions. That happened when this Gruenfeld Defense position began appearing in the 1980s.

Black to play

After White scored some quick victories, Black found a good defense in **1...b6** and began to reverse the score. Suddenly White's gambit seemed unsound.

After all, Black has two passed pawns. What does White have? He began to play **2 ♕c1 ♗b7** – and **3 ♗c4 ♕a4 4 ♗b5 ♕a2 5 ♗c4** to force a draw by repetition.

Eventually White came to his senses. There's going to be a lot of chess played before Black can carry out ...a1(♕).

White found he had excellent compensation in **5 ♖e1!**. After he scored a new string of victories, in which the a-pawn played no role, the evaluation changed once more. Black realized he had to fight back with more aggressive ideas, like 1...♗g4.

92
He who fears an isolated d-pawn should give up chess.

Pawn weaknesses matter most when all other factors are equal. When the other factors aren't equal – because one side has the two bishops or dominates an open file, for example – pawns take a back seat.

Experience shows that accepting an isolated d-pawn in return for freer play is fine for White in the Semi-Tarrasch QGD and for Black in the Tarrasch lines of the French Defense and Queen's Gambit Declined, for example. Not surprisingly #92 comes from Siegbert Tarrasch. His warning about overvaluing pawn structure applies to many other bad-pawn situations:

Ganguly – Barua
Calicut 2003

White to play

Black captured White bishops on d3 and d4 and enjoys superior pawns. Take off the heavy pieces and he is much better.

But the middlegame favors White – despite what computers say – because of his better king and development, e.g. **1 ℤfc1 ℤc8 2 ℤxc8+ ♝xc8 3 ♘h5** (3...g6 4 ♘f6 and ℤc1).

Black preferred **3...ℤg8 4 ♕f4 ♝d7** but had no play after **5 h4 ♕d8 6 ℤe1 ♝c6**. Then came **7 ℤe3!**, with ℤf3 in mind, and **7...g5 8 ♕f3 ♕a5 9 ♕f6 ℤg6 10 ♕h8+ ♚e7 11 ♕b8! ♕d8 12 ♕xa7 gxh4 13 ℤf3 ♚f8 14 ♘f4 Resigns**.

93

The real criterion by which to appraise closed positions is the possibility of breaking through.

Another fine perception by Richard Reti in *Masters of the Chess Board*. In open positions we can readily see who controls the important files and diagonals, or who will do so in the near future. But closed positions require greater powers of visualization. We have to assess the likelihood that a pawn advance will open the right line for the right pieces.

This skill is something of a blind spot for weak players and strong computers:

van de Wiel – Fritz SSS
Rotterdam 2000

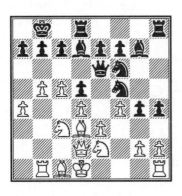

Black to play

Each side has a pawn storm in motion and the outcome seems to hinge on who breaks through first. White threatens c5-c6 and that's why 1...♗c8 is good (2 c6 b6).

Instead, Black played **1...h3??** and after **2 g3!** it had no chance of opening the side of the board on which it was strongest. White was able to take his time elsewhere – **2...♗e8 3 a5 ♚a8 4 ♔e1 ♗d7 5 ♔f2** – before breaking through and winning.

This and the example that accompanies #157 illustrate the difference between foresight and calculation. No one would dispute a computer's superiority in counting its way through forcing variations. But in quieter positions, what matters more is the ability to visualize the opening of files and diagonals through pawn captures and advances and to evaluate the consequences.

94

From computers you need variations. The evaluation you need to forget.

As an honored guest at the Tigran Petrosian Memorial in 2004, Boris Spassky spoke on a variety of subjects including the usefulness of computers to tournament players. With #94 he endorsed the view that programs can help spot tactics – but their assessments can't be trusted when there are no tactics. Computers tend to overestimate variables that masters know have little significance.

Rogozenko – Morozevich
Istanbul 2000

White to play

"Strangely enough, all chess programs 'think' that White is a bit better here," wrote Black in *New In Chess*. Why? Because computers exaggerate the significance of bad pawns. For that reason, a machine wouldn't like 1 ♗g4 and 2 ♗xe6, although it holds the balance.

Instead White began to get into trouble with **1 ♗e2?! ♗b3 2 ♖f4 ♔g7 3 g4 ♖d6 4 ♖e4 ♔f8**. Computers don't appreciate positions in which one side can steadily improve, which Black did: **5 ♖f4 a5 6 ♖e4 ♖d8 7 ♖f4 ♔e7 8 ♖e4+ ♔d6 9 ♗d1 ♗e6! 10 ♗e2? f5 11 gxf5 ♗xf5 12 ♖f4 ♔e5 3 ♖f3 b5! 14 e4? ♗e6.**

Here even computers recognize White is losing, **15 ♖c3 c4 16 f3 ♔f4 17 ♖c2 ♖d4 18 ♗d1 b4 19 axb4 axb4.**

He resigned after **20 ♗e2 ♔e3 21 ♖c1 ♖d2! 22 ♗xc4 ♖h2 23 ♗f1 ♖h1 24 ♖c2 ♗h3.**

95
After some moves, both players stand badly.

This recalls Howard Staunton's comment on a LaBourdonnais-McDonnell game: "I cannot see how it is possible for either player to save his game."

Staunton was being sarcastic. But Boris Verlinsky, an early Soviet master, was earnest when he wrote #95 about one of his own moves. Often a move will sharpen the position so much that it increases the winning chances for both players. That means it also raises the losing chances for both players, so that each seems to stand worse. If the two players could compare notes they would realize that only one of them had the inferior position. But since they can't, one player – or both – may play conservatively and a somewhat accidental draw may be the outcome. Take this example:

Morozevich – Makarichev
Moscow 1992

White to play

Black had offered a piece in order to play ...fxe5 last move. But after

1 gxf5 he saw how precarious he stood, e.g. 1...e4? 2 f6! wins for White (2...exf3 3 ♕xe8! ♖xe8 4 ♖xe8+ ♕xe8 5 fxg7).

He found **1...gxf5!** – and that convinced both players that they stood worse.

White chose the cautious **2 ♔h2** and the position petered out to a draw after **2...e4 3 ♗xg7 exf3 4 ♕xf3 ♕xg7 5 ♕xf5+ ♔b8 6 ♖xe8 ♖xe8 7 ♖g1 ♕b2**. "After the game it turned out that both players underestimated their chances," Black wrote.

96

There are two kinds of equal positions – equal positions you like to play and equal positions you can't stand the sight of.

Vishy Anand summed up the problem with calling a position equal. It means that if both players choose the best moves they have equal chances of winning. But that doesn't mean the best moves are equally easy to find. Some positions are simply much harder to play for one side rather than the other.

Another way an equals sign is misleading is when it is used to mean the most likely result is a draw. But the R+B-vs.-R endgame, for example, can be called "=" because it is drawn with best play. So here's some advice: In case you ever have a choice, take the side with the bishop.

Kramnik – Deep Fritz
Match 2002

Black to play

White sought this allegedly even position because one of his seconds "thought it wasn't that equal." He was right because White's superiority became clear after **1...♖ad8 2 ♗e3 ♖xd1+ 3 ♖xd1 ♗xc3 4 ♖d7 ♖b8**.

It may still be "equal" because the likely outcome remains a draw. But only White has winning chances. Instead of taking risks (5 ♗e4) White regained the pawn with **5 ♗xc6 bxc6 6 ♖xa7**. Black eked out a draw with difficulty.

Some positions are simply more equal than others.

CHAPTER SIX: **MISTAKES**

97

There is no such thing as a winning move.

David Hooper presumably meant to shock his *British Chess Magazine* readers when he used these words (September 1984) to express an old thought, that games are lost by bad moves, not won by good moves.

Hooper was explaining Wilhelm Steinitz's theory of balance. If both sides play correctly from move one the game must be drawn, Steinitz believed. Therefore, what we call a winning move is not possible without a previous error by the opponent, Hooper added. For example:

Salov – Piket
Wijk aan Zee 1991

White to play

A natural move for White is ♖a1, to win control of the file by trading rooks and bringing the other rook to a1. But Black was in time pressure and White didn't want to force matters. Instead he played quietly, **1 ♖fe1** and then **1...♘df6 2 ♕e2**.

Black replied **2...f4! 3 ♗f2 g5!**, and afterward called this "the more or less winning push." The trend became more evident following **4 ♖f1** (not 4 g4 ♘xg4!) **g4 5 ♗e1 gxf3+ 6 ♕xf3 ♗h6 7 ♗d2 ♖g8** and Black won in 10 moves.

But as Hooper – and Steinitz – would have said, what made the attack work were the mistakes by White at move one and two when ♖a1! would have been good enough to keep the Steinitzian balance.

It's true that 3...g5! put Black on the road to victory. But that didn't make it a winning move. Rather, failing to play 3...g5! would simply have been another, countervailing error that would help restore the balance.

98

To create a chess masterpiece you really need the generous participation of your opponent.

After Adolf Anderssen lost badly in a match in 1858, he was asked by a fan why he hadn't been as brilliant as he had been in his "Immortal" and "Evergreen" games. "Mr. Morphy won't let me," he explained.

Garry Kasparov wrote #98 when he cited the defense's errors in the "Evergreen" (*My Great Predecessors*). Kasparov's own "immortal" depended considerably on his opponent's cooperation:

Kasparov – Topalov
Wijk aan Zee 1999

Black to play

White offered a rook on d4 for a king-hunt which began 1...cxd4 2 ♖e7+! and was based on 2...♛xe7 3 ♕xd4+ ♚b8 4 ♕b6+ wins. Black had to play 2...♚b6 3 ♕xd4+ ♚xa5 4 b4+ ♚a4 5 ♕c3! and his king was lured to e1, when he resigned 16 moves later.

Kasparov believed it was the greatest combination ever played.

But if Black had declined the sacrifice with **1...♚b6!** White would not only have lost his chance for a masterpiece he might have lost the game:

Kasparov acknowledged that **2 ♘b3 ♗xd5 3 ♕xd6+ ♖xd6 4 ♖d2 ♖hd8 5 ♖ed1** was best play and he concluded the ending is equal. However, Alexander Belyavsky, among others, claimed Black is winning after **5...c4!**, e.g. **6 ♘c1 ♚c7 7 ♗g2 c3!**.

White to play

The threats of ...cxd2 and ...♗a2+ lead to a minor piece ending, **8 ♖d3 cxb2 9 ♔xb2 ♗c4 10 ♖xd6 ♖xd6 11 ♖xd6 ♔xd6**, that is clearly better for Black. The brilliancy would have been impossible without 1...cxd4??.

Quick wins, as well as sparkling ones, owe their origin to bad moves. "The root of brevity and brilliancy is blunder," James Mason said in *The Principles of Chess*.

99
Some part of the mistake is always correct.

Mistakes were a favorite topic of Savielly Tartakower and one of his most savvy comments was that every mistake, even a gross error, has some logic to support it.

This sounds like a labored attempt at irony. But it should be obviously true. When a master blunders there is almost always a good reason for his move. After Vladimir Kramnik allowed Deep Fritz to mate him in one move in an even endgame, the commentators agreed his blunder was eminently logical.

The more good reasons there are for playing a move, the less likely we will look for its tactical refutation.

1 d4 d6 2 c4 e5 3 ♘f3 e4 4 ♘g5 f5.

White to play

This is how **Muir – McNab**, 4NCL 2001 began.

White now chose a move that serves three purposes. It supports his center, opens lines for his queen and KB and prepares to complete his kingside development.

Unfortunately the move was **5 e3??** which lost a piece, **5...♛xg5!**.

And this wasn't the only time 5 e3 has been played in master chess.

100

To lose a game it is not enough to make only one mistake.

Miguel Najdorf reached a double-edged position shortly after the opening and wondered if he was lost. "Luckily I did not lose my head and remembered the saying of my old master Tartakower, that in order to lose a game it is not enough to make one mistake," he said.

Of course, this depends on the size of the mistake. A blunder that drops a piece is more than enough to put a game out of reach. The reason Tartakower's axiom rings true is that most mistakes are not gross errors. They are minor enough to keep the position within the perimeter of bad-but-not-lost.

Euwe – Rubinstein
Bad Kissingen 1928

Black to play

This is the forgotten second act to one of the great grandmaster gaffes. The first act opened with 1 ♘f3 d5 2 c4 e6 3 d4 ♘f6 4 ♗g5 ♘bd7 5 e3 ♗e7 6 ♘c3 0-0 7 ♖c1 c6 8 ♗d3 a6 9 cxd5 exd5 10 0-0 ♖e8 11 ♕b3 h6 12 ♗f4 and now 12...♘h5?? allowed 13 ♘xd5!, based on 13...cxd5 14 ♗c7, winning the queen.

The annotators consigned the rest of the game to the "matter of technique" file and made a big deal two years later when Akiba Rubinstein again lost the same pawn in a ♘xd5 trap like this. Yet he fought back so well he might have drawn if he had chosen **1...♔e6!**, which threatens a kingside (...♔f5-g4) raid.

If 2 ♔d2 ♔f5 3 f3 he can paralyze White with 3...♖b3!. Similarly, 2 e4 ♖b3 3 ♖d2 f5! and now 4 f3 fxe4 5 fxe4 ♖g3 also draws, as given by Oleg Stetsko.

Instead, Black made another error – the decisive one, **1...♖b3?**. White had time for **2 ♔d2 ♔e6 3 ♔c1! ♔f5 4 ♖c4!**, stopping the king raid (4...♔g4 5 d5+). He won after **4...g5 5 hxg5 hxg5 6 ♖xa4**.

Remarkably, the tournament book detected no improvements for Black and said the win was just "a matter of technique" after 12...♘h5??. This is remarkable because the book was written by Savielly Tartakower.

101
Proper punishment is proportionate.

Black's 12...♘h5?? was not bad enough to lose that game because chess follows a principle of proportion. Steinitz' students followed the principle by making minor concessions in defense when they were only slightly worse and by launching big attacks only when they had big advantages.

Emanuel Lasker applied the principle to mistakes and #101 expresses his view. In his *Manual* he cited a game of Richard Reti's that began **1 e4 ♘f6 2 e5 ♘d5 3 ♘c3 ♘xc3 4 dxc3**.

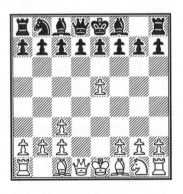

Black to play

Reti said 4 dxc3 weakens the center and hands Black a kingside majority after **4...d6 5 exd6 ♕xd6**

6 ♕xd6 cxd6!. He went on to claim (*Kagans Neueste Schachnachricten* for July-September 1925) that 4 dxc3 was a losing mistake. "The game will show how by modern chess technique a minute but clear positional advantage in the opening can be easily converted to a win," he wrote.

"Into a win?" asked the incredulous Lasker. Maybe to an advantage or initiative. But it simply isn't bad enough to lose the game. Chess is fairer than that, he felt.

In fact it was 5 exd6?, rather than 5 ♘f3, and additional errors that got White into trouble. But even if 4 dxc3 was a mistake as Reti claimed, it was unlikely to be severely punished because positional mistakes seldom are:

102
A tactical mistake involves a much heavier punishment than a strategic one.

Max Euwe's insight, in *Strategy and Tactics in Chess*, underlines the gravity of a tactical error. It is punished quickly. A strategic error, on the other hand, is a long-term mistake. If you choose the wrong side of the board to attack, you're committing a strategic error and you may eventually lose. But if you hang a pawn – or a king – it's worse.

X3D Fritz – Kasparov
Match 2003

White to play

White has two good queenside plans: Targeting the a-pawn with c5-c6 or breaking through on the b-file with b4-b5. He could further both plans with 1 ♕c4.

But the machine played **1 cxd6?**, which limits him to one plan. After **1...cxd6 2 b5 axb5 3 ♕xb5 ♗h6** and then **4 ♕b6 ♔h7 5 ♕b4** it became clear it was out of ideas.

Black concluded he had a big advantage. But we know (from #100, #101 and #102) that this cannot be true: White has made only one error. It wasn't a big one. And it was positional, not tactical.

Nevertheless Black went for the kingside kill with **5...♖g7??**. He overlooked **6 ♖xe5! dxe5 7 ♕xf8**, which cost a pawn and the attack. He resigned five moves later. His tactical error counted much more than White's positional muff.

103
Defenders blunder more than attackers.

This is the simpler form of the Rudolf Spielmann quotation that goes, "Practical play adduces evidence that errors occur far more frequently in defense than in attack." What he meant was serious errors, the kind that change the course if not the outcome of a game.

When the attacker errs, he may only lose time or the initiative. It may be a fatal error but it likely won't cause immediate defeat. Or the slip may be so slight that it isn't noticeable until the post-mortem. But when a defender errs, it is usually obvious. His punishment, say for missing a threat, is usually more abrupt and severe.

In practice, annotators rarely give a double question mark to an attacker's error unless it hangs a rook or queen. Defenders are judged much more harshly, as in this example:

Sutovsky – Greenfeld
Haifa 1996

Black blundered with **1...a5??** and resigned after realizing **2 ♖xg4!** had been threatened (2...hxg4 3 ♖xf6! and 4 ♕h5+ and mates).

Black to play

104
The winner is the one who makes the next-to-last blunder.

The subtext to this Tartakowerism is that the winner, as well as the loser, makes mistakes. It is the timing of errors that matters. Next-to-last isn't as bad as last.

When Mark Taimanov was asked to predict the outcome of the 1963 World Championship match he said, "Botvinnik will play better. But Petrosian will play without mistakes." Petrosian won.

Making the final mistake also decided Botvinnik's 1951 title match. He played many more good moves than challenger David Bronstein, according to analysis by Alexander Khalifman. But the most evident reason the match was drawn was the three game-losing blunders by Botvinnik.

This also explains Rustam Kasimdzhanov's long-shot victory in the 2004 (FIDE) World Championship. He didn't play nearly as many good moves as his leading rivals. But Kasimdzhanov won because he rarely made the last error.

Adams – Kasimdzhanov
FIDE World Championship 2004

Black to play

This was the decisive game of the tournament. Black had been outplayed but kept alive with **1...♞a8!**, threatening ...♞c7.

He should still be losing after 2 ♖a7 ♞c7 3 ♗a4. But White began a series of errors with **2 ♖a4? ♞c7**.

Since 3 ♗c4 ♞xc6 is getting bad, White returned his material edge with 3 ♖xb4 ♛b8 4 ♖xd4 ♗xd4 5 ♛xd4 ♛xb5 6 f5 ♖c8.

This led to an even ending after **7 ♗h6?** (7 f6!) ♞e8 8 e5 ♖xc6 9 exd6 ♖xd6 10 ♛e5 ♛xe5 and was followed by more missteps that cost him the game and title.

105

If you attack the opponent's pieces ten times in a row, he will blunder something on move 11.

Garry Kasparov, who said this policy worked for him, attributed it to "the old masters" (on World Chess Rating.com, 2003). The rationale is that constant threats can expose a defender to tactical fatigue. "The simple strategy of attacking your opponent's pieces and creating threats on every move has a cumulative effect," said another Soviet-trained GM, Vladimir Malaniuk. "In 5-6 moves it reaches a critical mass and brings about the collapse of his defense."

Some rivals of Judith Polgar say she's already an "old master." "After my game with Polgar I realized that the main thing in chess is to attack various enemy pieces with every move," Alexander Grischuk said sardonically after the following game. He didn't blunder but he made enough inexact moves to let White slip away:

J. Polgar – Grischuk
Linares 2001

White to play

It's not obvious yet but White is in deep trouble in view of the c-file, ...d4 and ...♘f4. She threw defense to the wind and made threats with virtually every move – **1 ♗f5 ♖c1+ 2 ♔f2 g6 3 ♘b3! ♖c4 4 ♗d3 ♖xb4 5 g3!**. By stopping

5...♘f4 White threatens ♖e2-c2-c7!, with winning chances.

Black replied **5...♘g7?** (5...♗c8!) and there followed **6 ♖e2 ♗c8 7 ♖c2! ♗xh3 8 ♖c6 ♖a4 9 g4!**. White threatens to win the bishop with ♔g3. But Black would have won easily after 9...♘e6 10 ♔g3 ♘f4.

Even after he played **9...h5? 10 ♘c5! ♖xa2+ 11 ♔g3 hxg4 12 fxg4** he had 12...♖a3! 13 ♔xh3 ♘e6. But after he played **12...♘e6? 13 ♘xe6 fxe6 14 ♗xg6** the win was gone.

By making a series of threats you may prevent a dangerous opponent from making his own threats. But against a lower-rated opponent there's an alternative policy:

106
Don't try to force the issue
until you are sure of winning.

The stronger player often becomes excited when a lower-rated opponent errs. He tries to crush him. But that puts his opponent in the somewhat easier position of having to find forced replies.

Instead, the stronger player should not try to punish the first mistake. He should play solidly and wait for more mistakes, Simon Webb said in *Chess for Tigers*, where he wrote #106. Ideally the next error will be committed in another sector of the board and provide a second weakness:

Petrosian – Trikaliotis
Siegen 1970

White to play

Black mishandled the hanging pawns and had to push one to c4. White could obtain a better endgame with 1 ♕xe7+ and bxc4/♘d4.

But that might not be enough to win. White waited for a second error with 1 ♕b2! ♖ac6 2 ♘d4 ♖c5 3 h3. At various later points after this he could have liquidated into a heavy-piece endgame with ♘xe6(+). But that too would ease Black's defense. Instead, White hoped to trade rooks, after ...cxb3?,

into a very good Q+B-vs.-Q+N ending.

Black failed to make that error and continued **3...h6 4 ♕d2 ♔g8 5 ♖3c2 ♕b7**. White gave him a new way to go wrong, with **6 g4!**.

Black complied with **6...♕e7 7 ♔g2 h5?**. Instead of making White's kingside weak, it gave him the needed second error. After **8 ♕e2 hxg4 9 hxg4 g6**:

White to play

White crashed through on the h-file, **10 ♖h1 ♔g7 11 ♕f3 ♖h8 12 ♖xh8 ♔xh8 13 ♖c1 ♔g7 14 ♖h1**. **Black resigned** after **14...♕g5 15 ♘xe6+ fxe6 16 ♕h3 ♖c8 17 f4 ♕d8 18 ♕h7+**.

107

A two-move trap in the sixth hour is often more effective than a ten-move combination in the second hour.

One way of looking at this remark, by Georg Marco and Carl Schlechter in the *Karlsbad 1907* tournament book, is that players are more prone to err when they get tired. Fatigue seems to effect tactical sight more than logic, intuition or one's sense of strategy and general principles.

There's an additional reason that sixth-hour traps succeed. As the game approaches an end, players become more and more convinced of its likely outcome. This can blind them to two-movers.

Taimanov – Fischer
Candidates match 1971

White to play

White was close to victory for several moves but realized here that

1 ♖xf6 would allow 1...♖a2 2 ♕f4+ ♕xf4 3 ♖xf4, when 3...♖c2! would likely draw.

He couldn't find a way of improving on 1 ♖xf6. But since he hadn't scored a single half point in the match up to this point, he was content to register a psychological victory. He decided to force Black to fight for a draw in the pawn-down ending.

But after 1 ♖xf6?? ♕d4+ 2 ♖f2 ♖a1+ there was no endgame.

108
Mistakes are like accidents.
They don't come singly.

"It is well-known that a mistake never comes alone" Kasparov said, alluding to Tarrasch's #108. One inaccuracy is usually followed by another. Or the mistakes become progressively worse. Often this is the result of worsening time trouble or increasing despair. A player realizes he's made a bad move and that unnerves him, leading to an avalanche of error.

Tkachiev – Piket
Cannes 2000

Black to play

Black sacrificed his queen soundly and has a choice of ways to demonstrate his winning edge. One is to open a path for the b-pawn with 1...cxb2 2 ♕xb2 ♘c4 (3 ♕b3 ♘a5 and ...b3). Also promising is the kingside attack of 2...♘f5 3 ♗f4 g5! 4 ♗e5 f6 5 ♗xh2 g4.

But he played **1...♘c4??** based on 2 bxc3 b3! and ...b2. He didn't think 2 b3! was playable because of 2...♘d2 and 3...♘xb3. Suddenly he realized 3 ♕d1! was legal.

Black would still hold the upper hand following 2...♘a3. But the disappointment of **2 b3!** was emotionally crippling. "I could not recover from this blunder," he recalled in *New In Chess* and lost soon after **2...♘b6? 3 ♗d6 ♔d7? 4 ♗c5! ♖b8 5 ♕f2 ♘c8 6 ♕g3!** in view of **6...g6 7 ♕f4 ♔e8 8 ♕f6.** This confirms another bit of general folk wisdom: "Bad things come in threes."

CHAPTER SEVEN: MOVE SELECTION

109

Never play a move without a reason.

During the 2007 China-Russia match, fellow grandmasters were watching Ernesto Inarkiev try to save a complex endgame. "What a good move!" one of them exclaimed when he sacrificed a pawn. "Yes, perhaps," replied another GM. "But what's the idea?"

"None in particular. It's just a good move!" was the reply. In fact, there was an idea. There always is for a grandmaster's move — even if the GM who played it has to think one up later to justify it.

#109 has been attributed to several early authors, including Damiano in the 16th century and even Al-Lajlaj, the 10th century Baghdad master who reputedly wrote the first major analysis of openings. It's a warning to novices who often play moves without a shred of purpose.

J. Polgar – Topalov
Hoogoveen 2006

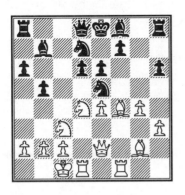

White to play

Masters play multi-purpose moves. There were three reasons

for **1 ♕f2!**. First, it takes indirect aim at f7, e.g. 1...♘b6?? 2 ♗xe5 threatens ♕xf7 mate.

Second, it discourages natural replies such as ...♕c7, in light of 2 ♗xe5 ♘xe5 3 ♕f6 ♖-moves 4 ♘xe6!. Third, it clears e2 for a good ♘ce2-g3-h5 maneuver.

Play continued **1...♖c8 2 ♘ce2! ♗g7?! 3 ♘g3 ♖h7 4 ♘h5 ♗h8 5 ♔b1 ♘c5?** and now 6 ♘f5! exf5 7 ♗xe5 ♗xe5 8 ♕xf5 and ♕xh7 would have won quickly.

110
Anyone can be brilliant
if he is a knight ahead.

This forgotten quip from George Mackenzie, quoted in the *American Chess Magazine* (August 1899), is one of many that relate the strength of a player's position to the quality of move he can play. While Siegbert Tarrasch had said bad moves appear in bad positions, others noticed that good moves appear in good positions. "Tactics flow from a superior position," said Bobby Fischer.

In a dead-won position, you can take liberties and look for the dramatic finish. Mackenzie anticipated David Bronstein, who said, "In a winning position it is easy to play pretty moves." The rationale is that when there is little doubt about the outcome of the game it is easier to look for an attractive way to finish off, such as with a sacrifice. That was the case here:

Ki. Georgiev – Grischuk
Heraklion 2007

White to play

Almost anything wins eventually. But in a position this good, it's fun to look for the flashy. White looked and found **1 ♖g6+!**.

Black resigned in view of 1...♔xg6 2 ♘xf4+ and 1...♛xg6 2 c8(♛).

111
A move is made in four stages.

Adrianus de Groot, the psychologist/master, explained that the first of four steps when seeing a new position is orientation. This means acquainting yourself with its main features. This is followed by step two, a wide search for candidate moves that recommend themselves for further attention. The third step is to investigate each candidate, and the fourth is to confirm that analysis. A mistake can be made at any stage. When you see an annotated game in print it's often difficult to determine where the error occurred, particularly if, as in the following example, there were several appealing candidates.

Rowson – Ramaswamy
Edinburgh 2003

White to play

White must have misjudged the two obvious candidates, 1 ♘xc5 and 1 ♕xc5, which would have kept an edge, when he chose

1 ♘c3?!, the move he played. He also failed to appreciate the fourth candidate, 1 ♕f5!, which would have given him a powerful, if not winning position in lines such as 1...b6 2 ♘c3! and ♘d5.

The other great psychologist/master, Nikolai Krogius, wrote #111 but came up with a different four stages. In *Psychology in Chess* he said they come at the end of the selection process: "Decide on a move, write it down, check it and only then move it." This allows more reliable control over "even the most obvious idea," he said, and safeguards against a rush to judgment.

112
It is more important to look around than to look ahead.

Cecil Purdy meant that looking ahead – the "if he goes there, I go there" analysis – is not as valuable as the more general examination of the board that you make before that. In de Groot's terms, the first two steps are more important than the latter two. But in our haste to look ahead, we often end up looking foolish.

P. Nikolic – Tisdall
Reykjavik 1996

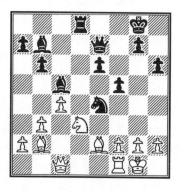

Black to play

Black's position improved so much in the previous few moves that he was sure there was a killer here. He thought 1...♗d6, eyeing a sacrifice on h2, might be the murder weapon.

But when he calculated 1...♗d6 it didn't look lethal at all. He became

frustrated and eventually chose another explosive idea, **1...♖xd3? 2 ♗xd3 ♕h4**, with the idea of 3...♗xf2+ and hopes of 3 ♗xe4?? ♕xe4 and mates.

However, the simple **3 ♕e1** was more than adequate, and after one more error of frustration, **3...♕g5?**, the game was over (**4 ♔h1! ♘d2 5 ♕xe6+ ♔f8 6 ♖g1 ♘e4 7 ♗xe4 ♗xe4 8 ♗d4 Resigns**).

Black had misevaluated. His position wasn't as good as he thought. But he lost because he didn't look around to find a somewhat obvious candidate, **1...♗d4!** and 2 ♗xd4 ♖xd4. Black would have good winning chances after 3 f3 ♖xd3 4 ♗xd3 ♕c5+ 5 ♔h1 ♘f2+ 6 ♖xf2 ♕xf2.

113

A master player looks at every more he would *like* to make, *especially the impossible ones.*

Irving Chernev's discerning comment, in *Logical Chess Move by Move*, seems to contradict what we know about the efficiency of masters. Don't they examine fewer candidates than non-masters, as #15 indicated?

Yes, they do. But they also have a well-honed appreciation of what the positionally correct move looks like. That's why they won't automatically reject a move because it seems tactically "impossible."

What is truly wasteful is rejecting, out of hand, the move that they would like to make:

Shirov – Gelfand
FIDE World Championship 2000

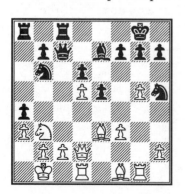

White to play

White's knight is attacked. General principles tell us to look first at 1 ♘c1 and only later at 1 ♘a1. There's little to calculate in

either case. White might play 1 ♘c1 as soon as he sees how the knight can get to the nice b4 square via a2.

But this is wrongheaded. Since he can't calculate far anyway, White should think in general terms. Then he will recognize that the best outposts for his knight are e4 and f5 and he will see **1 ♘c5!** allows him to reach e4.

White didn't automatically reject it because of **1...dxc5.** He looked further and saw that 2 d6 favorably regains the piece. He won, soon after **2...♗xd6 3 ♕xd6 ♘f4 4 ♗xf4 exf4 5 ♗b5 g6 6 ♖ge1**, because he considered the attractive, impossible move.

114
Always look for ways of ignoring threats.

With these words, Cecil Purdy underlined the limits of knee-jerk advice. Novices are told they must try to see if their opponent's last move made a threat. If it did, their first priority is preventing the threat from being executed.

This is good advice – for novices. It has helped many players with three-digit ratings reach four digits. But they become dependent on reacting, not acting. To improve they need to see if the threat can be ignored.

Here's an example of a safety-minded Black taking precautions with his king that are immediately fatal. In the post-mortem analysis he realized the threat could be safely ignored.

Kasparov – Kengis
Riga 1995

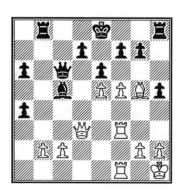

Black to play

While White was bulking up on the f-file Black picked off the a-pawn. Black looked for ways he could be punished and concluded that fxe6 and ♖xf7 is a threat.

But his cure, **1...0-0??**, was worse than the disease in view of **2 ♗f6!**. Black couldn't take the bishop (2...gxf6 3 ♖g3+ ♔h8 4 ♕e2 and mates).

He didn't last long after **2...♕b5 3 ♖g3!**. For example 3...♕xd3 4 ♖xg7+ and 5 ♖g5+ mates or 3...g6 4 ♕d1! exf5 5 ♖xf5 and ♖xh5.

The best response to the threat was not to respond. After **1...♖xb2! 2 fxe6 ♕xe6** White has nothing better than **3 ♖xf7 ♕xf7 4 ♖xf7 ♔xf7**. Black's king can reach safety and he can think about winning with his a-pawn.

115

A master sweats and squirms to find the right square for a piece. The grandmaster tosses a piece in the air and it lands on the best square.

Olaf Ulvestad, as quoted in *New Ideas in Chess*, was highlighting the power of intuition. Relying on intuition is the squirm-free alternative to sifting through several candidate moves.

But what is intuition? To Vishy Anand it's "the first move I think of." To other GMs it's the first move they *feel*. They experience the urge to play a particular move without thinking. "Intuition is the moves my fingers make when I give a simultaneous," Arthur Bisguier said.

Bisguier added (*Overboard* 1974) that intuitive feelings cannot be put into words: "Take someone like Sam Reshevsky. I'm sure he's going to explain why he made a move. Well, you better believe me when I tell you that he's just trying to figure out some nice reason why he made the move, when the move had occurred to him immediately."

Sakaev – Belov
Krasnoyarsk 2003

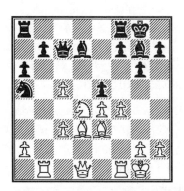

White to play

White felt he was better but quickly concluded 1 fxe5 ♗xe5 and 1 ♘e2 ♖ad8 offered nothing. His intuition pointed to 1 f5. But there were too many variations to prove the sacrifice was sound.

He followed the advice of Rudolf Spielmann: "The expert chessplayer must be good at analysis, but he must not overdo it."

White played **1 f5!** and **1...exd4 2 cxd4 ♖fe8 3 f6**, and this was validated much later with a crushing victory.

Vasily Smyslov said intuition was the "main characteristic of talent." Yet it's a talent based on pattern recognition and that suggests it can be acquired. De Groot concluded that a player's potential is based on how many patterns he can familiarize himself with. "The most important factor in determining a player's ceiling, in general, appears to be the scope of his memory capacity," he wrote in *Thought and Choice in Chess*.

116

Counter-intuitive moves require nerves and calculation.

"When intuition does not betray you, chess is easy and beautiful," Vlastimil Hort wrote. But sometimes it does betray you. The intuitive move in many positions doesn't pass the tactics test. Your analysis tells you a downright ugly alternative may be best.

Computers can play ugly moves with a clear conscience because they haven't the slightest bit of intuition. When humans consider a candidate move that doesn't seem right, the cool precision of a machine is needed.

Karpov – Kramnik
Vienna 1996

White to play

If White tries to do more with his knight he allows ...&xb4. He can free the knight with 1 a3 but that

puts both queenside pawns on the bishop's color and endangers both. "Good nerves and faith in your calculations (are) needed to make such moves," White said in *New In Chess*.

He went ahead with **1 a3!** and play continued **1...♔f5 2 ♘e3+ ♔g6 3 ♔f3 ♗e5 4 ♘d5 ♔g7 5 ♘e7!**. Black won both pawns, **5...♖c3+ 6 ♔g4 ♖xa3 7 f4 ♗c3 8 ♔h5! ♗xb4**.

But White had seen further – **9 ♘f5+ ♔g8 10 ♖a8+ ♔h7 11 ♖a7 ♔g8 12 ♘xh6+ ♔f8 13 ♖xf7+ ♔e8 14 ♔g6** – and won with the h-pawn.

117

Except for the mating move, there is no move that does not weaken some part of the position.

Siegbert Tarrasch's proverb is often repeated but infrequently applied. There are two good ways to use it.

First, it warns us that any candidate we consider has a downside. "You have several options in any situation, you can choose only one, and each has a shortcoming," David Bronstein said. Therefore, it's essential to know what – and how serious – the shortcoming is.

Another way to use #117 is realizing that no matter how strong your opponent's last move appears, it is bound to have a drawback. It may not be a major one, but if you don't look for it...

Pengxiang – Inarkiev
Nizhny Novgorod 2007

White to play

White played **1 g4** to expose f7. This wasn't really dangerous in view of 1...♘xe7 2 ♖xe7 ♖f8.

However, Black looked for a way to ignore the threat and play for a win. He chose **1...♖c3**. Its drawback is disconnecting Black's rooks. That may sound like an abstract observation – until White looks for a way to exploit the unprotected rook at a8.

He refuted 1...♖c3?? with **2 ♖e3!** and won after **2...♖xe3 3 ♕xa8+** and **3 gxf5**.

118

Never make a good move too soon.

James Mason didn't mean moving a piece hastily – that is, without thinking enough – but moving it too early. A good move in the position you are looking at will probably still be a good move on your next turn. Chess positions simply don't change that radically from one move to the next. Mason's rule tells us to consider whether waiting is worthwhile.

This applies to positional moves as well as to attacking ones. In the following example, the positionally desirable knight advance is also an excellent attacking move. But it can be played too soon.

Svidler – Nakamura
Santo Domingo 2002

White to play

The position cries out for 1 ♘d5. The knight will occupy a splendid outpost, threaten ♘xe7+ and look for a chance to play ♘f6+ to open the g-file. White's superiority would be indisputable after 1...♗d8 2 ♖g2 or 2 g6.

But as good as ♘d5 is, this is too soon. It can be improved by 1 ♗e3!. Then 1...♕xe3 2 ♘d5! is stronger in view of 2...♕c5 3 ♘xe7+ ♔h8 4 g6! and wins.

Also, by delaying ♘d5 White can get his QR into play faster. The game went **1...♕c8 2 ♕h5 ♕e6** and now **3 ♘d5!** is much stronger than before, e.g. 3...♖fe8 4 g6! ♘f6 5 ♘xf6+ ♗xf6 6 ♖af1! and wins

119

In a sound position there are at least two alternatives that are "the only move."

It is rare when one aphorism is born in answer to another. With #119 Aron Nimzovich was telling off his blood-rival, Siegbert Tarrasch.

Tarrasch tried to bring clinical correctness to chess and concluded that choosing a move was a scientific puzzle. "Each position must be regarded as a problem, where it is a question of finding the correct move, almost always only one, demanded of that position," he wrote in *The Game of Chess*. "In a game of chess, secondary solutions are almost non-existent."

Nimzovich diametrically disagreed. Unless you are faced with major threats, your position isn't a puzzle at all, he said. There is more than one right answer.

Anand – Karpov
Wijk aan Zee 2003

White to play

White concluded he had no choice but to destroy Black's center with **1 ♕xd5**. After the best defense, 1...♕xd5 2 ♗xd5 ♘xc3, he would have good winning chances.

After the game, however, he realized that he had two reasonable alternatives – **1 ♖d1** and **1 ♘d2!**, which is best (1...e4? 2 ♘xe4 or 1...♖cd7 2 c4).

Bear in mind that in some positions there may be two, not one, "best" moves. In other positions there may be none. All the alternatives can be equally good or bad. That's why excellent advice is:

120

Don't worry about finding the best move. Seek always to find a good move.

This was Bobby Fischer's common sense approach (*Atlantic Chess News*, September-October 1988). In many positions there is no way of proving that one move is distinctly better than the others – at least not without an unlimited amount of time and/or help of a computer.

Another saying often quoted by masters is, "If you can't find a good move, don't play a bad one." This is useful because it's often easier to tell if a move is bad than if it is good:

Svidler – Leko
FIDE World Championship
2005

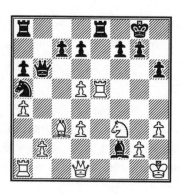

Black to play

Black tried for more than half an hour to find the best move. But

1...f6, which is probably best, didn't impress him.

As so often happens, he became frustrated and played a move he hadn't calculated at all, **1...d6?**. If he had looked longer he would have realize it's simply bad – **2 ♖xe8+ ♖xe8 3 b4! ♘b7 4 ♖a2! ♗g3 5 ♖e2**. Black's knight has no future because d6 is occupied by his own pawn. Black's queen is locked out of play. On the other hand, White's knight has a great future because 1...d6? created a hole at c6. White won after **5...♖d8 6 ♘d4** and **7 ♘c6, 8 ♗d4** and so on.

121

Timid moves are the reckless ones.

"Timidity loses out in chess as in life," Cecil Purdy added. He was warning against the natural temptation to play conservatively when things are going well. If the position is dynamic to the slightest degree, cautious moves carry a hidden risk of missed opportunities.

Kramnik – Kasparov
World Championship 2000

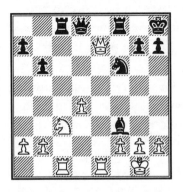

White to play

This was the critical moment in the match that made Vladimir Kramnik world champion. He was enjoying a one-point lead with no more than seven games left and could have gone into a pawn-up ending, 1 ♕xd8 ♖cxd8 2 gxf3 ♖xd4. He thought that would give him a 50 percent chance of winning and virtually no chances of losing.

The alternative was **1 gxf3 ♕xd4**, staying in a middlegame that could be dangerous because of his mangled king position. But he sensed Black would have the greater problems after **2 ♘b5**.

Should he go into the endgame with the assurance he'd keep his match lead? Or should he go for what could be the knockout? He chose the latter and was proven right after **2...♕xb2? 3 ♖xc8 ♖xc8 4 ♘d6!** and **4...♖b8 5 ♘f7+ ♔g8 6 ♕e6! ♖f8 7 ♘d8+! ♔h8 8 ♕e7 Resigns**. His two-point lead won the match.

Post-game analysis showed that even after **2...♕f4!** White would have the better chances (3 ♖xc8 ♖xc8 4 ♘d6) and they are greater than in the timid 1 ♕xd8 endgame.

122
It's better to falsify your ideas than to verify them.

Masters distinguish themselves from the other 98 percent of players in many ways but among the criteria that stand out is their ability to cast doubt on their candidate moves. They are better at second-guessing.

"Mistrust is the most necessary characteristic of the chessplayer," is the way Tarrasch put it. Jonathan Rowson's version in *Chess for Zebras* was #122. "Falsify" may sound strange to non-scientists but here it means confirming your candidate is good by making an honest effort to prove that it isn't. The proper attitude is "I'm not sure about ♗f5, let me see if there's a flaw" – rather than "I like ♗f5. I'll try to prove it works."

Kramnik – Topalov
World Championship 2006

White to play

White has a nice game and initially felt that either 1 dxe5 or 1 g3 was best. The first move is thematic because after 1...♘xe5 2 ♘d4 White threatens to mobilize his kingside majority with 3 f4 and 4 e5.

But when he checked further he saw that 2...♖cd8! and then 3 f4 ♘eg4 4 e5 ♗c5! might be a big problem.

He turned to candidate No.2. The appeal of 1 g3 is that White can put his KB to work on h3. But he rejected this too because it was impossible to calculate what happens after 1...exd4 2 ♘xd4 b4 3 ♘a4 c5 with the idea of ...♗xe4.

In the end White found the best move behind door number three, 1 ♕d2!. It threatened 2 dxe5 ♘xe5? 3 ♕xd6 and, unlike the alternatives, it had no major drawback. He obtained the edge after 1...♖cd8 2 ♕g5 and eventually won, thanks in part to his second-guessing of 1 dxe5 and 1 g3.

123

The most difficult thing in the chess world is to choose one from among several apparently equally good moves.

It's an embarrassment of riches when you have more than one attractive candidate. One may win material but an alternative promises an initiative. Or one path guarantees a superior pawn structure while another severely restricts enemy pieces. Siegbert Tarrasch, in his game collection, gave us #123 but didn't offer advice on how to choose.

Benjamin Blumenfeld did: Play the candidate that is easiest to calculate. "Easiest" can mean the one whose bottom line you are more certain of. Or it can mean the one you don't have to calculate as far as the alternative.

Bareev – Korotylev
Moscow 2004

White to play

White's instinct told him that either 1 &xd7, grabbing a pawn, or 1 &e2, developing a piece and eyeing an attack on the h5-knight, would lead to an edge.

But after half an hour of calculating he couldn't prove it, e.g. 1 &xd7 &fd8 2 &xd8+ &xd8 3 &c3 f6 offers Black some compensation for a pawn. Is it enough? White couldn't tell.

Eventually he opted for a third possibility, 1 &d6 so that 1...&xd6 2 exd6. This would give him visible advantages, the two bishops and better pawns, and, more important, it didn't require calculating further.

His judgment was confirmed after play went 2...f5 3 &e2 &f6 4 0-0 &d8 5 &e5 &f7 6 &xf7 and White was clearly better.

124
If you see a good move, look for a better one.

This maxim has been attributed to everyone from Damiano to Emanuel Lasker and is particularly good advice in favorable positions. Candidate moves tend to look better in good positions than in bad ones, and a player with the edge often errs by rushing to play the first attractive one he sees.

"I played this rather quickly," Peter Svidler said of a move that made his position clearly superior in his final game with Garry Kasparov. But after the game was drawn he discovered he "completely overlooked" a simple alternative that would have won a pawn and the game.

Heeding #124 not only turns draws into wins but can shorten games by a dozen or more moves.

Nisipeanu – Dorfman
Cap d'Agde 2000

White to play

White's **1 ♗a5!** set up a winning threat of 2 ♖d8+ ♕xd8 3 ♗xd8 ♔xd8 4 ♕xf7. Black tried to keep the game going with **1...♖f8**, hoping to survive the Q-vs.-R+B ending.

The hopes were dashed when White looked beyond 2 ♖d8+ and found **2 ♕f6!**, which threatens to mate with 3 ♖d8+. **Black resigned** rather than play the feeble 2...♕xf6 3 exf6 ♗e7.

125
Reserve the greater option.

This was a Purdy mantra: If you have a choice between two candidates and one of them is a move you are likely to make in the next few turns anyway, play it. In that way you leave yourself with more options on the next move. Your opponent's response to the first move will help determine your follow-up.

One of the more common errors a player will make is trying to preserve as many of his options as possible. But this refusal to make a commitment enables his opponent to retain his own valuable options, as in this case:

Ivanchuk – Sadvakasov
Skanderborg 2003

White to play

White is bit better thanks to his ability to open part of the h-file. But once he trades on g6 he gives up another option, the cramping h5-h6. He decided to delay a decision about the h-pawn.

But after 1 ♖d2? and 1...c5! 2 ♕d1 c4 Black stood well. He met 3 hxg6 with 3...fxg6! and used the half-open f-file to win. (Not 3...hxg6? 4 ♘g5! with its threat of 5 ♖h8+! and ♕h1-7 mate.)

White's error was trying to retain all his options. That allowed Black to keep his own options when it came time to retake on g6. If White had played **1 hxg6!** – and reserved the greater options – Black should avoid the reply 1...fxg6 because of the pin on the b3-g8 diagonal (2 ♘e4! and 3 ♘eg5).

That would limit Black to 1...hxg6, after which 2 ♖h4! c5 3 ♖dh1 is a much faster White attack than in the game.

126

One should never prevent one's opponent from making weak moves.

This is an echo of Napoleon's "Never interfere with your enemy when he is destroying himself" and appeared in the *Karlsbad 1907* tournament book of Georg Marco and Carl Schlechter. It applies best to pawn moves.

When your opponent is preparing to push a pawn, there is a natural tendency to restrict him. But from a psychological as well as a strategic point of view, it pays to consider letting him have his way:

Morozevich – Topalov
FIDE World Championship
2005

Black to play

Black had been on the defensive on the queenside but now has a chance for 1...b5. Instead, he played the sly **1...♕c6!**.

He hinted that he wanted to play 1...b5 but wanted to rule out ♘d6 as a reply. White took the opportunity to secure the position of his knight with 2 a4.

But 1...♕c6 was designed to allow White to make that bad move, since after **2 a4?** his c3-knight is tied to the defense of the a-pawn and couldn't eliminate the d4-knight with ♘e2.

Black was able to improve his position steadily, **2...b6 3 ♖e3 f6! 4 ♖h3 ♖f7** and obtained a winning positional edge after he inevitably got ...b5 in (5 ♗e3 ♖d8 6 ♖e1 ♘f8 7 b3 a6! 8 ♘e2 b5 9 axb5 axb5).

127

When in doubt, move a piece, not a pawn.

A pawn is more likely to make an irreparable mistake because it can't move backward. Yet #127 is often violated, even by the positional-minded players who should know better. Viktor Korchnoi said they are the ones likely to "play with their pawns" in time trouble.

In passive positions it is tempting to change matters and the easiest way to make a change is push a pawn. But *zeitnot* is the worst time to make an irrevocable decision that could turn out to be an error.

Chernin – Psakhis
Beer-Sheeva 1993

Black to play

Time pressure prompted Black to become active at the wrong time, **1...h5?**. White didn't try to exploit the weakness at g6 immediately. He waited for another error, with **2 h4 ♖d8 3 ♗d5 ♕d6 4 ♕c2 ♖d7 5 ♕c8 ♖d8 6 ♕a6**.

On the final move of the time control a pass like 6...♖d7 was best. But Black again pushed, **6...f5?**, based on tactics (7 exf5?? ♕xd5).

He was in big trouble after **7 ♗c4!**, in view of 7...fxe4 8 ♖f7+ and ♕b7!. Black couldn't take back the weakening move and had to make do with **7...♕c6 8 exf5! ♖f8 9 ♗d3 gxf5 10 ♗b1 ♖f7**.

White to play

Compare this with the previous diagram and it's no wonder that White was able to penetrate on the kingside after **11 ♕e2**, intending ♔h2 and ♖xf5 or ♖f4. **Black resigned** after **11...♗c7 12 ♕d2! f4 13 ♕xd4+ ♖f6 14 ♕d3! ♔f8 15 ♕h7 ♗e5 16 ♕h8+**.

128

One of the hallmarks of very strong players is the ability to recognize when they should try to do something and when it is better to play a move which just simply improves their position.

Unless your position is very bad, there is bound to be a move that makes it better in some way. There usually are more than one of these "little" moves available. On the other hand there may – or may not – be a "big" move, one that changes matters in a significant way.

You can waste a lot of time and energy looking for something "big" when it doesn't exist. With #128 Nigel Davies was underlining the value of appreciating when to look and when to satisfy yourself with "little."

Agdestein – Ekstrom
Bad Wiessee 2000

White to play

Znosko-Borovsky said a player tries from move one on to increase the number of non-forced candidates he has to chose from. "Whenever this number begins to

grow less it is a sure sign that the position is deteriorating and that the pieces are becoming correspondingly less effective," he wrote in *The Middle Game in Chess*.

The number for Black here is getting less and less. If it were his turn, 1...exd4?? would lose the queen to 2 exd4. In addition, castling kingside would be risky in view of 2 h5!.

That indicated to White that he should just strengthen his position, with **1 ♖e2!**, protecting his d2-bishop. Black obliged with **1...0-0-0?! 2 g5 ♘fd5** and was losing after **3 dxe5!** (3...♕xe5 4 ♕xf7 or 3...♗xe5 4 ♘xd5 and 5 ♗xa5).

129
Before making the move you've chosen, take one last look, with the eyes of a beginner.

This was another Benjamin Blumenfeld rule, beloved by Soviet-trained teachers. It is the ultimate weapon against chess blindness:

Once you've decided which candidate to play, look at the position one last time. Ask yourself if it would allow mate in one move. If it doesn't, look to make sure your queen isn't going to hang as a result of it. If that's no danger, check out the possibility of losing a rook. And so on.

"The majority of (rated) players know Blumenfeld's rule well but in the heat of battle they often forget it," Mikhail Krasenkow wrote in *Shakhmaty v SSSR* in 1991.

Epishin – Rustemov
Dos Hermanas 2003

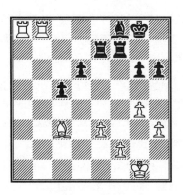

Black to play

Black played **1...♖a7??** and as soon as his hand left the rook he saw 2 ♖xf8+! ♖xf8 3 ♖xa7. He said he forgot Blumenfeld's rule because he was engrossed in how to get rooks off the board.

But he didn't lose. White, in time trouble, expected another move, 1...♖b7. When the rook went to a7 instead, he instantly replied **2 ♔g2??**. The game ended in a draw after **2...♖xa8 3 ♖xa8 ♖d7**.

130

When you have eliminated all the plausible moves, you'd better play what you have left quickly before you lose on time.

Tony Miles acknowledged the debt to Sherlock Holmes when he offered this practical advice (*Tony Miles: It's Only Me*): Once you've decided that a move is forced, there is no reason to spend more time on it. Play it and get your opponent's clock moving. There's no point forfeiting over an "only" move.

Kasparov – Psakhis
Murcia 1990

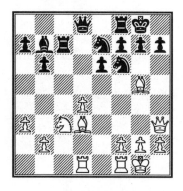

Black to play

Black quickly realized that ♗xf6 followed by ♕xh7 mate was threatened. He saw that **1...♘g6** was "absolutely the only move."

Yet he squandered 25 minutes before playing it because he wanted to figure out what he was going to do on **2 ♗xg6 hxg6 3 ♕h4** followed by ♖d3-h3.

He should have gone ahead with 1...♘g6 and worry about 3 ♕h4 when it happened. There's always a chance it won't happen – and that's the case here. White didn't like the looks of **3...♖xc3! 4 bxc3 ♕d5**, which threatens mate and gives Black good queenside counterplay. Black's search beyond an "only" move was wasted.

CHAPTER EIGHT: **OPENING**

131
Your only task in the opening is to reach a playable middlegame.

Lajos Portisch was an opening maximalist. He spent hundreds of hours preparing his favorite lines. But he put things in perspective when he wrote #131 in *How to Open a Chess Game*. All you really need from the opening is to get out of it in reasonable shape.

This attitude doesn't get proper attention because opening books take the maximalist approach. But Vladimir Kramnik demonstrated its power when he adopted the Caro-Kann Defense for the first time in his tournament career. He didn't want to have to fight in the opening and after 1 e4 c6 2 d4 d5 3 e5 he avoided the complex main lines in favor of the modest 3...c5!? and 4 dxc5 e6.

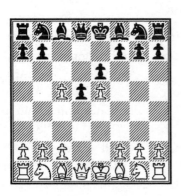

White to play

This is a kind of French Defense in which White was given an extra tempo (compared with 1 e4 e6 2 d4 d5 3 e5 c5). But the tempo is the double-edged dxc5. Who is better? Nobody knows for sure, and it didn't really matter to Kramnik. If he was worse, it's only slightly, and the real battle would come after move 10.

He stood well after **5 ♗f4 ♗xc5 6 ♗d3 ♘c6**, not even trying for advantage with 6...♛b6!? 7 ♗g3 ♛xb2. The game, against Alexey Shirov, didn't really begin until the middlegame, and that's where Black won.

132

The best opening is the opening your opponent doesn't know.

Any sound opening, from the Abrahams Variation to the Zinnowitz, is a good weapon against an opponent who is unfamiliar with it, according to this ancient adage. The trouble is there is no foolproof way of guessing correctly what your opponent doesn't know.

Mikhail Botvinnik's advice was: "To avoid what everybody knows, it's necessary to know what nobody knows." When Botvinnik adopted the Winawer Variation of the French Defense (**1 e4 e6 2 d4 d5 3 ♘c3 ♗b4 4 e5 c5 5 a3 ♗xc3+ 6 bxc3 ♘e7**) it had appeared in fewer than a half dozen master games. Simply by playing it when no one else did, he became the world's Winawer expert.

His game with Milner-Barry from Hastings 1934-35 went **7 ♘f3 ♘bc6 8 ♗e2 ♗d7 9 0-0 ♕c7 10 ♖b1 c4**.

White to play

An attack on the base of the chain, **11 ♘e1?! 0-0-0 12 f4?**, seemed logical. But f4-f5 was easily stopped (**12...f6 13 ♘f3 ♘f5 14 ♕e1 h5! 15 ♘h4 ♘ce7!**) and after much maneuvering Black won.

Improvements were found, of course. But Botvinnik kept ahead of his opponents by learning more about the Winawer. Nick deFirmian summed up this approach. "First you learn the theory," he said in *How to Get Better at Chess*. "Then you learn the subtleties of this theory and finally you create your own ideas."

But this may take more time than an amateur can afford. He has to choose his openings based on how much preparation is required. So, keep in mind:

133

It's impossible to play the Dragon only from time to time.

Spoken by a true Dragonista, Gennady Sosonko. Openings like the Dragon Variation of the Sicilian are so theory-driven that it is virtually impossible to play them successfully unless you stay constantly in touch with the latest TNs, or new moves.

TNs were introduced, on average, at move 17 in the Dragon, according to a survey of recent *Informant* games. That's a very late stage and indicates that a Dragon player has to master an awful lot of theory. It makes no sense to employ such a high-maintenance opening only occasionally. (For "Dragon" in #133 you can substitute "Sveshnikov" or "Meran" or any number of mega-theory lines.)

This is why most non-masters rely on a low-maintenance arsenal of one or two defenses to 1 e4 and one or two to 1 d4. They also depend to some degree on memorization despite what teachers say.

134

Understanding is good, understanding is impressive but it is memory that does the work.

A psychiatrist and avid amateur player, Kenneth Mark Colby, offered this renegade point of view in *Secrets of a GrandPatzer*. (He acknowledged he was borrowing from Mark Twain's quip about thunder and lightning.)

It's an exaggeration, of course. But we all depend on memorization at the start of a game. Relying solely on understanding is possible only in caveman openings.

"Memorization is enormously powerful," Bobby Fischer said in a 2006 radio interview. "Some kid of 14 today or even younger could get an opening advantage against Capablanca, and especially against the players of the previous century, like Morphy or Steinitz. Maybe they could still be able to outplay the kid. Or maybe not..."

"The kid" would still need enough understanding to know what to do after a new move was played. It is relying exclusively on memory that is fatal. Vladimir Kramnik admitted he lost a key game in his 2004 World Championship match because he only thought a moment about a blunder before playing it. The move was based on faulty computer analysis that he memorized just before the round.

135

If God played the Benoni against God, I believe White would win. But at the human, even World Championship, level, practical chances are about equal.

Some openings violate all sorts of thing we've been taught about how to play the game. In a heavenly test, they would surely be refuted, as C.H. O'D. Alexander said of the Benoni in #135 (*Fischer v. Spassky Reykjavik 1972*). But without divine intervention, we'll continue to use these lines because they work too well.

What mortals say isn't enough to discourage us. A game at Moscow 1935 began **1 d4 ♘f6 2 c4 g6 3 g3 c5**:

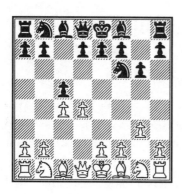

White to play

"This move cannot be recommended," the tournament book warned, "since now a position is reached characteristic of the 'Benoni Gambit,' 1 d4 c5?, which is condemned by nearly all theoreticians (in view of the reply 2 d5!)."

In other words, **4 d5** in the diagram cramps Black. But 3...c5 was revived in the 1950s and Black began to win games, thanks to those equal "practical chances."

There are several variations in vogue today that were routinely denounced a generation or so ago, like the Slav Defense line that goes 1 d4 d5 2 c4 c6 3 ♘f3 ♘f6 4 ♘c3 a6!?. Anatoly Karpov predicted it would remain popular until it is tested in a world championship. Perhaps only then, when God faces God, will Black's violation of opening rules be punished.

136
It is better to know less but to know it better.

If you try to study every opening, "you will learn them all superficially and none of them deeply," Benjamin Blumenfeld said. The right policy is #136, said Mark Taimanov in his game collection. This follows a checker maxim attributed to Tom Wiswell, "It is better to know less and understand more."

The best examples of it today are games of Vladimir Kramnik. He has the narrowest repertoire of any world champion since Jose Capablanca. He plays what he knows, and what he knows he knows better than his rivals.

Kramnik – Sadvakasov
Astana 2001

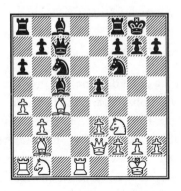

White to play

Kramnik improved on the book 1 h3 with 1 ♘c3. It's hardly a deep conception. Anyone who takes the time to study the position would recognize White is slightly better developed and might benefit from a quick ♘c3-d5 and ♖ac1.

But it was Kramnik who introduced **1 ♘c3!** and he won quickly after **1...e4 2 ♘g5 ♗d6** and then **3 ♘d5! ♘xd5 4 ♖xd5** with ♕h5 to come (**4...♗xh2+ 5 ♔h1 ♗e5 6 ♕h5 ♗f5 7 ♘xf7! ♖xf7 8 ♕xf5!** because 8...♖xf5 9 ♖d8 is mate).

Larry Christiansen tackled the title subject in *How to Get Better at Chess* by saying, "Probably the easiest way to go about it is to become very well acquainted with just a few openings, maybe going as far as 15 moves deep."

137

The most important novelties are hidden in the games of the old masters.

Savielly Tartakower's facetious comment about retro-openings is confirmed today in the games of players like Alexander Morozevich, and earlier by Bent Larsen and Bobby Fischer. When Larsen revived the Bishop's Game, one commentator noted how his opponents were armed with the latest analysis from Isaac Boleslavsky "but Larsen studied Greco and Philidor!"

Old openings have the advantage of being well-tested and ill-remembered. They are often dismissed because they haven't been endorsed by recent games or Fritz analysis. But many good ideas don't require that.

Spassky – Fischer
World Championship 1972

Black to play

Modern thinking says Black's d-pawn belongs on d6. But after **1...d5!** and **2 exd5 exd5 3 0-0 ♗d6** Black equalized immediately. He explained that he got the idea from an Adolf Anderssen game in 1877. It had disappeared from master chess for 95 years.

Why did it disappear? The answer is fashion. Openings fall out of vogue for reasons that often have nothing to do with their merit. Lines that were popular in the 1980s, such as the Stonewall Dutch, the Old Indian Defense and the Bird Variation of the Ruy Lopez were rarely played after 2000 – for reasons no one seems to recall today.

Another good source of novelties lies in openings that are not just unfashionable but "unplayable":

138

Any opening is good enough to be played if its reputation is bad enough.

Like many a Tartakowerism this one has two layers of meaning. On the first layer, it says that many good ideas lie hidden in lines that are considered refuted. This makes sense because virtually every opening with a name, and many without, was tested decades ago. The ones that were considered good have already been analyzed past move 15. To find something new before move 15 you have to look at the other openings, the ones that have poor reputations.

The success of the Soviet school was due in part to a fundamental precept: "If an opening cannot be refuted by concrete variations, it is playable, even when it appears to be on the verge of catastrophe," as Yuri Averbakh put it.

The second point of #138 is psychological. By using a line that has a bad reputation you can instill a sense of unjustified optimism in your opponent. "The best variation to use in a tournament is not a merely good line but more exactly a line which, though good, is considered to be bad," Aron Nimzovich wrote.

Nimzovich achieved excellent results by reviving the Caro-Kann and Philidor Defenses as Black and 1 b3 attack and the 3 e5 French as White. Each of those lines had become discredited to some degree in the generation before Nimzovich. And by the time that those openings were once again considered dubious, after 1970, they were resurrected and made respectable again by players who appreciated the wisdom of #138.

139

The defense always catches up
with the offense.

Every few years a powerful new approach to a major opening appears. It wins game after game. Weaker players beat stronger ones with it. This was the case of anti-Dragon attacks in the 1950s, the 3 e5 line of the Caro-Kann in the 1980s and the English Attack in the Sicilian during the 1990s, to name a very few.

But inevitably an antidote for Black is found. The defense catches up according to #139, a rephrasing of Laszlo Szabo. He noted in his game collection that there was a parallel between how innovations evolve in chess and warfare: "A new attacking weapon only gives an advantage for a short time because as soon as one is introduced, new defensive systems are worked out."

White to play

In this standard position in the Semi-Slav Defense, White used to play 1 b3 or 1 ♗d2, with an eye to 0-0-0. Black castled quickly and obtained counterplay with ...dxc4/...e5.

But in the early 1990s White began to win with **1 g4!?**. For example, 1...0-0? 2 g5 ♘h5 3 ♗d2 b6 4 e4! with a quick attack. White scored 25-8 in the first 33 games that 1 g4 was played, according to one database.

Yet within a few years, improvements were found, such as **1...♘xg4 2 ♖g1 f5!? and 3 h3 ♘gf6 4 ♖xg7 ♘e4!**. The string of White victories was over. The defense had caught up.

The same goes for a great new defensive system, like the Benko Gambit in the 1960s and the various Hedgehog lines that appeared in the 1970s. After an initial run of success, antidotes are found. The offense catches up with the defense. Will the defense make a comeback in those lines? Yes, if history repeats.

140
Help your pieces help you.

Paul Morphy's predecessors understood how an opponent could be knocked out in the first dozen moves with tactical shots. But they tried to accomplish this with two or three pieces, such as the queen, KB and KN, before castling.

What distinguished Morphy's approach was getting all of his pieces into play before his opponent. In some of Morphy's fastest victories he had four or more pieces engaged in attack when his opponent had only developed two pieces. He was credited with #140, an explanation of why rapid development worked so well. Today every beginner learns the Morphy principle. Yet it keeps beating the strongest players.

Topalov – J. Polgar
Bilbao 2007

White to play

Development is roughly equal. But it shifted sharply in White's favor after **1 ♘e4! ♗xf4 2 ♗xf4 ♛xf4 3 g3 ♛e5?! 4 0-0-0** with a threat of 5 ♘d6+ and 6 ♛xe5.

Play continued: **4...♚e7?** (4...♚f8) **5 ♛f3 ♘f6 6 ♛a3+ c5 7 ♘xc5 ♘d5 8 ♗g2**. Black, still trying to get pieces off the first rank, was lost after **8...♘b4 9 ♘d3 ♛e3+ 10 ♚b1 ♖b8 11 ♖he1! ♛b6 12 c3**. Morphy would be pleased.

141

Superior development increases in value in proportion as the game is more open.

Richard Reti called this "another of Morphy's perceptions" because it was demonstrated over and over in his games. Having more pieces developed than your opponent usually doesn't matter in a closed position. As superb as Morphy was in 1 e4 e5 games, he had difficulties making his pieces work best in positions in which the center was somewhat blocked. Adolf Anderssen appreciated that and used 1 a3 against Morphy in their match after he had been outplayed in the Ruy Lopez. Morphy opened the center as soon as possible but only scored a win, a loss and a draw.

But when the center is at least partially dissolved, the significance of an advantage in development expands sharply:

Svidler – Jakovenko
Foros 2007

White to play

White's better developed pieces should favor him but only after the center was opened, **1 d4! cxd4 2 ♕xd4!.**

A trade of queens, 2...♕xd4 3 ♗xd4, would make Black's queenside vulnerable, e.g. 3...b5 4 ♗c6+.

Black tried **2...♕b5.** But after **3 ♘d6+ ♗xd6 4 ♗xd6** he was headed downhill, **4...♕d3 5 ♖ad1 ♕xd4 6 ♖xd4** and eventually lost.

142
Develop as well as possible
– but not as quickly as possible.

This was Miguel Najdorf's advice, cited in *Najdorf: Life and Games*, to justify moving a piece twice in the opening. It challenges the conventional maxim, "Move every piece once before you move any piece twice."

As players gain experience they discover that when the middlegame begins, around move 12 or 14, one or more of their pieces are usually misplaced. Taking an extra tempo or two before then to rectify the situation is often a wise investment.

Sutovsky – McShane
Malmo 2003

Black to play

White would love to open the position with d2-d4 and Black's willingness to fall further behind in development, **1...♘g4!?**, seemed odd. It threatens a mate, 2...♘xf3+ and 3...♕xh2 but that can be parried by **2 g3**.

Black's idea is that **2...♘xf3+ 3 ♕xf3 ♘e5** and **4 ♕d1 e6 5 f4 ♘c6!** stops d2-d4. Then White has no way to open the position favorably. He's still ahead in development but Black was at least equal after **6 e5 d5 7 exd6 ♗xd6 8 ♘d5 ♕d8 9 ♗g2 0-0.**

143

You know where the knight belongs before you know that much about your bishop.

This was Wihelm Steinitz's explanation of why knights should be developed before bishops. Knowing what to do with knights is easier because they have fewer options. In practice a knight usually has one or two good squares for its first move. A bishop may have three or four.

Deciding what to do with a bishop is often delayed until the pawn situation is clarified and you can see the good diagonals – and the better ones.

van Wely – Jakovenko
Foros 2007

White to play

It's no secret in the Queen's Indian Defense that g2-g3 prepares ♗g2. But there are lines in which White waits for the center to be changed so that he can attack with ♗d3!? instead. A third option arose here when White played 1 ♗h3!, with ideas of ♗xe6 or ♘xe6.

Because he waited to decide what to do with the bishop he was able to launch a winning attack after **1...h6 2 ♘xe6! fxe6 3 ♗xe6+** and **4 ♘e5.**

144

Move the queen only one square, to the file that is least likely to be opened.

This suggestion from Cecil Purdy is a grandchild of the early-19th century recommendation that White should always play ♕e2 and Black should imitate him with ...♕e7. Since 1 e4 e5 was automatic in those days, "your King's second square" was regarded as the best place to develop the queen, around move six to eight, as J.H. Sarratt wrote in 1808.

Today the ideal first square for a queen is typically on a file that cannot be easily opened from the other side. A common situation arises in the Semi-Slav, 1 d4 d5 2 c4 c6 3 ♘f3 ♘f6 4 ♘c3 e6 5 e3 ♘bd7 when White posts his queen at c2 and looks for e2-e4. Once Black threatens to open the file from the other end (...c5), he has to consider moving the queen a second time.

145
Making the king secure is at least the equivalent of a strong developing move.

Rudolf Spielmann, who knew a thing or two about king safety, was responding with #145 to the mistaken view that castling wastes a tempo that could be better used in advancing a piece. Quite the contrary: Castling is the most efficient of all opening moves because it performs two functions, securing the king and developing the rook.

A more valid charge of wastefulness can be made against "castling by hand," which usually means spending two king tempi to safeguard it. But it makes sense when you want the rook to remain where it is.

Rustemov – Vallejo Pons
Dos Hermanas 2003

White to play

Development seems to be equal and neither king has a truly safe haven. Black can open the kingside (...hxg4) and appears to have more options in the center (...cxd4 or ...c4).

White found a good plan in 1 ♔f1! and ♔g2. He can meet 1...cxd4 with 2 ♘b5!, when the threat of ♘c7+ gains time for a favorable 3 ♘xd4.

Black played **1...hxg4 2 fxg4 ♘h6** but even though it cost White two tempi to secure his king after **3 ♔g2**, it was well invested in view of the advantageous 3...0-0 4 ♘f3 and 3...0-0-0 4 ♘a4! ♕c6 5 b4.

In the game Black tried to blow the kingside up with **3...f5** but he was worse **4 ♕f3! fxg4 5 hxg4 ♘f6? 6 ♗e5** – thanks in part to White's rook still being at h1.

146

Castle because you will or because you must – but not because you can.

This was Harry Nelson Pillsbury's "formula for castling," according to his friend William Ewart Napier in *Amenities and Background of Chessplay.*

Castling is wrong when it puts the king in a more vulnerable zone ("castling into it") or when you have better things to do at the moment. "Castling cannot be bad but its timing can," goes the Russian saying:

Grischuk – Kasparov
Moscow 2002

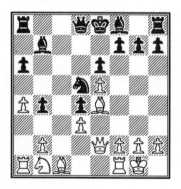

Black to play

White loosened the enemy queenside with a2-a4/...b4 and is two moves away from establishing a fine position with ♘d2-c4.

That's why 1...♗e7 and 2...0-0 would be wrong. Black correctly sensed the urgency of the situation and played **1...♕c7!**, threatening the e-pawn.

The best defense was **2 f4** but again Black delayed castling in favor of **2...♖c8!**. White discovered he was clearly worse after **3 ♘d2 ♘e3 4 ♖f3 ♗xe4!**.

He avoided 5 ♘xe4 ♕xc1+! 6 ♖xc1 ♖xc1+ in view of 7 ♔f2 ♖c2 8 ♘d2 b3 and 9...♗b4.

By the time Black castled, he was winning, **5 dxe4 d3! 6 ♕xd3 ♘c2 7 ♖b1 ♘e1 8 ♕xa6 ♘xf3+ 9 ♘xf3 ♕c4 10 ♕b5+ ♕xb5 11 axb5 ♗c5+ 12 ♔f1 0-0**.

147

Now I know why it's called castling long. It's carried out in two steps: 0-0-0 and ♔b1.

This was one of Eduard Gufeld's jokes in his game collection. Queenside castling alone doesn't make the king secure. A second, prophylactic move, ♔b1, is needed to complete the process.

If the king is left on c1, it fails to protect the a-pawn and may be vulnerable to tricks along the c1-h6 diagonal. This is why ♔b1 is often played immediately after 0-0-0. In the following example, White's delay in making the king move gave Black a tactical possibility along the dark diagonal. But once Black missed his chance, White was able to correct the error and have the better game.

Kasparov – Anand
Linares 1998

White to play

White has just castled and should continue 1 ♔b1!. He can meet the plan of 1...♗f6 and 2...♘e5! with 2 ♗f4 ♘e5 3 ♕e4!, with advantage.

But after the inexact **1 ♖he1?** ♗f6! Black would stand well. A key difference is 2 ♗f4 ♗g5! exploits the White king's position, e.g. 3 ♗xg5 hxg5 4 ♕e3 ♘b6! (5 ♘xb6+ ♕xb6 6 ♕xg5 ♕xf2).

However Black erred too, with **1...♖ge8?**. Then the belated **2 ♔b1!** favored White in view of **2...♗f6 3 ♗f4** again.

148

Whilst it is vital to develop your pieces effectively, it is even more important to restrict your opponent's development.

When Louis Charles de LaBourdonnais is remembered it is dimly and in the same breath as Alexander McDonnell, his opponent in the celebrated series of tactics-heavy matches. But his legacy includes this positional observation. Denying your opponent good first-move squares for his pieces has an impact that can last well into the middlegame.

Kasparov – Tal
Brussels 1987

Black to play

If Black retreats the attacked bishop, White has time for the non-developing f2-f3!. That takes g4 away from Black's QB and e4 away from his knight. His developing moves might then be limited to ...♗e6 and ...♕d7, while White could expand powerfully with ♗f4, g2-g4, ♔h1, ♖g1 and ♘g3.

Black avoided that with **1...♗xc3 2 bxc3 ♘e7**, to prepare 3...♗f5!. But White was still able to hamper his development with **3 ♕c2!**.

Black's pieces were passive after **3...♗d7 4 ♗g5 ♘g6** and that allowed White a winning attack after **5 f4 h6 6 ♗xf6 ♕xf6 7 f5! ♘e7 8 ♘g3 ♘c8 9 ♖f4 ♘d6 10 ♕f2**, with a powerful threat of ♘h5xg7. Black resigned shortly after **10...♖fe8? 11 ♘h5 ♕d8 12 ♘xg7! ♘e4 13 ♗xe4 dxe4 14 ff**

149

With White I have a tempo more. With Black I have a tempo less, and that allows me to exploit the first weakness of the opponent.

This is how Aron Nimzovich claimed he was "always" able to play to win, regardless of who had the first move. If he had Black, he had the advantage of being able to wait for White to make the first weakening move.

He was joking when he cited **1 e4** as an example of an opponent's "first weakness." But he demonstrated how to exploit mistakes in a 1912 game that went **1...e5 2 ♘f3 ♘c6 3 ♘c3 ♘f6 4 ♗c4 ♗c5 5 d3 d6 6 ♗g5**. (Note that Black didn't try to punish White's fourth move with 4...♘xe4 5 ♘xe4 d5, as books recommend, because 6 ♗d3 dxe4 7 ♗xe4 is not enough of a "first weakness.") Now:

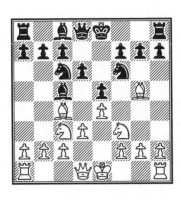

Black to play

It was time to break symmetry because 6...♗g4 7 ♘d5 favors White. Nimzovich chose **6...h6** and was rewarded with an error, **7 ♗h4 g5! 8 ♗g3 ♗g4 9 h3?** instead of the superior 9 h4!

Then **9...♗h5 10 h4 g4 11 ♘d2 a6 12 ♘d5 ♘xd5 13 ♗xd5 ♘e7!?** gave him a powerful initiative. He won after **14 ♗xb7 ♖a7 15 ♗d5 f5! 16 f4 gxf3 17 gxf3 ♘xd5 18 exd5 ♖g8 19 ♘f1 ♛b8!**.

150

If a new move is introduced, there are only two possibilities: either it's a genius move or it's an idiot move.

In case Miguel Najdorf's feelings weren't clear, he added, "A genius is born every hundred years, an idiot every day. So it's more likely that the new idea will be dubious than it should be good."

Of course, a new move is played at some point in every game. Najdorf was talking about new moves in the early opening. He was commenting on a game that began **1 d4 d5 2 c4 e6 3 ♘c3 ♘f6 4 ♘f3 c5 5 cxd5 ♘xd5 6 e3 cxd4 7 exd4 ♗b4**.

Najdorf – Portisch
Varna 1962

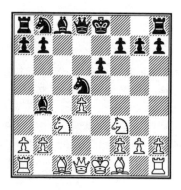

White to play

Black played the bishop move instantly and White realized its point. If he defends c3 with 8 ♗d2 the bishop gets in the way of his other pieces.

He chose **8 ♕c2** instead and was surprised by **8...♘c6 9 ♗d3 ♘xc3 10 bxc3** and now **10...♘xd4!?**

11 ♘xd4 ♕xd4.

But if 7...♗b4 was such a stroke of genius, why hadn't it become standard before, White wondered? Instead of cursing his ill fortune he looked for a refutation, just in case it was "an idiot move."

White obtained excellent compensation with **12 ♗b5!+ ♔e7** (not 12...♗d7?? 13 ♗xd7+ ♔xd7 14 ♕a4+) **13 0-0**. His attack was irresistible after **13...♕xc3 14 ♕e2! ♗d6** (14...♕xa1?? 15 ♗g5+) **15 ♗b2 ♕a5 16 ♖fd1 ♖d8 17 ♕h5!**.

This didn't refute 7...♗b4 because it can't be refuted. It was not an idiot move, after all, but quite a good one. It had just become "hidden in the games of the old masters."

CHAPTER NINE: **PAWNS**

151
Every pawn is a potential queen.

"Do not forget this," James Mason added for emphasis. But we always do, often until move 30 or 40.

Why? Perhaps because most chess thinking is short run. Typical tactics, like pins and forks, take two or three moves to create and exploit. Many good plans don't last much longer. But queening a pawn is a long-term idea. We think about it after we've stopped thinking of pawns as the ant-power of the board, the units we use to build centers, anchor outpost knights and break open enemy strongholds.

Hernandez – Anand
Merida 2001

Black to play

Black's position seems shaky. But he faces no immediate threat and, as per #35, has no reason to adopt purely defensive measures like ...♔e8. It was time to think about the long term.

His **1...♗xb2!** provided some compensation for the Exchange and gave his opponent something

to worry about: the b3-pawn is a potential queen.

White found a good answer, **2 ♕h2**, and then **2...♖b7 3 ♖h7+ ♔e8 4 ♖d1**. The escape route for Black's king is cut and White hints at 5 ♖h8+ ♗xh8 6 ♕xh8+.

Black's response, **4...♗d4**, seemed to plug up all the holes. White didn't find a good reply – because he forgot Mason's maxim.

White to play

He should start pushing his own passer with 5 a4!. Black's pieces are so tied up (5...♖a7 6 ♕b8+) that the pawn can win by itself. For example, 5...c3 6 a5 ♕e5 7 ♕xe5 ♗xe5 8 a6! ♖a7 9 ♖xe7+! ♗xe7 10 ♗xe7 ♔xe7 11 a7.

Instead, White played 5 ♖h8+? ♔d7! 6 ♖a8? and it was a Black pawn that brought matters to a close following 6...b2!.

For example, 7 ♕xc2 ♕h3+ 8 ♕h2 ♕xf3+. The game went 7 ♕h8 ♔c6 8 ♕e8+ ♕d7 9 ♕xg6+ e6 10 ♖a6+ ♔b5 11 ♖xe6 ♕h7+ and **White resigned** before a trade of queens and ...♘xa3/...b1(♕).

152
Pawns increase in value as they advance.

This, surprisingly, is a modern concept. Philidor, who made pawn play famous, warned against pushing pawns beyond the fourth rank (!) until the endgame. "Pawns, especially central ones, lose part of their strength by advancing to the fifth rank," he wrote in *L'analyse du jeu des Echecs*.

Wilhelm Steinitz agreed that advanced pawns are weak. "As a rule it is unadvisable to advance any pawn beyond the fourth rank," he wrote in *The Modern Chess Instructor*. A pawn on the fifth stands well only if protected by another pawn, he added.

The modern view holds that a pawn has a "lust to expand," in Aron Nimzovich's hard-to-forget phrase – and it becomes more valuable as it advances.

How much more? Eduard Gufeld offered an equation in *Chess Strategy*: A pawn not under attack increases by a factor of 1.5 as it goes above the third rank. This means it can be worth a piece on the sixth rank. This echoes comments by Akiba Rubinstein and (just about rook pawns) Siegbert Tarrasch.

Gufeld's formula also means a protected pawn on the seventh is worth a rook. If that sounds excessive, consider the following:

Khalifman – Ermenkov
Elenite 1995

White to play

White correctly rejected a draw by repetition (1 ♕b7 ♖b8 2 ♕a6 ♖a8). He played **1 b4! ♖xc6 2 dxc6** because two connected pawns on the sixth (2...cxb4 3 b6) must win.

Black preferred **2...e6 3 ♖ed1 ♕b8** but was caught in an avalanche of *peshki*, **4 bxc5 d5 5 exd5 exd5 6 ♖xd5 ♕e8 7 c7 ♕f7 8 b6! ♕xd5 9 b7 Resigns**.

153

Passed pawns must be pushed.

Another insight from that great lawgiver Anonymous. It is a natural application of #152 and is the way most endgames are won. When we don't push a pawn it's because we fear it would be beyond our ability to defend it or because it's performing better immediate service where it is.

Kramnik – Gelfand
Dortmund 2007

White to play

White's advantage lies in his passed c-pawn and minor pieces. But it is the pawn that makes his pieces superior to Black's, by denying d5 to the enemy knight and b5 to the bishop. To make progress White has to choose between #153 and "Do not advance a pawn which is already restricting your opponent's pieces" (LaBourdonnais).

He correctly chose **1 c5!**. Black's pieces were liberated but the pawn soared in value after **1...♗b5+ 2 ♔g2 ♕c7 3 c6**.

Black found nothing better than **3...a6 4 ♕c5+ ♔e8 5 b4 ♘d5 6 ♗xd5 exd5 7 ♕xd5** and lost when forced to give up the bishop for the c-pawn.

154

A superior pawn structure is a long term advantage.

Mikhail Botvinnik's observation, cited in *64* (September 2004), contradicts another view, expressed by Reuben Fine: "Pawn inferiority is usually relative to the amount of time to straighten them out."

Fine had in mind backward pawns. They are weak until they can be safely pushed and/or traded. But other bad pawns, such as an isolani or undissolvable doubled pawns, can't be repaired, Fine conceded. They remain long-term disadvantages, and that's why Botvinnik's postulate is the one to remember.

Kramnik – Ivanchuk
Monaco 2001

White to play

White's **1 e4!** is tactically justified by 1...♘xe4 2 ♖xc6! ♘xd2 3 ♘xd2 dxc6 4 ♗xc6+. Or 1...♗xe4 2 ♘xe4 ♘xe4 3 ♘e5 (3...d5 4 ♗xe4 dxe4 5 ♕g4) with advantage.

But the main point of 1 e4! is strategic. White threatens ♘d4xc6. The game continued **1...0-0 2 ♘d4 ♖c8 3 ♘xc6 dxc6 4 ♕e2 ♕c7 5 ♖c2**.

White's superior pawn structure is significant because it's an asset

that #154 places in a high category. According to one modern view, there are four types of advantage in chess:

The highest level is a material edge that is sufficient to win without exceptional effort. Two extra pawns or the Exchange are examples of this.

On the second level is a smaller material advantage, such as an extra pawn. It needs work to become decisive.

The third type of edge is a long-term positional one, like White's pressure against the c-pawn here.

Such an advantage requires a lot more work to convert than a material edge. But it is significantly more valuable than the fourth kind of asset, a temporary one such as Black's control of an open d-file after **5...♖fd8**.

The file was a minor factor – and the c-pawn was the main theme – in the rest of the game, which White won after **6 ♖fc1 h6 7 h3 ♘d7 8 ♘f3 ♛b6 9 e5 c5 10 ♘d2 ♘a5 11 ♘c4 ♘xc4 12 ♖xc4** and **13 b4!**.

155
Pawns alone form the basis of attack and defense.

This was Philidor's explanation of his declaration that pawns are "the very life" – he didn't say "the soul" – "of the game." Later writers elaborated:

Rudolf Spielmann, thinking mainly of attack, wrote, "The pawns are the steel structure of every position and ordinarily dictate the course of events." On the other hand, Evgeny Znosko-Borovsky said, "Pawns, used collectively, are the defensive force *par excellence*."

Bent Larsen said pawns are the key to combinations because you can spot tactical patterns in familiar pawn structures. And Yakov Neishtadt said pawns to a large degree determine piece activity. They decide whether a rook has an open file, a bishop has a good diagonal, a knight gets an outpost, and so on.

Zviagintsev – Dautov
Essen 2002

Black to play

Every diligent student goes through a Nimzovich period. (Most of us recover.) Under Nimzo's influence, we see Black having more control of the center, a blockading knight at f5, the better dark-squared bishop and a lustful d-pawn. He must stand well, right?

Wrong. The pawns make White's position far preferable. His b- and e-pawns render Black's other knight useless and the bishop weak. His kingside pawns make a strong atack possible with ♗d3, ♛e2 and g2-g4.

This became clearer after **1...a5 2 a3 axb4 3 axb4 ♛c6 4 ♗d3 g6** and White seized the initiative with **5 b5! ♛b7 6 c4**. He stood better after **6...♖xa1 7 ♛xa1 ♘d4 8 ♛d1 ♖a8 9 ♘xd4 cxd4 10 ♛g4** and won.

156
A pawn is best defended by a pawn.

The words come from *The Logical Approach to Chess* by Max Euwe, M. Blaine and J.F.S. Rumble. But the sentiment stems from #32, "The stronger the piece, the weaker the defender" and the Steinitzian principle of economy in defense.

"The pawn is a born defender," Nimzovich said. Its role in life is to perform the sentry duties that would be wasteful if performed by other pieces.

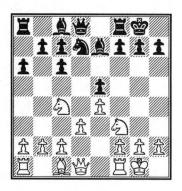

Black to play

In this Ruy Lopez position, Black's immediate concern is his e-pawn. It seems reasonable to defend it with 1...♗f6.

But Black's pieces get in a tangle, **1...♗f6? 2 ♗d2 ♖e8 3 ♗c3**. He cannot move his QN until he defends his e-pawn further or creates another weakness (3...b5? 4 ♘a5). In one celebrated upset, Yefim Geller found himself losing after playing the clumsy **3...c5 4 a4 b6 5 h3 a5 6 ♕d2 ♖e6 7 b3 ♕e8**.

However, with **1...f6!** Black solves his problems. His knight is liberated and can go on the offensive, after ...c5, and ...♘b8-c6-d4. Many amateurs are suspicious of 1...f6 because they've been scared into believing that all holes are bad. But e6 is not a hole if Black has the only light-squared bishop (cf. #80).

The guideline here comes with the usual caveat: A pawn is best defended by a pawn, all other things being equal. The caveat is significant in positions such as 1 e4 e5 2 ♘f3 when Black can choose between defending the e-pawn with 2...d6 or 2...♘c6. This time the pawn move has a drawback because it cramps Black's game somewhat.

157

Pawn chains are best attacked at the base.

This building block of middlegame strategy dates from the pre-history of chess. It must have been familiar to Gioacchino Greco because he gave examples in his manuscript circa 1620 of 1 e4 e6 2 d4 d5 3 e5 with the sole continuation being 3...c5. The logic is that ...cxd4 would open a file for Black at least half way, undermine the e5-pawn, and create the possibility of a passed d-pawn. The value of #157 is universally recognized today — at least by humans:

Kasparov – X3D Fritz
Match 2003

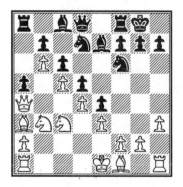

Black to play

Virtually everyone in the ballroom-full audience watching this game recognized that Black should attack the chain's base at e3, such as with 1...♘e8 followed by ...f5 and ...f4!. Otherwise Black can do nothing while White gobbles up the a-pawn and attacks the other base, at b7.

You could hear spectators groan as Black failed, move after move, to find the plan that every post-beginner is taught. It was clear after 1...♗d6 2 ♖b1 (not 2 cxd6??

♘xb6) ♗e7? 3 ♘xa5 ♘b8 4 ♗b4 ♕d7 that Black had no clue to the position.

Play continued 5 ♖b2 ♕e6 6 ♕d1 ♘fd7 7 a3 ♕h6 8 ♘b3 ♗h4? 9 ♕d2 ♘f6? 10 ♔d1 ♗e6 11 ♔c1 ♖d8 12 ♖c2 ♘bd7 13 ♔b2 ♘f8 14 a4 ♘g6 15 a5 ♘e7 16 a6! bxa6 17 ♘a5 and Black resigned 15 moves later in this position.

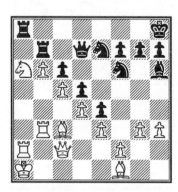

Black to play

This is what the attack-on-the-base strategy looks like when it succeeds perfectly. White can push the b-pawn to victory after ♖ba3, ♘b4 and the removal of the blockader at b7.

158

If you have a white-squared bishop, you need to place your pawns on black squares.

This is the Philidor quote that is often misunderstood, rather than mistranslated. His interest in pawns naturally led him to bishops because other pieces aren't affected nearly as much by pawn advances. (The others are, of course, affected by pawn *trades*.)

Philidor's counsel is sometimes taken solely as a warning against making a bishop "bad." But his concern, as he went on to explain in *L'analyse*, was maximizing the power of both the bishop and the pawns. They coordinate well when they separately control light and dark squares. Here's a case of each player making a major decision with their e-pawn. What makes one move good and the other bad are the bishops:

Andersson – Ermenkov
Cienfuegos 1975

Black to play

Black has an isolated pawn but a well-placed knight and some attacking prospects (...♕c8-h3). But he played **1...e5?**, devaluing both the pawn and his bishop.

White, on the other hand, appreciated the strength of **2 e4! ♘f6 3 f3!**. His pawns and bishop work together well: **3...♖ae8 4 ♔g2! ♖f7 5 ♕c4 h6 6 ♘c5 ♖fe7 7 ♗e3 ♘h7 8 b4! ♘f8 9 ♖d2 ♖d8 10 ♖fd1 ♖xd2+ 11 ♖xd2 g5 12 a4** and so on until he was able to crash through on the queenside.

159

When the opponent has a bishop, keep your pawns on squares of the same color.

This is Jose Capablanca's rule, in his *Primer*. It often clashes with #158 and that confuses inexperienced players. Why put pawns where they can be targets? The answer is that you are limiting the scope of the enemy bishop. If you put pawns on the other squares you are creating holes for the bishop to exploit.

Kasparov – Anand
PCA World Championship 1995

White to play

White, a pawn up, made a surprising draw offer as he played 1 ♗e3. Black quickly accepted and explained that a draw was fair

because once he puts his remaining pawns on the color of White's bishop (...b6, ...f6) "he cannot hope to play for a win." The bishop bites on granite while Black can seize the initiative on the light squares, with ...♕f7 and its threat of ...♗xc4.

This is why White should have played 1 ♗b2!. Then 1...f6 is again correct but can be answered by 2 e5! fxe5 3 ♖ae1, exposing Black's dark-square weaknesses. Better is 2...f5!, which violates #159 by necessity. It allows 3 ♖ad1 and ♖d6! when White would have winning chances because rooks get to play on 64 squares, not just 32

160
Nothing compromises a position like pawn moves.

Beginners learn this lesson when they weaken their castled position with pushes. A White king at g1 is typically most secure if the pawns remain at f2, g2 and h2. They have to be attacked at least twice before they are really threatened. "The best position for the pawns is the horizontal line," said Znosko-Borovsky in *The Middle Game in Chess*.

When Siegbert Tarrasch wrote #160, he added, "especially in the center of the board." Even a natural advance there has to be viewed with suspicion:

Carlsen – Aronian

Candidates match 2007

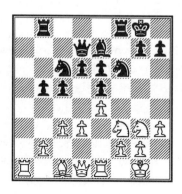

White to play

Quiet positions call for quiet moves. Here 1 ♗d2 or 1 ♗e3 are passive but good.

On the other hand, White's **1 d4?** was active but bad for three reasons: After **1...exd4 2 cxd4 c4!** Black undoubles his pawns, obtains a strong queenside majority and improves his bishop.

White tried to compensate with **3 ♗g5 h6 4 d5?!**. But his second bad move with this pawn put Black on the road to winning, **4...exd5 5 ♗xf6 ♗xf6 6 ♕xd5+ ♖f7 7 ♕d2 ♘e5!**.

161

Doubled pawns are healthy as long as they remain in their position, crouching like a frog.

Aron Nimzovich was addressing a natural question: What if you have slightly damaged pawns, such as a group of three that includes doubled pawns. Shouldn't you try to advance them in hopes of dissolving them?

His answer was "no" and he explained it by #161. He added another analogy, "It is no disadvantage for a man to be a limper as long as he remains seated."

Rahman – Speelman
Calcutta 1996

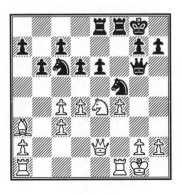

Black to play

White had correctly refrained from touching his "crouching" c-pawns in the previous eight moves. It is Black who should try to

change the pawn structure, and the standard strategy is ...c5. The thematic way of doing that is 1...♘a5 and 2...c5 so that the c4-pawn becomes a target after ...♖c8 and ...cxd4. But Black didn't like putting his knight on the edge of the board in case of 2 c5 bxc5. He prepared the push with **1...♘d8** instead.

White responded **2 c5?**, a positional blunder. He was worse after **2...bxc5 3 dxc5 d5! 4 ♘d2 ♘c6** and then **5 ♘f3 d4!**.

For example, 6 cxd4 ♘fxd4 and ...♘c2 or, as the game went, **6 ♖ac1 ♘e3**, with what proved to be a winning edge. (7 ♘xd4 ♘xd4 8 ♕xe3 ♘c2 9 ♕f3 ♘xa3 10 c4 e5!).

162

The essential disadvantage of the isolated pawn, its essential weakness, lies not in the pawn itself, but in the square in front.

What did the Hypermoderns leave us besides skepticism about pawn centers? Another important piece of their legacy is #162, in which Richard Reti overthrew a conventional view in *Masters of the Chess Board.*

An isolani, such as a White pawn at d4, is almost always a target. But a White rook at d1 or queen at d2 is often enough to defend it. The real problem with the isolani is it allows Black a wonderful outpost at d5 that White's heavy pieces cannot attack.

Nimzovich, another Hypermodern, was obsessed with blockading the isolani and other pawns as well. ("The passed pawn is a criminal, who should be kept under lock and key. Mild measures, such as police surveillance, are not sufficient.") The reasons are not just positional.

Sutovsky – van Wely

Amsterdam 2002

White to play

For 29 moves White had maintained the blockade on d4. But now he wanted to increase his advantage and didn't like 1 ♖xf5 because 1...♗d3 and ...♗e4 appeared too strong. (It isn't: 2 ♖f7+ ♔g8 3 ♖g7+ ♔f8 4 ♔g2! ♗e4+ 5 ♔f2 wins.)

Instead he played **1 ♗c5??** and was stunned by **1...d4!**. The dreaded Black bishop comes alive after all (2...♗d5 3 R-moves ♖h1 mate).

White replied **2 ♔g2** but he was lost, and **2...d3!** would have ended the game fastest.

163

Blockading an isolated pawn is outmoded. It should not be blockaded but taken!

This was Bent Larsen's improvement on Nimzovich's "First restrain, then blockade and finally destroy." Nimzo's successors argued that blockading an isolani was as good as winning it and that by leaving it on the board the pawn inevitably becomes weaker. But Larsen, who liked to play with or against an isolani, disagreed.

I. Sokolov – Short
Bled 2002

White to play

A standard policy in this position was 1 0-0 because White stands well in the opened position of

1...dxe3 2 fxe3 and then 2...♘e5 3 ♗xe5 ♗xa4 4 ♕b2!.

But better is **1 e4!** because White can blockade and encircle the d-pawn until it can be taken. He accomplished this with simple moves, **1...♗e8 2 ♘b2 ♘d7 3 ♘d3** and then **3...♗h4 4 c5! ♗xg3 5 hxg3 ♘de5 6 f4 ♘xd3+ 7 ♗xd3 h6 8 ♘c4 ♖c8 9 ♘d6 ♖c7 10 e5**.

The d-pawn is dead and the only reason White didn't stop to capture it was that he had a faster win, **10...f6 11 ♕e2 a6 12 ♕e4 f5 13 ♕e2** and **14 g4!**.

The news for the player holding the isolani is not at all bad. Six times in the 1974 Candidates finals match Viktor Korchnoi accepted an isolated d-pawn as Black in the French Defense. In four of those games his opponent, Anatoly Karpov, managed to capture it. In the other two he blockaded or restrained it. But all six games were drawn because Black consistently managed to obtain piece play as compensation. That's why a good guideline is:

164
Play the isolani like a gambit.

In the early part of a game, there is a tradeoff between the plusses and minuses of an isolani. It is an offensive weapon that supports outposts and may unleash pent-up power by advancing. But as the endgame approaches, these virtues count less and the pawn becomes more and more a liability.

Lev Alburt, in *Chess Rules of Thumb*, meant by #164 that the possessor of an isolated d-pawn should seek the initiative as if he were a pawn down. Otherwise his position slowly deteriorates.

Black to play

Black should play energetically even though **1...♘xf3+ 2 ♗xf3 ♕c7!** seems to doom his d-pawn.

For example, 3 g3 ♗e5 4 ♗xd5 ♘xd5 5 ♖xd5 ♗e6 is the kind of compensation a King's Gambiteer can appreciate.

White can be more cautious with **3 h3**. But again Black should handle the position as if he might be a pawn down at any moment, **3...♗h2+ 4 ♔h1 ♗e5 5 ♗d2 ♗e6 6 ♗e1 ♖fd8 7 ♕e2 a6 8 ♖ac1 ♖ac8 9 a3 ♕d7** (hinting at ...♗xh3).

After **10 ♔g1 ♗b8!** he has good play thanks to ...♕d6 and/or ...♗a7.

There's also a bit of folk psychology at work: When you lose a pawn, your position often seems to improve. This is an illusion, of course. Nevertheless, if you've spent several moves trying to protect a targeted d-pawn – and then manage to sacrifice it for some play – you may feel liberated at having been relieved of the defense. Your pieces, and mind, are freed to do other things.

165
Hanging pawns are a pair of isolated pawns.

Igor Bondarevsky's rationale for this perception (cited in *Shakhmaty v SSSR* 1991) is that hanging pawns are separated from other pawns and cannot be protected by them, just as an isolani is separated and vulnerable.

It's true that one hanging pawn can be protected by the other, when it advances. But then both are usually immobile and more vulnerable in the long run. If Black has hangers at d5 and c5 and protects one with ...c4 the laggard at d5 can be pounded by rooks and minor pieces the way an isolani would. And if you manage to exchange off one of the hanging pawns, you're not out of the woods – because you've created an isolani:

Yusupov – A. Sokolov
Interpolis 1987

White to play

There is no reason to complicate (1 ♕a4?! dxc4 2 ♖xd7!?) when White has strong quiet moves, such as **1 ♘e3!**. By forcing **1...d4**, his slight edge grew, **2 ♘ec4 ♗xc4 3 ♘xc4 ♕a6 4 e3!**.

Black must acquiesce to an isolani because 4...dxe3? 5 ♗xd7 is unsound. Play continued, **4...♘b6 5 ♘xb6 ♕xb6 6 exd4 cxd4 7 ♗c7! ♕c5 8 ♕xc5 ♗xc5 9 ♖ac1** and White's pressure mounted until Black lost the d-pawn and resigned.

If forced to make a choice of evils, some players prefer to have an isolani and others will take the hanging pawns. Nigel Short said he didn't understand why his colleagues avoided the hangers until he heard Ulf Andersson's tongue-in-cheek explanation: When you blunder away an isolated pawn, you no longer have any weaknesses. But when you blunder away a hanging pawn, you're left with an isolani – and that's much worse.

166

Trade rooks when you have an isolani. Avoid the trade when you have doubled pawns.

In general, any trade of pieces should hurt the side with weaker pawns because it lessens the chance of a tactic that would mask the strategic weakness. But this is not the case with an isolated pawn.

The presence of heavy pieces tends to increase pressure on an isolani because it can be attacked on its file. An illustration of rook finesses was:

Ivanchuk – Aronian
Morelia-Linares 2007

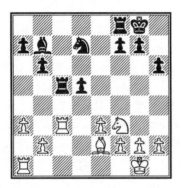

White to play

White's **1 ♖cc1!**, rather than 1 ♖ac1, looks bizarre if you're unaware of the principle. (If you understand it, you know that 1...♖xc1+! 2 ♖xc1 ♖c8! would have been a better defense.)

After Black met 1 ♖cc1! with **1...♖fc8**, White replied **2 ♖d1!** even though **2...♖c2 3 ♗b5! ♘f8 4 ♖ab1** made it look like he'd overdosed on passivity pills.

He saw that Black's rook will be kicked back by ♗a4, and that led to **4...♖2c7 5 ♗a4 ♘e6 6 ♗b3 ♔f8 7 h3 ♖c5**.

With **8 ♔h2!** White again kept rooks on (8 ♖d2 ♖c1+!) and made slow progress, **8...♔e7 9 ♖d2 ♖b5 10 ♗a2 ♖bc5 11 ♘e1 a5 12 ♖bd1 ♖d8 13 ♔g3 ♖b5? 14 f3 ♖c8 15 ♘d3**. The threat of 16 a4 led to **15...d4 16 ♗xe6 ♔xe6 17 ♘f4+** and White won after **18 ♖xd4**.

And what if you have doubled pawns? This time rook trades hurt. The reason is that when you make a doubling pawn capture, say 1 d4 d5 2 ♘f3 ♘f6 3 ♗f4 e6 4 e3 ♗d6 5 ♗g3!? ♗xg3 6 hxg3, some or all of the weakness is offset by use of the half-open file.

This was folk wisdom in the 19th-20th century. It was confirmed by a database analysis reported by IM Larry Kaufman in *Chess Life* (May 2005). Kaufman concluded that when a player still has both rooks, the "cost" to him of a doubled pawn is only 1/16th of a pawn. The rooks' ability to use the half-open file wipes out most of the weakness. But this cost grows to 1/4 of a pawn when a pair of rooks is traded and to 3/8th when both rooks are traded, he found.

167

Geniuses do not have to capture toward the center.

Irving Chernev's wisecrack could be applied to other pawn rules as well: If you understand when it makes sense to violate a rule, go ahead.

Philidor religiously captured towards the center, even when – as in a much-anthologized game with a certain Count Bruhl – it made more sense to violate the ancient rule. The proper, Chernevian attitude was demonstrated by Greco, nearly two centuries before Philidor.

Greco analyzed **1 e4 e6 2 d4 d5 3 e5 c5 4 c3 ♘c6** and showed how if White supports his center with **5 ♘f3 ♗d7 6 ♗e3**, Black can transfer his attack to a new base, **6...c4!?** and ...b5-b4.

One of his illustrative games showed White attacking the Black base, **7 b3 b5 8 a4!**. Then came **8...a6! 9 axb5 axb5 10 ♖xa8 ♛xa8**.

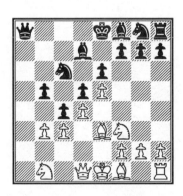

White to play

Now on **11 bxc4?** Greco gave **11...dxc4!** to clear d5 for Black's pieces.

He soon had a winning position – although White's play helped, **12 ♗e2 ♘ge7 13 0-0 ♘d5 14 ♗d2 ♗e7 15 ♘g5 ♗xg5 16 ♗xg5 0-0 17 ♗f3 ♘a5 18 ♗xd5 ♛xd5 19 f4 ♗c6 20 ♛d2 ♘b3 21 ♛c2 ♘xd4!**, in view of the 22 cxd4 ♛xd4+ 23 ♛f2 ♛xf2+ and ...♖a8/ ...b4 endgame.

The toward-the-center rule is so ingrained that Bobby Fischer had fun with it in *My 60 Memorable Games*.

Mikhail Botvinnik was following his opening preparation for a previous World Championship match when Fischer stunned him with a refutation:

Botvinnik – Fischer
Varna 1962

Black to play

With **1...♕xf4!** Black won a pawn (2 ♗xf4 ♘xc5). This looks so simple that there must be more to it.

There was. Fischer pointed out the desperado, **2 ♕xb6**, which seems to win a piece because both queens are hanging. But Black can reply **2...♕e4!**, attacking a rook. If White responds by attacking the queen, **3 f3 ♕h4+ 4 ♗f2** then **4...♕b4+** gains time for a capture on b6.

Fischer said that Black will win with **5...axb6!** and explained why this move deserved an exclamation point. It was "toward the center," he said.

CHAPTER TEN: **PIECES**

168

When two pieces coordinate in attack, their power is greater than the sum of the parts.

As Philidor observed in #6, you need to employ several pieces in an attack. Two pieces are better than one, three are superior to two and so on. But it was Emanuel Lasker, in his *Manual*, who popularized the idea that coordination multiplied the strength of pieces: Two pieces are more than twice as powerful as one.

This principle doesn't play a major role in the opening, when pieces are just coming off the first rank, or in the endgame, where they more often act independently. But coordinating the pieces "is the main feature of the middlegame," Jose Capablanca wrote. Even when few pieces are left they can produce magic together:

Gonzales Perez – Espinosa
Cuba 2004

Black to play

All four Black pieces take part in **1...♖xg2+! 2 ♔xg2 ♖g8+ 3 ♔h1** (3 ♔f2 e3 mate or 3 ♔h3 ♗c8!)

e3+ 4 ♗f3 and now **4...♕g2+! 5 ♗xg2 ♗xg2+ 6 ♔g1 ♗f3+** mates.

Lasker pointed out that pieces cooperate best when they are close to one another. But proximity alone isn't sufficient, as the example of a knight and a pawn shows:

Placing the knight in front of or alongside the pawn doesn't help much because they don't coordinate. But placing it directly behind a pawn doubles the attack on the squares diagonally in front of the pawn. And placing it diagonally behind a pawn creates a phalanx of four attacked squares in the rank ahead of the pawn.

169
You must attack with three pieces against two.

This was Garry Kasparov's advice (*British Chess Magazine*, December 1999) about certain endgames, such as when a player has two minor pieces fighting a rook. But it applies even more to middlegames. When there is a material imbalance, such as queen for three minor pieces, the best way for the player with the pieces to maximize their strength is to direct them against the king.

Polugayevsky – Torre
Biel 1989

White to play

Black has a slight material advantage – that "half-pawn." White could win a pawn with 1 ♗xb6, and thereby assume the lead in material.

But let's look at the board in simplest terms. We see four White pieces fighting three Black pieces. That's a numerical advantage and the way to use that advantage is attack.

Attack what? Well, the natural target is the square that only Black's king can defend, g7. That leaves us with **1 ♗d4!**, threatening 2 ♕f4 ♖-moves 3 ♕e5! and wins.

Black met that with **1...♘c4 2 ♕f4 ♖d8**. But he is out of useful moves after **3 h4!**. White won following **3...♕b4 4 ♕c7 ♖f8 5 ♗xc4 dxc4 6 ♕e5!** (e.g. 6...f6 7 ♕e6+ ♔h7 8 gxf6 ♕b7 9 ♘d5! gxf6 10 ♔g2 ♔h6 11 ♘xf6 etc.).

170

The less redundant two pieces are, the stronger they are in combination.

By redundancy Mark Dvoretsky meant the duplication of effort that plagues some pairs of similar pieces. A queen and bishop compete with one another for the same diagonals. That's why they don't work together as well as a queen and knight, he said.

Here's how to apply this principle:

Anand – Morozevich
World Championship 2007

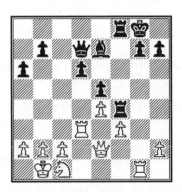

White to play

If White could quickly get his knight to d5 he would have an obvious advantage. That's why he looked at **1 ♕g2 g6 2 ♘e2**, when the threat of ♘xf4 gains time for 3 ♘c3.

But he rejected this after seeing **2...♖h4 3 ♘c3 ♕h3!** virtually forces a trade of queens. Many players would say the position after **4 ♘d5 ♕xg2 5 ♖xg2 ♗d8** is not only better for White but better than what he had in the diagram.

However, he rejected 1 ♕g2 because the bishop is no longer redundant in the endgame and, in fact, is stronger than the knight. White's chances would decline, not increase, in the 4...♕xg2 line.

Redundancy is everywhere in chess. Bishops are bad when they share the same squares as their pawns. The best strategy for the superior side in a 2R-vs.-R+N endgame is to trade a pair of rooks. Two queens are extremely redundant (#174). The worst pair of all are two bishops of the same color. But thankfully they only annoy us in compositions.

171

When you need to activate the king
– and when it's premature –
is a matter of "king feeling."

"King feeling" is a subtle sense of knowing when it is safe to bring your king out of its protective shell. This is not a matter of calculation because some positions when the king should be activated are impossible to count out accurately. And it's not a matter of applying rules because some kings are quite safe on the fourth rank in the late middlegame while others are unsafe on the second rank.

Shirov – Karpov
Linares 2001

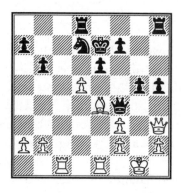

Black to play

Defense orthodoxy tells Black to keep the position closed (1...e5). But he wanted to counterattack, **1...♞e5! 2 dxe6 f5!**.

Then on **3 ♖c7+** he rejected 3...♚xe6 4 ♗xf5+! and had to choose between 3...♚d6 and the safety-minded 3...♚f6. The variations are hard to calculate.

But with the same excellent king feeling that led him to play 1...♞e5!, Black accepted the sacrifice **3...♚d6! 4 ♖xa7 fxe4**. He had a winning advantage soon after **5 e7 ♞xf3+ 6 ♚f1 ♖de8 7 ♕d7+ ♚e5**.

Describing this sense as a feeling is relatively new. "The king feels quite good in the center," Aivar Gipslis wrote when his king landed on c4 in a middlegame at the 1967 interzonal. Yuri Razuvaev praised a Soviet colleague for "subtle king feeling" in 1982 and Gregory Kaidanov helped popularize the term with #171 in *Shakhmaty v SSSR* in 1991.

172
Heavy pieces are strong only in attack.

This is a natural extension of "The stronger the piece, the weaker the defender" (#32). It's been expressed in many ways, such as "The rook is a major piece only in attacking" (Edmar Mednis in *Practical Middlegame Tips*). Rooks are good at gobbling pawns but poor at blockading and protecting pawns and minor pieces.

It's a similar story for the queen. Its strength often seems to be 90 percent offensive and 10 percent defensive. It can make double or triple attacks with minimal effort. A queen going just one square, say from e3 to d4, suddenly threatens pieces along the d-file, fourth rank and a1-h8 diagonal, while retaining its threats against pieces on the g1-a7 line.

But a queen's defensive power lies mainly in counterattack. When a Q-vs.-R+B+P imbalance occurs, the key issue is whether the queen can deliver checks. If it can't, the other side is better, wrote Lev Alburt.

Farago – Adorjan
Hungary 1978

White to play

Even if Black's c-pawn were on the kingside, say at g6 or h7, he would have some winning chances. As it stands, he has even better chances because the queen cannot

stop a simple plan: Get the rook to e2 or d2, advance the pawn to c2 and force a new queen after ...♗b2.

The queen can only counter-attack, **1 h5! ♖e4 2 ♕e8! c2 3 h6+**. By trading pawns White opens the way for a perpetual check, e.g. **3...♔xh6 4 ♕xf7 c1(♕) 5 ♕xf6+ ♔h5 6 ♕f7+** and draws.

Black improved with **4...♗g7! 5 ♕c7 ♖e2 6 ♕c4 ♔h7!** since he can promote after ...♗b2 or ...♗h6. Nevertheless, White should have drawn thanks to the queen's checking power after **7 ♔f3 ♗h6 8 ♔xe2 c1(♕) 9 ♕xe6**. (He lost due to a blunder.)

173
The queen is the Achilles
of the War of the Chessmen.

Ercole del Rio was alluding (in his book, *The War of the Chessmen*) to the late entry into battle of the most powerful piece. As noted earlier, the weaker the unit, the earlier it is typically developed. The queen often moves last because it can be driven back when attacked by anything other than the enemy queen.

According to the authoritative researcher Tim Krabbe, the latest a queen has made its first move was Alvarado-Carvajal, San Jose 2001. After spending the first 75 moves on d8, Black had run out of other useful moves and played 76...♛a8.

But Achilles was still quite a warrior when he showed up. In that 2001 game the queen's remarkable power was revealed when White promoted to a second queen. Black replied with a queen sacrifice that forced stalemate.

It can be argued that of all the first-rank pieces, the queen is the one that stands best where it does at the start of the game. Often there is no good reason to move it until after major changes in the pawn structure and piece configuration – simply because it has no better square to go to than d1 (or d8). In two recent World Championship events, the 2005 (FIDE) tournament and the 2006 reunification match, the queen took its first step at an average of the 14th move. In five of the tournament games, neither queen moved until the 20th turn.

174

The board is simply too small for two queens of the same color.

"They're in each other's way," Viktor Korchnoi added, as he described his game with Eugenio German at the 1962 interzonal. Korchnoi enjoyed an arithmetic material advantage, 2Qs+R-vs.-Q+2Rs+N. But the queen's offensive power plummets when two queens duplicate the work of one. Since he saw no way to force a trade of a pair of queens, Korchnoi agreed to a draw.

He put this knowledge to good use at Dortmund 1994 when he allowed Anatoly Karpov to promote to a second queen. Karpov's two queens and bishop were no match for Korchnoi's queen, rook and two bishops. In fact, post-mortem analysis indicated that Karpov's losing mistake was deciding to create a second queen, when he might have drawn by promoting to a knight instead.

In both of those games the semi-blocked pawn structure reduced the scope of the extra queen. A more telling example was:

Kosten – Zelcic
Bozen 1992

Black to play

White's material edge is substantial. Computers give him a winning (+3) advantage. Yet after 35 more moves of shifting the queens around White conceded he couldn't win. The board was simply too small.

175
Only a lonely queen fears two rooks.

Every beginner is taught that a queen is worth nine pawns or "units" and a rook is worth five. Conventional wisdom follows the arithmetic: If you give up two rooks to win your opponent's queen, you supposedly need an extra pawn to balance matters.

But a subtle distinction was discovered in the 19th century. J. H. Sarratt said it was only in an endgame that a queen needs an extra pawn to balance two rooks. Earlier it's the rooks who need an extra pawn, he said. This view was endorsed by Howard Staunton in his *Handbook* ("The power of the queen is wonderfully greater when she is aided and protected by other pieces than when she goes forth unsupported".)

But the distinction was largely forgotten until Bobby Fischer showed that when there are minor pieces present – even just one pair – the queen has no reason to fear the rooks, and #175 is a paraphrase of Fischer.

Wilder – Polugayevsky
Haninge 1989

White to play

Since pawns are equal, Black appears to be doing well. If there were no knights, he might consider playing for a win by engineering ...a4 or ...f5.

But with knights on, White is much better. This became clear after 1 ♕d1! f5 2 ♘b5, threatening ♘d4.

The coordinated queen and knight would be decisive after 2...♔f7 3 exf5 exf5 4 ♕d5+ ♔e7 5 ♘d4! or 2...fxe4 3 ♕xg4 d5 4 ♘d4 ♖d6 5 ♘xe6.

Black tried **2...a4** but lost soon after 3 ♘d4 ♖cc8 4 ♘xe6 ♖f7 5 ♘g5 ♖f6 6 b4 and 7 ♕d5+.

176

As the endgame approaches, rooks and pawns increase in value.

While the queen may lose some of its regal power as pieces are traded, rooks and pawns gain, said Cecil Purdy. Pawns become more important because most endgames are decided by promotion and because it is easier to advance them as the number of enemy pieces is reduced. Rooks also appreciate, partly because they are ideal for hunting pawns. "The rook is at its best when attacking pawns in an endgame," wrote Znosko-Borovsky. He might have had this in mind:

Reti – Bogolyubov
Bad Kissingen 1928

White to play

Count up the material and it's easy to see White has huge winning chances. But those chances are greatest in a middlegame (1 ♗d3).

It was a mistake to allow **1 ♗xe6? fxe6 2 ♕e2 ♖ac8** because 3 c3 fails to 3...♕b6 followed by 4...♕xb3 or 4...e5.

That meant White had to allow an endgame, **3 ♖d1 ♕xc2 4 ♕xc2**

♖xc2. He still had a theoretical advantage but the improved power of the rooks became apparent after **5 ♘d4 ♖d8! 6 ♗g5 ♖d7**.

There followed **7 b3 e5! 8 ♘xc2 ♖xd1+ 9 ♔f2 ♖b1** with a threat of ...♖b2 as well as ...♖xb3.

White to play

On paper, White is still materially ahead after **10 ♘e3 ♖xb3 11 a5**. But on the board Black has all the winning chances. He eventually won after one more White mistake.

177

A rook may possess an open file but it is of little use if there is no point of entry.

John Littlewood elaborated on his comment, in *How to Play the Middle Game*, by observing how frequently a player seizes control of a file on principle. His opponent, on principle, automatically shifts his own rook to the file. The result, Littlewood said, is "a series of mindless exchanges of the heavy pieces and a quick draw followed by the plaintive 'Where did I go wrong?'"

He went wrong by not appreciating why possession of the file counts. "The main objective of any operation on an open file is the eventual occupation of the seventh or eighth rank," Aron Nimzovich said. If occupation is not possible, because there is no point of entry, you get a situation like this:

Bologan – I. Sokolov
Pamplona 2002

Black to play

Black makes a threat (4...♘xd4! and 5...♖xc1) and prepares a trade of rooks that should ease his congestion. But **4 ♖b1!** revealed that Black's rooks are misplaced. They have no way of safely reaching c2 and cannot be exchanged off.

Moreover it was White who had a threat, 5 b3, e.g. **4...♖b8 5 b3 axb3 6 ♖xb3 ♕a8 7 ♖eb1** with advantage.

Black has a good plan (...♗d8!) of activating his bishop at b6 or a5. But instead he chose to mobilize his other under-used pieces, with **1...♖ac8? 2 ♕e2 ♖c7 3 ♗d3 ♖fc8.**

Black gave up a pawn (4...exd4 5 ♘xd4 ♘e5 6 ♗xb5 ♗xb5 7 ♕xb5) and might have drawn later on – if he had found better use for his rooks.

178

A castled rook is already developed.

Alexander Belyavsky and Adrian Mikhalchishin said #178 was handed down in the Soviet school to answer the age-old question of "Which rook?" That is, which rook should be moved first once you've castled. The answer, they wrote in *Secrets of Chess Intuition*, was "the other one" because the castled rook is already in play. "Certain chess coaches have expressed this even more emphatically by saying that it is the rook furthest away that should be brought to the center," they added.

The wisdom of this is obvious when a player castles queenside and his rook immediately enjoys control of part of the d-file. It's less clear when he castles kingside. But after 0-0, many GMs tend to look at "the other one":

Topalov – Kasimdzhanov
Linares 2005

White to play

White sought this position because his KR would be well developed after fxe3. But he found a better move in **1 ♖ae1!** since 1...exf2+ 2 ♖xf2 would give both rooks a file.

Black preferred **1...♗e6! 2 fxe3 ♘de7 3 ♘d6 b6**. Now that the pawn structure is set, White was free to make better use of his rooks, **4 ♖b1! f6 5 ♖b5 ♘e5 6 ♖f4** and then, **6...♘7g6 7 ♖d4 ♗d7 8 ♖bd5** with advantage.

179

A rook on the same file as your opponent's king and queen is always well placed, intervening men notwithstanding.

Edward Freeborough and the Rev. Charles Ranken were the authors of one of the first columnar openings books, *Chess Openings – Ancient and Modern* (1893). The analysis has long been out-of-date but much of their advice remains valid, and #179 is a good example – even if we replace the "and" with "or."

The rationale for it is the possibility – even if remote – of opening the file, and thereby attacking the king or queen with the rook.

Yermolinsky – Salov
Wijk aan Zee 1997

Black to play

When hedgehog pawn structures became common, Black often put his rooks at c8 to control the half-open file and d8 to defend the d-pawn. But the pawn rarely needs protection and the square d8 may be needed for a good ...♕b8/...♗d8-c7 maneuver.

Eventually, hog-lovers appreciated how well a rook stands at e8. Here it faces the queen on the other side of the barbed wire following **1...♖fe8!**. This became significant after **2 ♖ac1 ♖ac8 3 ♗e3 ♕b8 4 f3** since **4...d5!** is good.

White didn't like 5...dxe4 or 5...e5 but after **5 cxd5 exd5** he had tactical problems on the file. Best was 6 ♗f4 followed by 6...♗d6 7 ♗xd6 ♕xd6 8 ♕f2 and only then exd5.

Instead White played **6 exd5?** and allowed **6...♗a3! 7 ♖c2 ♖xc3 8 ♖xc3 ♘xd5 9 ♖cd3 ♘c5** with advantage to Black.

180
Strongest in Rear

This was Mikhail Tal's way of saying that the best arrangement of heavy pieces on an open file is for a queen to stand behind rooks. Having the rooks in front makes it easier to bully the enemy defenses with threats of trades or sacrifices.

Textbooks usually cite antique examples of #180, such as when Alexander Alekhine exploited an open c-file this way against Aron Nimzovich at San Remo 1930. A more recent case:

Adams – Zhang Zhong
Wijk aan Zee 2004

White to play

White's best chance lies on the h-file. But getting his queen to h2 or h4 and then hxg6 will likely mean no more than a queen check on h7.

White found the correct **1 ♖h4!** followed by **2 ♖dh2**. Then the ideas of ♘f6+ or ♕h1/hxg6 assured an advantage.

Note that Black would have no significant counterplay on the c-file until he engineered his own version of "strongest in rear." But by the time he got his queen to c8 and his rooks in front, it was too late: 1...♕f5 2 ♖dh2 ♖e7 3 a3 b5 4 ♕d2 ♖c4 5 ♕a5 ♕c8 6 ♘f6+! ♗xf6 7 gxf6 ♖ec7 8 hxg6 fxg6 9 ♕e1! and wins.

181

A firmly defended knight or bishop in the center is only slightly weaker than a rook.

There are other versions of this claim and this one, made by Grigory Levenfish in a 1941 issue of *64*, is the most optimistic. It only applies to the early stages of a game because by the ending par values are absolute, as Spielmann said, and the rook gains in strength, according to #176. In the middlegame, however, the pawn structure can limit rook mobility:

Mitkov – Rublevsky
Neum 2000

White to play

White pushed his pawn to f5 to attack g7 more easily. He played **1 ♖f3!?** with the idea of ♖g3/♗h6.

For example, 1...b5? 2 ♖g3 ♔h8 3 ♖xg7! ♔xg7 4 ♗h6+.

But hold on. Isn't the rook hanging after 1 ♖f3 ? Yes, but White banked on the opening of the g-file after **1...♘xf3 2 gxf3** – and the removal of that centralized knight – as compensation.

Black played **2...♔h8** but lost after **3 ♖g1 ♕d8 4 e5! dxe5 5 ♖xg7!** in view of 5...♔xg7 6 ♗h6+ ♔h8 7 ♗g5 ♗e7 8 fxe6 and ♗xf6+/♕xh7 mate. Analysis indicated chances are balanced after the best defense, 2...♗xd4! 3 ♗xd4 e5, so this test of #181 appears sound.

182
Knights are at their weakest when defending each other.

This observation from Boris Spassky (cited in *101 Tips to Improve Your Chess*) is based on redundancy and mobility. Knights that protect one another lose their ability to do other things. Often they don't dare move because that would break the mutual defense.

This is a familiar concept in endgames. In the pawnless Q-vs.-2Ns ending, the knights usually lose quickly if they defend one another. They serve best when standing next to one another, protected by the king. The situation in the middlegame is more subtle:

Leko – Morozevich
FIDE World Championship 2005

White to play

Black's queenside attack looks promising. But after **1 g5 ♘ec4 2 ♗c1! b5** the knight on a5 blocks his best chance for progress (that is, ...b4, ...a5-a4 and ...b3).

And since the knights were more or less frozen in place, White could ignore them and go to work on the kingside, **3 f4 b4 4 ♘ce2** with ideas of f4-f5 or g5-g6!?.

Black fought back with **4...♕b6 5 ♖h2 d5!? 6 exd5 ♗c5 7 ♕f3 ♖ad8**, trying to exploit the White knights' inability to do anything except protect one another.

When White tried to free his knights, **8 ♘b3?**, he allowed Black to solve his knight problem, **8...♘xb3 9 axb3 ♘e3 10 ♗xe3 ♗xe3**. He drew the endgame with his two bishops after several ups and downs.

183

The pawn is the knight's worst enemy.

James Mason's observation in *Principles of Chess* makes sense when we compare the knight to other pieces. Unlike a bishop, rook or queen, it cannot attack a pawn from a distance nor stop its advance. If it gets close enough to halt a pawn, it can't also capture it, as a king, rook or queen can. And while long-range pieces can battle two distant pawns, the knight can never dance at two weddings.

Sutovsky – Erenburg
Tel Aviv 2002

White to play

The knight seems to have the queenside pawns stopped. Draw? No, because of **1 a6! ♘xa6 2 b5**. The knight can't stop the pawn from reaching b7 and can only guard the queening square.

That means White can win on the kingside where he has an extra pawn, **2...♘b4 3 b6 ♘c6 4 b7 ♔e7 5 ♔g5 ♔f7 6 e6+! ♔f8** (6...♔xe6 7 ♔g6 and ♔xg7) **7 ♔g6 ♔g8 8 b8(♕)+! and 9 e7**.

But it can also be argued that a knight is a pawn's worst enemy. Knights are superb blockaders and are agile enough to exploit fixed pawns. Here, for example, 1 ♔f5?? would allow 1...♘e6! 2 a6 ♘xd4+ 3 ♔f4 ♘b5 and Black is the one trying to win.

184
He who has the bishops has the future.

Knights may have more of a presence in the present. They are usually the more valuable minor pieces in the opening. But the bishops have the future because they inevitably grow in range as pawns are traded.

Campora – Goldin
Cali 2001

White to play

The slightly blocked pawn structure helps the knights and White should develop (1 ♕e2) without disturbing it. But he wanted to change the structure with **1 f4?**.

If he had gotten to play 2 f5, White might have held things in balance. But **1...c4!** opened things up for Black's QB and **2 dxc4 ♕d4+ 3 ♔h1 exf4!** helped its brother.

Black's superiority was obvious after **4 ♗xf4 ♕xc4** and following **5 ♕d3? ♕xd3 6 cxd3 ♗a6 7 ♖fd1 ♘e5! 8 ♗xe5 fxe5 9 a4 ♖ad8** he was winning easily.

"The facetious Tarrasch" said #184 around 1900, according to Alexander Alekhine (although Savielly Tartakower called it "an old motto" in *500 Master Games of Chess*).

185

The player with the two knights should try to open the position.

In the last example White violated what Anatoly Karpov called "Nimzovich's rule" – The position should be closed when your opponent obtains the two bishops. John Watson challenged this in *Secrets of Modern Chess Strategy*:

"Given that a game is in the opening or early middlegame stage (i.e. that not too many pieces and pawns have been traded), it tends to be desirable for he who has acquired the two bishops to immediately close the position, and for he who gains the knights to immediately open it."

Watson later tweaked his rule: the player with the two bishops should try to prevent the position from being opened, not necessarily trying to close it.

The rationale for either version is that a player usually has to invest a tempo or two to get the 2Bs. This loss of time helps his opponent – provided his opponent follows the Morphy principle of opening the position when he has time on his side. Otherwise the lead in development evaporates and all that is left are the favorable bishops.

Leko – I. Sokolov
Odessa 2007

White to play

Here **1 f3!** was good for the same reason that 1...exf3? was bad. Black should keep matters closed with a 1...e3 2 ♕e2 0-0-0 sacrifice.

He only lasted five moves after **1...exf3? 2 ♖xf3 ♕h5** and then **3 ♕e2 ♗f5 4 ♖af1 g6 5 ♕c4 ♖f8 6 d5 ♘d7 7 ♘xd7 ♗xd7 8 d6 Resigns**.

But if an opponent gives you the two bishops for nothing, it usually pays to open the position. In Morphy's most famous game, he was given both the two bishops and a lead in development after 1 e4 e5 2 ♘f3 d6 3 d4 ♗g4? 4 dxe5 ♗xf3 5 ♕xf3 dxe5. No wonder he won.

186

If you have the two bishops, play on the squares of the missing enemy bishop.

Josif Dorfman made some farfetched claims in his book, *The Method in Chess*, but he was on solid ground when he wrote: "When you have the bishop pair, it is logical to develop play on the squares of which the opponent does not have a bishop." This had been expressed in other forms before and is illustrated in games like:

Short – Salov
Madrid 1995

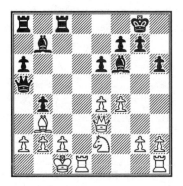

Black to play

Black is a pawn down and might be expected to throw himself into a queenside attack involving ...a5-a4. Instead, he tried to exploit the squares of White's missing bishop. White's queen masks his color weakness but not after **1...♕c5! 2 ♕xc5 ♖xc5** and then **3 ♘g3 a5 4 ♗a4 ♗h4 5 ♖he1 g5! 6 fxg5 ♗xg5+ 7 ♔b1 ♖d8**.

Black's bishops coordinated well, **8 ♖d3 ♗a6 9 ♖xd8+ ♗xd8 10 ♖e3 h5! 11 a3 h4**, and after

12 axb4 ♖g5! 13 b5 ♗b7 14 ♖d3 ♗b6 he was winning.

A corollary to #186 is: If you have to surrender the two Bs, you should trade the bishop on whose squares you can defend more easily.

In most cases you won't have a choice of bishops to trade. But when you do:

Radjabov – Ivanchuk
Odessa 2007

White to play

Thanks to the knight fork White must relinquish one of his bishops

With **1 ♕g3? ♘xd3 2 ♕xd3** he surrendered the wrong one.

He was soft on the light squares after **2...♗e6 3 ♖ad1 ♗c4 4 ♕f3 d3** and within a few moves Black dominated the board (**5 ♘g3 a5 6 ♗d6 ♕f6 7 ♕e3 axb4 8 axb4 ♕c3 9 ♖d2 ♗d4**).

The right policy was **1 ♗xe5!**. Black is better but not by much because White isn't soft on the dark squares.

187
If no one has the two bishops, the minor pieces are roughly equal.

Or as Cecil Purdy put it, "Once a player no longer has both his bishops, knights and bishops become practically equal." His premise was that 2Bs-vs.-B+N is an advantage but the edge disappears when reduced to B-vs.-N.

This can be used as a guideline when considering whether to give your opponent the two bishops. If you can be assured that one of those bishops will be traded in the near future, you should have nothing to fear.

Krivoshey – Teske
Aschach 2002

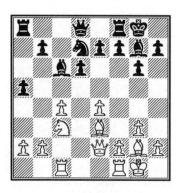

Black to play

It seems natural to play **1...♘c5?**. But White can favorably play **2 ♗xc5! dxc5** because he can immediately prompt another trade with **3 e5!**.

Following **3...♗xg2 4 ♔xg2 ♕c7 5 f4** Black's remaining bishop is worse than the knight.

We see this theme in openings such as 1 e4 c5 2 ♘f3 d6 3 c3 ♘f6 4 ♗d3 ♘c6 5 ♗c2 ♗g4 6 d3 g6 7 ♘bd2. White's last move enables him to recapture on f3 with a knight and pursue his plan of d3-d4.

However, 7...♗h6!? exploits White's last move. After 8 h3 ♗xf3 9 ♘xf3 ♗xc1 the two-bishop edge is gone and chances are roughly equal.

188

There are good "bad" bishops and bad "good" bishops.

Traditional thinking tells us a bishop whose scope is limited by its own pawns must be inferior to one with greater scope. This belief has inspired a number of witticisms, including Yuri Razuvaev's "Only a good bishop can be sacrificed. A bad bishop can only be lost."

But Steven Mayer in *Bishop versus Knight: The Verdict* argued with #188 that there were good "bad" bishops who performed better service than bad "good" ones. Pawn-bound bishops, if otherwise well-placed, can be excellent pieces, he said. That's the case with White's dark-squared bishop in the next example.

Anand – Bareev
Linares 1993

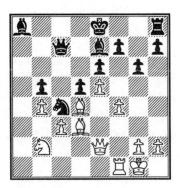

White to play

White traded a poor piece for a good one with **1 ♘xc4!**. Black's **1...bxc4!?** looks bizarre because it passes up a chance to make his bad

bishop good and hands White a protected passed pawn.

But White explained that after 1...dxc4 he would continue 2 ♗e4 ♗xe4 3 ♕xe4 and penetrate on the a-file with ♖a1-a7. Black's remaining bishop is "good" in a technical sense. But it is not nearly as effective as White's bad one, which controls a7. He would win with little effort.

Black's 1...bxc4!? follows the "not according to the rules" principle of defense. It forced White to come up with an alternative winning idea. (He did it with 2 ♗c2 ♗c6 3 ♕e3 0-0 4 f5! exf5 5 ♗xf5!.)

189
Bad bishops protect good pawns.

The words are Mihai Suba's but the thinking goes back to Philidor. The Frenchman said a good way to defend pawns was to put them on the same color as your bishop. Today we call that heresy. But if the pawns are *already* fixed on squares of a specific color, a bad bishop can perform important defensive duties.

Trading off such a bishop may benefit your overall piece mobility but cost you pawn after pawn. Here's a case that illustrates how a good bishop would be a good attacker and a terrible defender, as per Boris Gulko's comment in #10. But this time it's the defensive role that counts:

In this example from *Shakhmaty v SSSR*, Igor Bondarevsky pointed

out that Black wins if he has a dark squared bishop, say at h4. White may get to play ♔xb6 but Black protects the other pawns with ...♗b4 and then gobbles up White's pawns with his king.

But if Black had a light-squared bishop, say at h5, it's a different story. The bishop can win White pawns but can't defend its own, **1 ♔e5 ♗d1 2 ♔d6 ♗xb3 3 ♔c6** draws. And finally:

190

The worst bishop is stronger than the best knight.

This Russian joke, cited by Garry Kasparov among others, challenges the viewpoint popular in the early 20th century that the two pieces are relatively equal. The modern view is that a bishop is superior in far more cases than it is inferior. We may disagree about how many cases that means but we tend to agree that it is a significant number.

Bareev – Lautier
Enghien les-Bains 2001

Black to play

A natural move, 1...♕e7, began Black's downward spiral. He should have eliminated the unsightly bishop first (1...♘xd2! 2 ♕xd2 ♕e7 and 3...♘f6).

This would benefit him in two ways. He would solve his redundancy problem because he would have only one knight to occupy e4. Secondly, Black would have good queenside prospects after ...♖fc8 and ...♗b4.

In the game White's kingside play counted more thanks to the bishop, **1...♕e7? 2 ♗e1! ♖fc8 3 g4! ♘df6 4 ♗h4! ♕e8 5 gxf5 exf5 6 ♔h1 ♔h8.**

White could ignore the pressure against a4 and c3: **7 ♖g1 ♖c7? 8 ♗xe4 ♘xe4 9 ♘xe4 ♗xe5? 10 ♘f6!.** Then 10...gxf6 11 ♖xc7 ♗xc7 12 ♗xf6 mate or 10...♗xf6 11 ♖xc7 ♗xh4 12 ♖gxg7 and wins.

The Russian terms for bishop and knight are *slon* (elephant) and *kon'* (horse). That inspired a favorite line of Eduard Gufeld: "If you don't believe that a *slon* is stronger than a *kon'* – go to the zoo and compare."

CHAPTER ELEVEN: **PSYCHOLOGY**

191

On the chess board people fight, not wooden pieces.

This was Emanuel Lasker's simplest observation about the human and fallible element in chess and one that is taken for granted today. "Very often in choosing a move you need to consider the peculiarities of the opponent's style, the manner in which he is playing in the competition and how he stands in the scoretable," Vasily Ivanchuk said in a 2007 ChessPro interview. "Analyzing a position, you can't just calculate chess variations."

David Bronstein explained, in *David Against Goliath*, how a move that was "purely psychological" led to one of his greatest combinations. He tried to exploit how Viktor Korchnoi's mind worked:

Bronstein – Korchnoi
Moscow-Leningrad match 1962

White to play

With **1 ♕b6** White attacks the rook and invites it to d2. "I made use of the fact that Korchnoi knew me," Bronstein wrote. He knew Korchnoi would initially assume

Bronstein had figured out a way to take advantage of the rook's absence from the first rank.

But when Korchnoi looked at **1...♖d2 2 ♕b8+ ♔h7** and couldn't find any tactical follow-up, he would conclude Bronstein had miscalculated and go into that line to punish him for taking liberties. He got careless after **3 ♖e8** and played **3...♕xf3** (rather than 3...♖xb2!).

But this was a blunder that lost to **4 ♖h8+ ♔g6 5 ♖xh6+!!**. The tactics are cute (5...♔xh6 6 ♕h8+ ♔g6 7 ♕h5+/8 g5+/9 ♕xf3 or 5...gxh6 6 ♕g8+ ♔f6 7 ♕f8+ and 8 ♕xf3). But the pieces didn't play the moves. People did.

192
Winning isn't everything
but losing is nothing.

This sounds like a poor imitation of what Vince Lombardi, an American football coach, said ("Winning isn't everything. It's the only thing."). But what Edmar Mednis meant by #192 is that the pain of defeat is greater than the elation of victory and it influences your fighting spirit more in later games.

"I don't like to lose and when I win, I'm rather satisfied but not happy. I don't know why," Svetozar Gligoric said in *How to Get Better at Chess*. Another veteran grandmaster, Florin Gheorghiu, said, "I feel badly if I lose a game, especially if I was doing well...When I win, I feel normal."

When a player wins a game, the good feelings are temporary. He quickly begins to focus on the next round. But a defeat may remain in his consciousness, causing him to have flashbacks, hours and even days after a game, about that losing blunder or missed opportunity. "It's not the loss that's dangerous but the depression that follows," as Anatoly Karpov said (*Shakhmaty v Rossii*, March 1995).

Mednis' point is there is more at stake when fighting to draw a bad position than when trying to win a favorable one. In both cases the reward of success is a half point. But the emotional cost of failure is not the same.

193

The most difficult opponent for me was me.

Mikhail Botvinnik, Boris Spassky, and Lev Polugayevsky, among many other GMs said this. During a game they had to argue with themselves about moves and overcome their fears, habits and prejudices. "Every player struggles against an opponent and at the same time against himself," Tigran Petrosian said.

I. Sokolov – Macieja
Reykjavik 2003

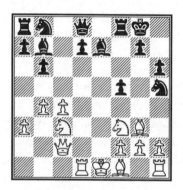

White to play

On the previous move Black had a choice of recaptures on f5. He chose ...exf5 because he didn't want to open the c2-h7 diagonal after ...℥xf5 and ♗d3. But that decision gave White another light-squared diagonal to exploit, with **1 c5!**.

Black realized that he would have problems after 1...bxc5 2 ♗c4+ and 3 ♘d5. He found the best move, **1...♗xf3!**, but only "after a big fight with myself," he recalled in *New In Chess*.

It was a fight because on principle he didn't want to give up an excellent bishop. Eventually he convinced himself he'd have equal chances following **2 gxf3 ♘c6! 3 b5 ♘a5**. A fighting draw followed.

It makes sense to learn more about your "most difficult opponent." As Grigory Levenfish told his students:

194
Get to know yourself.

Levenfish advised young players to find out what kind of positions they liked, what kind they disliked and in which they performed well or poorly. This was a novel thought in an era when players were told they must adopt a "universal style" so that they could play any position. Levenfish recognized that you can't play equally well in all positions.

Self-knowledge is most important when choosing an opening. Some are inherently tactical, others reduce tactics to a minimum. Some demand "best" moves to be successful. Others like the Exchange QGD need only "good" moves.

"The best openings to play are the ones you are most at home in," Irving Chernev wrote in *Logical Chess Move by Move*. Yet many players insist on playing lines that don't suit them. Take the case of Mikhail Tal and the French Defense:

Tal was clearly uncomfortable when he met 1 e4 with 1...e6. His game with Lajos Portisch at Oberhausen 1961 went **1 d4 e6 2 e4! d5 2 d4 d5 3 ♘d2 ♘f6 4 e5 ♘fd7 5 f4 c5 6 c3 ♘c6 7 ♘df3 ♕b6 8 g3 cxd4 9 cxd4 f6 10 ♗h3!** and then **10...fxe5 11 fxe5 ♗b4+ 12 ♔f1:**

Black to play

Tal played an un-Tal-like move, **12...♘f8?**, rather than 12...0-0 13 ♔g2 ♘dxe5!? 14 ♘xe5 ♘xe5. His pieces were so passive after 13 ♘e2 ♘g6 14 ♔g2 0-0 15 ♗g4 ♗d7 16 h4! that when he did sacrifice, at move 22, it was much too late.

There's nothing wrong with the French, of course. But it wasn't the opening for Tal. "At that point my 'French career' came to an end," he wrote. The French requires Black to play with great accuracy "and this is a quality I never had a great measure of."

This sounds like Tal finally got to know Tal. Yet he later resumed his "French career" – and scored only a half point in three games.

Another case of a great player who didn't know himself was the young Garry Kasparov. He adopted the Caro-Kann Defense in large part due to the influence of his trainer, a Caro-fan. Kasparov dropped it only after Eduard Gufeld called him a coward for playing an opening that was so inappropriate for his style.

"Look at you, shining eyes, such dark hair, you must be a Sicilian Mafioso!" Gufeld told him. "You must play the Sicilian!" The rest is history.

Self-knowledge goes beyond the choice of openings. As Bobby Fischer matured he rid himself of certain lines with which he had mediocre results, such as the Two Knights Variation of the Caro-Kann Defense. But he also learned that he was significantly stronger than his opponents in certain kinds of endgames, such as with rooks and bishops of opposite colors.

Levenfish's main point, in *Shakhmaty v SSSR*, 1940, was that players hurt their chances for improvement by not looking objectively at their own play, both strengths and weaknesses. He cited the case of the ever-optimistic Yefim Bogolyubov.

One day after a round during the great Moscow 1925 tournament, Levenfish and Bogolyubov walked back together to their hotel. The subject of Jose Capablanca came up and Levenfish praised the Cuban's endgame artistry. "But I play the endgame significantly better than Capablanca," Bogolyubov exclaimed. That's when Levenfish realized Bogolyubov would never get better than he was then.

195

The greatest skill in chess lies in not allowing the opponent to show what he can do.

The person sitting opposite you at the board is most dangerous when he gets a chance to play his kind of move, the type that utilizes his strengths. The ultimate skill, as Kasparov said in #195 (*My Great Predecessors Vol. 1*), is denying him the opportunity.

When Kasparov played his first match with Anatoly Karpov he was favored to win. He seemed to have surpassed his opponent in most of the categories of expertise, such as calculation, intuition, conducting an attack and active defense. But Karpov nearly won the match in the first three weeks because he was able to keep Kasparov from showing what he could do in those categories.

Karpov – Kasparov
World Championship 1984

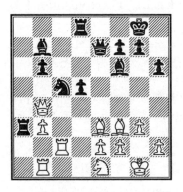

Black to play

White threatens a rook as well as a pawn (♗xc5). Black had prepared a typical "Kasparov move," **1...d4!**. He would have been happy to play 2 ♕xa3 dxe3 and 3 fxe3 ♕xe3+ or 3 ♕c1 ♗d4!.

Karpov had defended more difficult positions than those in his career. But he didn't play into his opponent's strength when he could liquidate the danger, **2 ♗xd4!**. On 2...♗xd4? 3 ♕xa3 White has the upper hand (3...♗xf2+ 4 ♔f2 ♘d3+ 5 ♘xd3 ♕xa3 6 ♗xb7 is Q-vs.-R+B+N).

Black found another Kasparov move, **2...♖xb3!**. But all that did was head from a dicey middlegame towards a pawn-down endgame, **3 ♖xb3 ♖xd4 4 ♕xb6 ♘xb3 5 ♖c7 ♖d7 6 ♖xb7**. That's when White got a chance to show what he could do.

It wasn't enough and the game was drawn. As William Napier said in *Amenities and Background of Chessplay*, "The greatest difficulty of the game is to play as well as one knows how."

196

The threat is stronger than the execution.

This is often misattributed to tobacco-phobe Aron Nimzovich, who exclaimed it when he feared an opponent was about to light up a cigarette at New York 1927. But Nimzovich was quoting what was by then a familiar thought. Edward Lasker, for example, explained Emanuel Lasker's "never make a purely defensive move" philosophy by saying that when you make a threat, even a minor one, it usually disconcerts the opponent "more than its execution."

Why should it? One explanation is that a threat is a distraction. "An insignificant threat which persists for a certain length of time and burdens our play, forces us to bear it in mind, and to try to guess at what precise moment the enemy will choose to set it in motion," wrote Evgeny Znosko-Borovsky.

Nikolai Krogius said a threat isn't just an annoyance but a source of "fear and uncertainty" that skews rational thought. "In thinking only of safety a player involuntarily exaggerates the opponent's chances and deliberately curbs his own aggressive tendencies," he wrote in *Psychology in Chess*.

Kosashvili – Yudasin
Haifa 1995

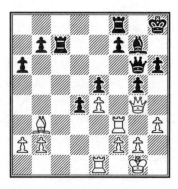

White to play

White prepared a kingside buildup with **1 ♖f5!**. But Black, a pawn ahead, was far from lost following **1...♗f6 2 ♕f3 ♔g7**.

It was when the threat of h3-h4 became more visible – after **3 g3 ♖e8 4 ♖d1 ♗d8 5 ♔h2** – that he panicked with **5...f6? 6 h4 ♗e7?**.

After **7 h5!** he saw 7...♕h7 8 ♖xe5! fxe5 9 ♕f7+. Instead, he managed to reach an endgame, but it was lost, **7...g4 8 ♕e2 ♕h7 9 ♕xg4+ ♔h8 10 f4 ♕g7 11 ♕xg7+**.

The psychology of #196 is a familiar one. Movie director Alfred Hitchcock explained why he carefully built tension in his films. "There is no terror in a bang," he said. "Only in the anticipation."

197

An attack is against a castled position, weak pawns and, most of all, against the mind of the opponent.

Players attack because they like to and defend because they must. Forcing an opponent to defend is the easiest way to put him off stride, as Savielly Tartakower intimated with #197.

That was Vladimir Kramnik's thinking in one of his first games with Kasparov. He opted for a risky sacrifice rather than grab a pawn. "When I play Kasparov I personally like to attack because Kasparov, strong in attack, doesn't like to defend," he explained.

Korchnoi – Salov
Belgrade 1987

White to play

White attacked a castled position and weak pawns with **1 h5**. But **1...g5 2 ♘g6!?!** was an assault on Black's psyche.

After **2...hxg6 3 e5 fxe5 4 dxe5 ♕c5 5 ♕xg6+ ♔h8** White obtained two pawns and an initiative for the sacrificed knight. But what counted more was that Black was reeling from the surprise of 2 ♘g6. Once the forcing moves were over he had to make difficult choices. He missed winning chances, then drawing chances and eventually lost.

Veteran attackers get flustered when they are on the other side of the psychology of #197. After Mikhail Tal's king came under fire from Viktor Korchnoi's queen and bishop in a 1968 Candidates match game he acknowledged he had misjudged something. But he wasn't sure what. "I either underestimated the queen or the bishop or Korchnoi," he said.

198

It is easier to win a slightly inferior position than an absolutely equal position.

Jan Hein Donner's quip was answered by Tigran Petrosian, who said "Make a note: It's much easier to play for a win from an equal position than from a bad position!"

The difference between the two attitudes lies in how you think victories come about. If you believe games are won, then you'll prefer equal positions because they allow you to try to accumulate advantages with minimum risk. But if you believe that games are lost – that is, by mistakes – then a slightly inferior position may be more promising because it can prompt errors of overconfidence.

"My own opinion, is that if you reach an equal position as Black, then it is usually a draw," Bent Larsen said in a 1990 *Chess Horizons* interview. "If you obtain a slightly inferior position, then you have good chances to win!" He said Paul Keres "discovered for himself how true this paradox is" at the 1959 Candidates tournament. Keres only scored 50 percent with White because his opponents carefully tried to equalize. But he rolled up a 12-2 score with Black.

Another great player who exploited his opponents' overconfidence in superior positions was Viktor Korchnoi.

Boersma – Korchnoi
Leeuwarden 1977

White to play

In his first Dutch Championship, Korchnoi "confidently accepted bad positions" and went on to win, Donner wrote in *The King*. Here, for example, White could have maintained his edge with a variety of quiet moves such as 1 ♔e2. Instead, he thought he should restrict Black with **1 g4**.

But he overlooked that **1...♘xg4! 2 ♖g1 h5 3 h3 ♘h6** costs a pawn in view of **4 ♖xg7 ♘f5**. Black won.

199

Inferior positions are often easier to play than equal ones.

The rationale for this bit of folk wisdom is that a player with a slight advantage labors under a psychological burden. He knows that unless his edge becomes greater, the most likely outcome is a draw and he will have wasted an opportunity. As a result, he sweats to find the best moves (even though a "best" move may not exist).

His opponent often has an easier time. In some openings, such as the Benko Gambit, Black can play his first 12 moves on auto-pilot. White has more choices and consequently a more difficult task. No one would dare claim Black, a pawn down, has the advantage in the Benko. Few masters would feel a typical early position is equal. Yet it is easier to play Black.

Mikhail Tal made the same point about symmetry:

Portisch – Tal
Candidates match 1965

White to play

It would be ridiculous to think Black is better, Tal said. Yet his position is easier to play because he gets to decide whether to follow White's lead.

He could have safely imitated White's move, 1 ♕c1. But Black did better with 1...♖c8!, following the principle of lining rook up against queen (#179).

He seized the open file and the advantage after 2 ♗h6 ♘d4! 3 ♘xd4 ♗xh6 4 ♕xh6 ♖xc3 5 ♕d2 ♕c7 6 ♖fc1 ♖c8.

200

Of the two evils, under-estimation and over-estimation of one's own strength, the former is much the more harmful.

It's usually a mistake for a 1200-player to believe he is capable of carrying off a speculative rook sacrifice or multi-stage positional plan. He is overestimating his ability. But the basis for Tal's #200 runs this way:

If you think a candidate is the best move, it is a tragedy to pass it up simply because you don't regard yourself as capable of finding the right follow-up. After all, you acquire skill so that it will point out such a candidate to you. Why waste it?

van Wely – Piket
Wijk aan Zee 1992

White to play

White was right in thinking 1 ♖h1 was best. It seizes an open file that cannot be contested (1...♖h8?? 2 ♗xh8) and prepares to invade with 2 ♖h7+.

But he convinced himself that his technique wasn't up to winning such a position. Instead he went in for 1 ♖xc6!? ♗xc6 2 ♖xc6, which threatens a mating attack (♗h5+) at slight material cost.

That's not a bad decision. But he underestimated his own ability and this could have hurt him after **2...g4! 3 ♗d1 ♖d6!**, which is unclear. (In the game Black misplayed, with 3...♖ac8? 4 ♖a6, and eventually lost.)

201
Self-confidence and strong nerves are more important in chess than ideas.

Donner made this claim in *The King* and said it explained why Lasker was greater than Tarrasch and Capablanca was superior to Rubinstein. Confidence and optimism helps you deal well with the strain of play.

Optimism makes some players stronger, wrote C.H. O'D. Alexander. Pessimists are plagued by self-doubting. "It is difficult for such players, however gifted, to reach the top or stay there for long if they do," he wrote. A classic case of optimist versus pessimist:

Spassky – Fischer
World Championship 1972

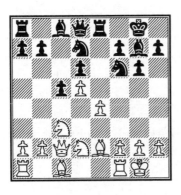

Black to play

In the first game of this match, Fischer defended a Queen's Gambit Declined and equalized easily. But the next time he had Black, trailing 0-2 against an opponent he had never beaten, he chose the much sharper Benoni. When the diagram was reached he played **1...♘h5!?**.

It's an amazing choice considering the match situation and the likelihood that **2 ♗xh5 gxh5** would be an irreparable weakness. But it was White who was riddled with doubt.

He began to play weakly, **3 ♘c4 ♘e5 4 ♘e3 ♕h4 5 ♗d2?** (rather than **5 ♘e2!** with advantage). He lost and that began the turnaround that decided the match.

When the 12 finalists of the 2006 Russian Championship were asked by an interviewer if they considered themselves optimists, pessimists or realists: Four said they were optimists and four said realists. One replied he was an "optimistic realist." Another said he was a "tactical realist" but a "strategic optimist." Two gave unclear answers. None was a pessimist.

202

The player who "must" win is at a disadvantage.

Nikolai Krogius noted this phenomenon when he described how players impose unnecessary pressure on themselves. If a player convinces himself that he must get a full point he tends to reject moves that might lead to a draw, even though he suspects they are the best moves. This is a common reason for higher-rated players being upset by weaker ones. Siegbert Tarrasch called this "the silent odds" of tournament chess. The stronger player feels he must take risks that he wouldn't normally accept.

Krogius cited the case of IM Georgy Ilivitsky and his one chance for stardom. Ilivitsky needed to beat two stronger opponents at the end of the 1955 Soviet Championship in order to advance to an interzonal.

His opponents were at a disadvantage because they were even more desperate for victory. Vasily Smyslov was leading the tournament and needed a win to assure himself of first prize. He ran short of time, blundered and lost. In Ilivitsky's last-round game, the winner would qualify for the interzonal.

Ilivitsky – Furman
Moscow 1955

Black to play

Black had sought this position because of 1...罝xb4. But now he saw that 2 罝c8+ 罝xc8 3 豐xc8+ 含g7 4 豐c3! would lead to a drawish ending.

He chose **1...豐b2??** instead and after the simple **2 罝b1 豐e5 3 豐c4 豐f5 4 罝b3** White consolidated his position, later captured the a-pawn and won. Ilivitsky's improbable success, he told Krogius, lay "precisely in the fact that they wanted to beat me more than I wanted to beat them."

203

In chess there is only one mistake, overestimating your opponent.

We've all been warned, many times, not to expect our opponents to make mistakes. We question our candidate moves by looking for the strongest possible replies. We assume that our opponents will play like supermen. But then we make sure they prove it over the board.

Overestimating an opponent's ability is a cardinal sin, as Savielly Tartakower said in #203. The most dramatic examples of it occur when a player resigns early. He gives up because (a) he believes his position is objectively lost and (b) he assumes his opponent will find the best moves. The (a) may be true but not necessarily the (b).

Deep Blue – Kasparov
Match 1997

White to play

Black's position had been in positional meltdown for several moves. But the computer's strange-looking response to the queen check, **1 ♔f1**, should have given Black hope.

It didn't. He saw that 1...♛xc6 2 bxc6 is a lost endgame. So he played **1...♖b8** and resigned after **2 ♖a6**.

The next day he was told that **2...♛e3!** would have drawn because of **3 ♛xd6 ♖e8!** followed by ...♛xe4 or perpetual check.

Of course, that's an extremely difficult line to see. But against a human opponent Garry Kasparov would surely have tried 2...♛e3 and waited for White to prove that he was winning. Kasparov incorrectly assumed the computer had seen everything when it chose 1 ♔f1 and therefore there was no reason to doubt that 2 ♖a6?? was crushing.

204

It is a well-known fact that during a practical game, players often do not check variations entirely but just trust each other.

David Bronstein was one of the greatest calculators ever. But in *Sorcerer's Apprentice* he admitted with #204 that he and other GMs take the easy way out.

Against a weaker player it pays to verify that his last move is sound. But when facing relative equals we tend to feel that checking is a waste of time. We're willing to have faith in our opponents.

Dreev – I. Sokolov
Sarajevo 2002

White to play

White felt it was time to increase his edge and had a choice between 1 ♘b5, which threatens ♘d6 or ♗d6, and 1 ♗xf6.

He saw that **1 ♘b5 ♗xe5 2 dxe5 ♘xe5!** leads to a favorable endgame after **3 ♖xd8 ♘xg4 4 ♖d6!**.

There were many more tree limbs to calculate after the alternative,

1 ♗xf6 ♕xf6 2 ♘e4 ♕e7 because after **3 dxc5** White threatens **4 ♖d7! ♕xd7 5 ♘f6+**. Black has resources such as 3...f5 and 3...♘e5. But none works, e.g. 3...f5 4 ♕g6 fxe4 5 ♖d7! and wins.

Nevertheless, White trusted that his opponent had something up his sleeve and went into the 1 ♘b5? endgame. He won – but only 42 moves later.

Before one of his World Championship games with Bronstein, Mikhail Botvinnik wrote a note to himself that read: "Calculate carefully – Don't believe him – he may miscalculate." After the game Botvinnik was upset because he believed Bronstein when he allowed him to win a pawn. Botvinnik didn't take it and the game was drawn. "He deceived me!" he wrote.

205

When one player starts to play worse, his opponent starts to play better.

Vladimir Kramnik cited "this phenomenon" in an interview on *KasparovChess.com*. He didn't explain why it happens but experience gives us some explanations. In some cases a player on the ropes gets a surge of fighting spirit and starts finding better moves. His opponent, expecting an easy point because of his advantage, begins to play weakly. This shift in fortune may occur several times in the course of a long game, with the advantage swinging from one side to the other, and then back again.

Tseshkovsky – Kasparov
Moscow 2004

White to play

Black was outplayed with **1 ♗e4! b5? 2 ♘d4! g6?**. Analysis showed that 3 axb5! and 4 f5 might have won.

But it was White's turn to be outplayed. After **3 f5?? exf5** Black managed to reach an unclear position after **4 ♗xd5 dxe5 5 ♘xf5!? ♗xf5 6 ♖xf5 gxf5 7 ♕h5 ♗f8 8 ♕xf5 ♗g7 9 ♖a3? e4! 10 ♖h3**.

The tide shifted again. Black rejected **10...♖e5! 11 ♕xh7+ ♔f8** in favor of **10...h6??**. White had a chance to turn the tables with **11 ♕g6!** and ♖g3 or ♖xh6. He missed it but found enough good moves to mount a last-ditch attack.

The outcome was decided according to a Tartakowerism. Black blundered six moves later. But White made the final mistake, three moves after that, and lost.

206

Lack of patience is probably the most common reason for losing a game.

Bent Larsen, one of the great chess psychologists, made this point and added that impatience was also the most common cause of drawing a won game.

The reasons for impatience in the two instances are slightly different. The player with advantage often hurries to convert his edge because he wants to get the game over as soon as possible. He may feel discomfort but not distress if the game lasts longer than he expected. But the defender who tries to force matters towards a draw is usually suffering. He is trying to avoid the helplessness one can feel when conducting a more patient defense:

Khalifman – Chiburdanidze
Bazna 2007

Black to play

Black can put up resistance with 1...♖ee7. But she preferred the more active 1...e5. Many computers agree with the way she played, **1...e5?? 2 ♖d8 ♖xd8 3 ♖xd8+ ♖f8 4 ♖xf8+ ♔xf8 5 fxe5 ♔f7** until they reach **6 ♔f3 g5 7 h4!.**

Only then does it become evident that zugzwang is nigh, 7...h6 8 hxg5 hxg5 9 e4 ♔e6 10 exf5+ ♔xf5 11 e6! ♔xe6 12 ♔e4 and wins.

Black also lost due to zugzwang in the game, **7...♔e6 8 hxg5 ♔xe5 9 g4 f4 10 a4 c4 11 e4** and so on.

207

When your opponent fears something, you have to strive for it.

This shrewd observation, by Anatoly Karpov in *New In Chess*, is a natural way to exploit your opponent's emotions. If it's obvious he is trying to avoid some major change in the position, like a pawn push or a trade of rooks, you should try to confront him with his worst fear.

The change in the position may not be as bad as he thought. But there is a good chance he'll be unnerved by the prospect of it coming about.

Karpov – A. Sokolov
Brussels 1988

Black to play

Both players began to evaluate a timely g3-g4 by White because it can create a passed e-pawn. Black was afraid of it and that's why he rejected 1...♔h6 2 ♔f3 g6 3 h3 ♖a4 in view of 4 g4! hxg4+ 5 hxg4 fxg4+ 6 ♔g3! (not 6 ♔xg4? a5!).

Then he has nothing better than 6...a5 7 bxa5 ♖xa5 8 ♔xg4, which he feared may be lost.

Instead, he continued **1...♖a2 2 h3 ♖b2**. The pawn liquidation is again in the air, 3 ♔f3 ♔h6 4 ♖b6+ g6 5 g4. But this time White avoided it because he thought the result was drawish.

When the opportunity arose one more time, after **3 ♖b6! g6! 4 ♔f3 ♖a2**, White should have taken the plunge, he said. Even if it weren't the best theoretical try, **5 g4** and then **5...hxg4+ 6 hxg4 fxg4+ 7 ♔xg4** was the best practical chance — because that's what Black was trying to avoid, White concluded.

And finally:

208

When you think too much about your opponent you might forget about playing good moves as well.

So much has been said about psyching out an opponent that we tend to forget what ultimately decides chess games is one's own moves, Joel Lautier reminded us with these words in *Interview with a Grandmaster*.

It's nice to know in advance that your next opponent plays badly against 1 d4 and or that he's weak in middlegames with an isolated pawn or in an endgame with bishops of opposite colors. But if you've never played 1 d4 yourself – or you are weak in the same areas as he is – this information won't help much.

It's the condition of your own mind that counts. "One's own psychology is more important than the opponent's," as Vladimir Kramnik said on *www.chess21* in 2005.

CHAPTER TWELVE: **SACRIFICE**

209

In order to achieve success you have to try and demonstrate that two times two is five.

Mikhail Tal meant that to beat players who know basic principles and priorities – the arithmetic of chess – you have to violate them. Tal did this with sacrifices, which are in a sense a violation of arithmetic. You try to defeat a bigger army with a smaller one.

Kramnik – Topalov
Wijk aan Zee 2005

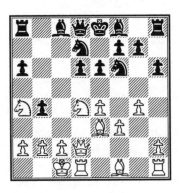

Black to play

When this opening position began to appear after 2001 Black tried 1...d5. It follows some basic principles, like countering a wing attack with a center thrust. But it violates others, by opening the position when behind in development. After 2 exd5 ♘xd5 3 ♗c4 and ♖he1 White's attack is too strong.

Then came **1...♘e5!**, which seems to make no sense. Black is sacrificing a pawn (**2 ♕xb4 ♗d7**) even though he's behind in development. He's moving a piece a second time. And he's weakening b6, which can be occupied by White's queen, knight or even bishop.

Nevertheless, 2+2=5. In this game White lost quickly (**3 ♘b3 ♖b8 4 ♕a3 ♘xf3 5 h3? ♘xe4**) and the sacrifice proved to be sound in other tests.

210

A sacrifice is best refuted by accepting it.

This maxim, which also appears as "The only way to refute a gambit is to accept it," is ascribed to Wilhem Steinitz. It's an exaggeration, as we know from games like the example that illustrated #98. But there is ample evidence that it applies well to openings.

For example, if there is a refutation of 1 e4 e5 2 f4, it begins with 2...exf4. "The refutation in any gambit begins with accepting it," Bobby Fischer wrote in his "Bust to the King's Gambit."

A minority view was voiced by Richard Reti, who claimed 2...d5 was best. Today that is regarded as somewhat dubious – but only after 3 exd5!, that is by accepting the Falkbeer Counter Gambit.

Modern gambits typically occur when material is offered much later. Take the case of a line in Queen's Indian Defense (**1 d4 ♘f6 2 c4 e6 3 ♘f3 b6 4 a3 ♗b7 5 ♘c3 d5 6 ♗g5 ♗e7 7 ♕a4+ ♕d7 8 ♕xd7+ ♘bxd7 9 ♘b5 0-0?!** and then **10 cxd5 ♘xd5**).

White to play

Black has good compensation for the pawn after 11 ♘xc7 ♗xg5! 12 ♘xd5 (12 ♘xa8 ♗d8!) ♗xd5 13 ♘xg5 ♖ac8. When the sacrifice was introduced around the turn of the 21st century it performed well, confirming the "old rule" cited by William Napier, "All gambits are sound over the board."

But Anatoly Karpov, citing the only-way-to-test-a-gambit maxim, accepted the pawn in a simpler way, **11 ♗xe7! ♘xe7 12 ♘xc7!**.

Then Black's initiative slows to a halt, e.g. 12...♖ac8 13 ♘b5 ♖c2 14 ♖b1 ♗e4 15 ♘g5! ♗g6 16 e4 and ♗d3. After a series of White victories the gambit disappeared from master practice.

211

Real sacrifices are those which cannot be gauged exactly in practical play, and can only be estimated.

"Sacrifice," like "defense," entered the English language from French after 1250, according to the etymologists. It enjoyed a broad chess meaning that included any kind of offer of material, from a Muzio-like gambit to a primitive last-rank combination of the 1 ♕e8+ ♖xe8 2 ♖xe8 mate type.

But in *The Art of Sacrifice in Chess*, Rudolf Spielmann said offers like 1 ♕e8+ are "sham" sacrifices because there is no risk. In contrast, the Muzio is a genuine sack, according to his #211, because White can only count on somewhat nebulous compensation. "In real sacrifices the player gives up material but is unable to calculate the consequences with accuracy; he has to rely on his judgment," Spielmann wrote.

Maroczy – Tartakower
Teplitz-Schonau 1922

Black to play

Before Spielmann, a sacrifice such as **1...♖xh2!! 2 ♔xh2 ♕xf2+ 3 ♔h1 ♘f6 4 ♖e2 ♕xg3** was looked upon suspiciously. Black gets three pawns, not immediate threats, for the rook.

But no improvements were found for White after **5 ♘b1 ♘h5 6 ♕d2 ♗d7 7 ♖f2 ♕h4+ 8 ♔g1 ♗g3 9 ♗c3 ♗xf2+ 10 ♕xf2 g3 11 ♕g2 ♖f8** and Black won impressively following **12 ♗e1 ♖xf1+! 13 ♔xf1 e5 14 ♔f1 ♗g4**.

He only received the third brilliancy prize, not the top one. The prize jury didn't believe a sacrifice as clearly speculative as 1...♖xh2 should be encouraged. Today, however, we recognize that all true sacrifices are speculative.

212

Many sacrifices do not require any concrete calculation at all.

This was Tal's most famous comment about his stock in trade. "A glance at the resulting position is sufficient to realize the sacrifice is correct," he added. By "correct" he didn't mean absolutely sound but sound enough for him to play with confidence.

Each player has his own zone of confidence that he needs to reach in order to go ahead with a move. Some players would need to examine lots of limbs on a tree of analysis to proceed with a sacrifice. Tal was comfortable with a glance above the trunk.

Tal – Winants
Brussels 1987

White to play

White spotted **1 ♘xe6** and then **1...fxe6 2 ♖xd6**. He saw 3 e5 and to a lesser degree 3 ♖xe6 would be threats.

But he felt guilty about playing 1 ♘xe6 without seeing something more concrete. He felt it was like taking a mathematics exam in which he knew the right answer but needed to do the calculations on paper to show how he derived it.

He satisfied his conscience by calculating one variation in detail. If

Black stops the threats with **2...e5** White can intensify the pin on the d-file with **3 g3! ♖c7 4 ♗h3 ♗c6 5 ♕d2**.

When Tal saw that a reasonable defense like 5...♖e8 could be defeated by another sacrifice, **6 ♘f5! gxf5 7 ♗xf5+ ♔g7 8 ♕g5+**, he felt satisfied enough to play 1 ♘xe6.

It didn't seem to trouble him when it was discovered after the game that 5 b5! wins faster in that line. Nor did it matter that Black could have defended better (2...♖c6!, instead of 2...e5, and then 3 e5 ♖xd6 4 ♖xd6 ♘xe5! 5 ♖xd8 ♘xf3+ offers reasonable chances).

What mattered was that what he saw in his glance met his standard. This approach shocked onlookers in the 1950s. "With such play, believe me, a player has no future," Pyotr Romanovsky remarked about an early Tal game. But it is Tal's view that enjoys widespread currency today.

213

The cost of a positional sacrifice tends to be much cheaper than a tactical one.

This observation, from Eduard Gufeld's *Chess Strategy*, reflects the difference in thinking behind the two kinds of sacrifices.

A tactical offer burns bridges. When you give up a piece for a pawn to get at the enemy king you appreciate that there may be little chance of saving the game if the attack fails.

But in a positional offer, the sacrificer usually gives up only a pawn – or "half-pawn" – and is expecting strategic plusses as compensation. If his judgment is wrong and the sacrifice is unsound, he may still have drawing chances.

Seirawan – Kozul
Wijk aan Zee 1991

White to play

White had no doubt that **1 ♕g4!** was correct, even after seeing **1...♕xg4 2 hxg4 e4!**. He evaluated **3 ♗e2! ♗xa1 4 ♖xa1** as winning for him.

Winning? Isn't he just down the Exchange? No, there are other factors:

The Black b-pawn is a permanent target, his bishop is shut out and

his rooks lack files. White can pick off the e3-pawn when he wants and reduce the material deficit to a half-pawn. Moreover, he has a simple plan of getting his king to f4 followed by ♖h1, g4-g5 and ♖h6, with a kingside bind.

His evaluation was correct – and Black agreed with it because after **4...♖ab8 5 ♔h2** he played **5...h5!** to avoid the bind.

There followed **6 gxh5 ♗f5 7 ♔g3 ♔g7 8 ♔f4 ♗h7 9 g4**.

Black to play

Black's pieces are still shut out while White can improve his with ♘c3-d1xe3 and perhaps g4-g5 and ♘g4-f6. He broke through with another strong idea, sacrificing a pawn to create a winning passer (9...f6 10 ♘c3 ♚h6 11 ♘d1 ♖be8 12 ♘xe3 ♖e5 13 ♖f1 ♖g8 14 ♗d1 f5 15 ♗e2 ♖g5 16 c5! bxc5 17 b6 etc.).

214

Sound pawn sacrifices are harder to find than sound piece sacrifices.

Mikhail Tchigorin wrote in *Niva* in 1901, "Little sacrifices (all of one pawn) sometimes define the knowledge, art and talent of a player more accurately than the announcement of mate in five moves." But Siegbert Tarrasch took that a step further with #214.

Good piece sacrifices are usually based on calculation. Tal's "glance" took him seven moves into the future in the example we saw. Sound pawn sacks, on the other hand, may demand sophisticated intuition instead because the consequences simply can't be foreseen with the same accuracy.

"It is normally impossible to calculate the consequences of a pawn sacrifice," wrote Alexander Belyavsky and Adrian Mikhalchishin in *Secrets of Chess Intuition*. This thinking is what prompted David Bronstein to exaggerate: "The only real sacrifice in chess is a pawn sacrifice" (*64*, 1990).

Karpov – Taimanov
Moscow 1983

White to play

Black intended to push his pawn to d4 to liberate his b7-bishop. He counted on 1 ♘f3 d4 and then 2 ♗xf5 ♗xf3! to give good play.

He was surprised by **1 ♗xf5! exf5 2 ♘f3** because it left a pawn hanging. But after **2...♖xc2 3 ♗d4** he realized White's idea. "Blockade at any price," he wrote.

To play this way White must have prepared an answer to 3...♕xb3. After all, two pawns is two pawns, and that does require calculation. (White had seen that 4 ♕h4! would give him an overwhelming attack.)

His judgment was confirmed when Black backed down, **3...♕c6**, and then **4 ♕h4 ♖e8 5 e6! fxe6 6 ♘e5 ♕c7 7 ♘xg6!**. White went on to win.

215

If you play the King's Indian, don't be afraid to be a pawn down.

This was one of Garry Kasparov's morsels of advice for students who attended the Botvinnik-Kasparov school in the final days of the Soviet Union, according the *Shakhmaty v SSSR*. Like another of his sayings, "If you are afraid of the move a4-a5, don't play the Benoni," it's a warning that certain openings demand that you take risks. In the King's Indian, Black's position is so naturally cramped that he must have active counterplay to survive.

Black to play

Extensive tests of such positions since the 1950s show that relying on positional ideas, like 1...a5? to secure c5 for a knight, will get Black killed after 2 ♕d2 ♘c5 3 g4 followed by ♘g3, 0-0-0 and h2-h4-h5.

He needs dynamic play, even at the cost of a pawn, e.g. **1...♘h5 2 g4 ♘f4! 3 ♘xf4 exf4 4 ♗xf4 ♘e5** and **...f5!** with good compensation.

If White refuses to accept the offer, Black can get good play with 3 ♕d2 a6 4 ♘g3 ♘c5 – and another sacrifice, 5 0-0-0 ♗d7 6 ♔b1 b5!, e.g. 7 cxb5 axb5 8 ♘xb5 ♕b8 9 ♘c3 ♕b4 and ...♖fb8.

One of the best guidelines for making a pawn sacrifice was proposed by Tarrasch in *The Game of Chess*:

216
Three tempi are worth a pawn.

"A gambit in which for the sacrifice of a pawn one obtains an advantage in development of three tempi is well worth playing," Tarrasch wrote. He applied this to openings and implied that pawn-grabbing is good if it only costs two tempi. Jose Capablanca said as much in his *Primer*:

"Should the opponent offer any material, even a pawn, which in your estimation you may capture without danger, it is advisable to take the offered piece, even if as a result full development is retarded for one or two moves."

But if development is delayed by more than two moves "it is doubtful whether the capture should be made," he added.

Timman – Huebner
Candidates match 1991

White to play

White saw that **1 d6!** would tie up Black until the pawn was removed. But can extra tempi help White much in such a closed position?

The answer took shape after **1...♕f6 2 d3 ♕xd6 3 ♗f4 ♕a6**. White had gained two tempi and will pick up another from the forcing ♖e1.

Tarrasch's guideline was confirmed after **4 b4 ♗d8 5 ♖e1 ♖f8 6 ♕h5**. White's compensation is more than enough because Black cannot coordinate his pieces – **6...d6 7 ♗d5 ♗d7 8 a4! ♖c8 9 ♗e4 g6 10 ♕f3 ♖c7 11 b5 ♕b6 12 ♗h6**. White won because **12...♖e8** allows **13 ♗d5 ♗e6 14 ♗xe6 fxe6 15 ♖xe6! ♖xe6? 16 ♕f8 mate**.

217

Before the endgame, an Exchange sacrifice is less expensive than a pawn sacrifice.

When the ...♖xc3 sacrifice in the Sicilian Defense began to appear, around 1907-8, Black got at least one pawn in return for the Exchange. Today Black may be content without any extra pawns if he gets an initiative. This makes sense because the loss of the Exchange doesn't affect matters much until queens are off the board.

"Do not be too much afraid of losing a rook for an inferior piece," said *An Easy Introduction to Chess* (1813), based on Philidor. "It seldom comes into play so as to operate until the end of the game."

Cecil Purdy offered a moden version, "In the opening and in the middlegame, the loss of a rook for a minor piece and one pawn is usually less serious than the loss of a pawn." Even without the extra pawn thrown in, the Exchange is less expensive.

Korchnoi – Karpov
World Championship 1978

Black to play

White is a pawn ahead but he also threatens to win the Exchange with ♘e6 and then ♘xf8 or ♘c7. On paper, the loss of the Exchange would seem more costly.

However, if Black had met the threat with 1...♕e7, White can seize the initiative with 2 e4!, e.g. 2...d4 3 ♘e6 ♖fc8.

Then 4 f4 gives him good attacking chances (4...axb5 5 fxe5 ♘xe5 6 ♗g5! or 4...♘xe4 5 ♘xe4 ♗xe4 6 fxe5 followed by ♕g4 or ♕b3/♗g5).

Black made a good decision, **1...axb5!**, and enjoyed good compensation after **2 ♘e6 c4!**. "Of course, Black gives up the Exchange without hesitation." Tal wrote, adding that "the worst is now behind him."

And finally, when it comes to sacrifices:

218

A player is braver after the game.

No matter how courageous someone is during a game, he is willing to take more risks in the post-mortem, when nothing is at stake. This is true of offering a sacrifice or accepting one. As Ljubomir Ftacnik wrote (*Inside Chess* 1991): "Since you cannot win or lose a game when annotating it, many players are much more courageous annotating than they are when playing. They come up with daring, sometimes paradoxical moves."

Often when one player is daring during the game, his opponent is braver afterwards.

Anand – Piket
Dortmund 2000

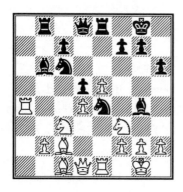

Black to play

With only seconds left in a bad position, Black took a desperate plunge, **1...♖xe5**. White replied 2 ♘xe4 and after 2...♖xe4 3 ♗xe4 dxe4 4 d5 ♘e5! the game could have been difficult.

Only in his annotations did White "play" **2 dxe5!**. He admitted it would have won easily, e.g. 2...♗xf2+ 3 ♔f1 or 2...♘xf2 3 ♕xd5 ♘d3+ 4 ♔f1.

CHAPTER THIRTEEN: STRATEGY

219

Capture of the adverse king is the ultimate but not the first object of the game.

Once you've been playing chess for a few years you forget how sophisticated the object is. Chess is a war game but victory is not defined by annihilating the enemy army or capturing its king. No, the game ends when you make an unstoppable threat to capture the king.

That's a fairly complex concept. Wilhelm Steinitz took it to another level when he made the distinction in #219. Players before him had won games by promoting a pawn. But this was their Plan B, which they turned to only after their Plan A, a mating assault, was thwarted. Steinitz began his career as an attacker but finished it by making mate his Plan B.

Steinitz – Schallopp
Nuremberg 1896

White to play

Before Steinitz, a standard plan in the Queen's Gambit Declined was to attack with ♗d3, ♘e5 and ♕f3. But he often played his bishop to

e2, with the option of ♗f3 to attack the d-pawn.

Here he obtained an advantage after 1 ♗e2 ♗b7 2 0-0 ♘h5 3 ♗e5! ♘d7 4 ♘e1!. His knight is headed for f4 to add pressure on d5.

After 4...♘hf6 came another few deft moves, 5 ♗g3 ♖c8 6 ♘d3 ♘e4 7 ♘xe4 dxe4 8 ♘f4 c5 9 ♗g4!, and White was on the road to a positional crush.

Max Euwe put Steinitz's teaching in similar words: "Whoever sees no other aim in the game than that of giving checkmate to one's opponent will never become a good chessplayer."

220

Tactics is what you do when there's something to do. Strategy is what you do when there's nothing to do.

Savielly Tartakower is credited with both this and "The tactician must know what to do when something needs doing. The strategist must know what to do when nothing needs doing." Both renditions shortchange strategy.

Strategy is not about "nothing." The strategist pursues concrete goals, just as the tactician does, but without a sense of urgency and with a greater reliance on maneuvers. Both the tactician and strategist hone their skills through pattern recognition. But the strategist thinks in broader terms.

Dvoiris – Vaulin
St. Petersburg 1999

White to play

White recognizes two typical weaknesses, the hole at d5 and the backward pawn at d6. But his d3-bishop gets in the way and that means there isn't "something to do."

So, White began by stopping ...b5 counterplay with **1 a4!**. This also allows him to meet ...♞b6 with a4-a5! before Black can carry out ...d5.

Play continued slowly – **1...♖ac8 2 ♖f2! ♖fd8 3 ♗f1 ♕c5 4 a5 ♔h7 5 ♕e1** – but that's par for the strategic course. White was advancing his plan, which simply means getting closer to a position he had in his mind back when he played 1 a4. As Cecil Purdy said:

221

The essence of planning is the visualization of a future position of some or all of your pieces.

The position White likely had in mind when the previous diagram arose was an idealized one with a rook on d1, his knights on c3 and d5 and a cramping pawn on a5.

He didn't have to see where Black's pieces would be then. Nor did he have to calculate the moves leading to the one he visualized. "You do not worry much about your opponent's replies except to make sure your plan is feasible," Purdy said, according to *His Life, His Games and His Writing*, which cited #221.

We left off the last example here:

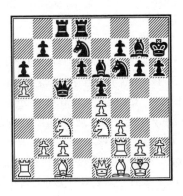

Black to play

Black played **5...♕a7**, and White took relatively simple steps towards his ideal position:

6 ♔h1 h5 7 ♖d2! ♕c5 8 ♖d1 ♕c6 9 ♖a3 ♗h6 10 ♘a2!.

This may not look like much. But White is close to playing ♘b4-♘d5. That was enough to prompt Black to trade his bishops, **10...♗xa2 11 ♖xa2 ♗xe3 12 ♗xe3 d5**. White's superiority is obvious after **13 exd5 ♘xd5 14 ♗g1** and c2-c4/b2-b4.

The only real calculating he had to do was back at the diagram. He had foreseen that Black couldn't dissolve his weaknesses, e.g. 5...d5 6 ♘exd5 ♘xd5 7 exd5 ♗xd5 leads to 8 ♗e3 ♕c6 9 ♘xd5 ♕xd5 10 ♖d2 and a solid positional advantage.

His minimal calculation is explained by:

222
The strategist plays by touch.

Max Euwe made this comment when reviewing his world championship victory over Alexander Alekhine in 1935. A strategist, like Euwe himself, likes to choose "principled" moves that he can play based on his sensitive "touch." Masters of touch include Vladimir Kramnik, Tigran Petrosian and Anatoly Karpov.

Karpov – J.Polgar
Linares 1994

White to play

If you had to explain why Black is worse you might name four factors: his inferior bishop, his dark-square weaknesses, his three pawn islands and his insecure king. White dropped the last of these from the list when he played **1 ♕d4!**.

He relied on the principle we saw in #83: Black's other positional problems will be exacerbated in the endgame. White's advantage became more visible after additional "touch" moves, **1...♘f5 2 ♕c5 h5 3 ♘d2 f6 4 exf6 gxf6 5 ♗b4 ♔f7 6 ♖a4! ♕xc5 7 ♗xc5**.

To # 222, Euwe added "The tactician has the harder task but if he can indeed calculate all the possibilities, he is at an advantage." But this is only true when there's something to calculate. Here there isn't and White could play principled moves – ♖fa1, f2-f3, ♔f2, b3-b4, ♘b3-a5 – almost without looking at Black's side of the board. He won with ease.

223

Opponents always have some kind of weakness in their position, even if imperceptible. Against that you have to play.

This profound insight by Tigran Petrosian deserves to be called Petrosian's Law. He had faith in a logical basis of chess: There is a rational foundation for every attack and your job was to find it, "even if imperceptible."

For example, in the Petroff Defense, **1 e4 e5 2 ♘f3 ♘f6 3 ♘xe5 d6 4 ♘f3 ♘xe4 5 d4 d5** the position is symmetrical except that Black's knight is on e4, not f6. That would seem to favor Black.

But experience shows that the knight and/or its support pawn can be attacked. They are the only possible weaknesses. Characteristically, when Petrosian played the Petroff he avoided 5...d5 and chose moves that gave White less of a target, such as **5...♘f6**.

Petrosian's Law is a useful reminder when it seems you're in one of those nothing-to-do positions.

Yudasin – Sagalchik
Kemero 1995

White to play

Chances would be nearly equal if Black's c-pawn could retreat to c7.

But because it's at c6, his d-pawn and b6 squares are weak. That justifies an attack beginning with **1 ♕b4!**, which wins after 1....d5? 2 ♕b6 ♖d7 3 ♕a7.

Better is **1...♕d5** but after **2 b3 h5 3 ♖ad1!** Black faces a threat of 4 c4 and 5 ♗xd6 or 5 d5.

Since 3...c5 4 dxc5 ♕xc5 5 ♕d2 is ugly, he preferred **3...b5**. But that's as desperate as it looks: **4 ♕a3 ♔b7 5 c4! bxc4 6 bxc4 ♕xc4 7 d5! ♗xd5 8 ♖e7+ ♔c8 9 ♗xd6 ♖d7 10 ♕b2! ♖xe7 11 ♕b8+ Resigns**. And all because of the c6-pawn.

224
Make a plan which conforms to the position.

This is how Max Euwe's characterized "the fundamental principle of Steinitz." The selection of a strategy should be consistent with specific features of the position. Siegbert Tarrasch put it more directly: "To play correctly, we can never do what we *wish*. We must do only what we are *forced* to do, what the position demands."

What the position demands may conflict with many of the maxims in this book. When that happens, the position – and its plan – takes precedence because it is specific, and maxims are general. "All general considerations must be entirely forgotten" and "only that which contributes to the execution of the plan selected is of any avail," Alexander Alekhine wrote.

Aronian – Carlsen
Candidates match 2007

White to play

This position doesn't demand White follow a particular plan. Rather it suggests three of them. One is swapping rooks on the open file. That would lead to an ending in which his two bishops count more than they do now.

Another plan is 1 f3 followed by e3-e4 to take d5 away from Black's knight and make his bishop ineffective.

Instead, White found a third plan, exploiting c6, Black's only real weakness. After **1 &a6!** Black didn't like 1...♘b8 in view of 2 &xb7 ♛xb7 3 ♘b5, threatening ♘d6.

There followed **1...&xa6 2 ♛xa6 ♖xc1+ 3 ♖xc1 ♘b8 4 ♛c4**. In four moves White had converted his two-bishop advantage into control of the c-file and a better knight.

He ground Black down after **4...♖d8 5 h3 ♘e8 6 b5**. His decision to play against c6 follows Petrosian's Law as well as one of Emanuel Lasker's:

225

Take the initiative always on that side of the board on which one has more territory or greater fighting force.

Edward Lasker quoted his distant relative this way in *Secrets I Learned From the Chess Masters*. The logic supporting it is typical of the second world champion: An initiative will be successful if it can apply superior force at the point of attack. Common sense tells us the appropriate point of attack will most likely lie in the neighborhood where you have superior force to begin with.

Rublevsky – Goloshchapov
Siliviri 2003

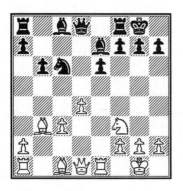

White to play

White might be tempted by 1 d5 exd5 2 ♗xd5 because it opens lines for his bishop and rook. But his initiative would disappear after 2...♗b7 and the isolated c-pawn he

created may count more (3 ♘e5 ♘xe5 4 ♗xb7 ♕xd1 5 ♖xd1 ♖ad8).

Instead, White detected a looming mismatch on the kingside. If he can shift his pieces to that area, they will outgun the only apparent defender, the e7-bishop.

To start, he offered a pawn, **1 h4!**, so that he could plant pieces on g5. It's based on the quick attack that would follow 1...♗xh4 2 ♘xh4 ♕xh4 3 ♖e3 and ♖h3.

Black declined but he was worse after **1...♗b7 2 ♘g5! ♘a5 3 ♗c2 ♗xg5 4 hxg5 ♗d5 5 ♕d3 g6 6 ♕g3 ♘c4 7 ♗f4** and ♖ad1 and soon lost.

226
Don't move pawns where you are weaker.

Eduard Gufeld called this "one of the classic rules of chess," although it's another exaggeration. We know pawns gain in offensive value as they advance. But they also lose some of their defensive ability with each push. Therefore you should be wary of making pawn moves where you are already weaker, i.e. where you have less operating room, fewer pieces or a chronic weakness.

Pawn chains are a good illustration. Each player has a strong side of the chain, where he has more space. We know we should attack a chain's base, that is, on the strong side. The converse is that it's often bad to push on the weak side.

Ponomariev – Ivanchuk
FIDE World Championship 2001-2

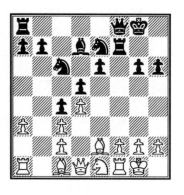

Black to play

Black has a choice of areas in which to expand. He selected the kingside, **1...g5**, and stopped 2 f4. But the kingside is where White has more space, and it was no surprise he could carry out his push favorably, **2 g3 ♘f5 3 ♘g2 ♕g7 4 f4**.

Black is naturally stronger on the other wing. That's why **1...b5!** was more solid, e.g. **2 f4 a5 3 ♘f3 ♘f5** with an excellent game.

227
Mobility creates its own plan.

This was Fred Reinfeld's interpretation of what Siegbert Tarrasch said about mobility and space. Tarrasch believed an advantage not only required you to launch an initiative, as Steinitz had said, but pointed your initiative in the right direction. You should attack in the area of your advantage. "When you have more mobility and more space, the game plays itself," Reinfeld said, channeling the Tarrasch spirit. "For the possession of the initiative carries the duty of maintaining and intensifying that initiative," he wrote in *Tarrasch's Best Games of Chess.*

Erdos – Belyavsky
Hungarian Team Championship
2003

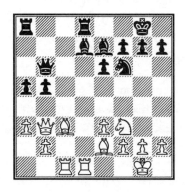

Black to play

The position is almost symmetrical. But Black's advanced b-pawn gives him more space and

an idea, **1...a4!**. Then 2 ♕c2 ♖ac8 and either ...♗c6-e4 or ...b4 are unpleasant for White.

He preferred **2 ♕a2**, after which the difference in mobility became evident, **2...♗c6 3 ♘d4 ♗d5 4 ♕a1**. That handed Black a plan of **4...b4!**, to expose a target at a3 or b2.

After **5 ♗xb4 ♗xb4 6 axb4 ♕xb4 7 ♗f3 ♗xf3 8 ♘xf3** Black's game had begun to play itself – **8...♘e4 9 h3 g6 10 ♘d4 ♖d6 11 ♕b1 ♕b7**. He won after **12 ♘f3? ♖b6 13 ♖d4 ♘xf2!** (14 ♔xf2 ♖xb2+).

228
Big edge, big plan.

This is another corollary to the Lasker/Steinitz principle of proportion. If you have a tiny advantage or none at all, the only plans that are likely to succeed are modest. But if your edge is substantial, you may be shortchanging yourself by trying to grind out a win slowly. You should think about a knockout.

"Sometimes the only logical way to utilize a given advantage is to attack your opponent's king," wrote John Littlewood in *How to Play the Middle Game in Chess*.

Topalov – Kramnik
Novgorod 1996

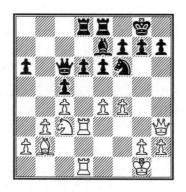

White to play

White might look for a positional plan that would exploit the d-pawn.

But he reckoned his edge in space and piece activity was manifest enough to justify a mating attack. He began with **1 ♖g3! ♔h8 2 ♖e1 ♕c8 3 ♖ee3**, with thoughts of ♖xg7.

Then came **3...♖g8 4 ♘d1 ♖d7 5 f5!** with a new threat (6 ♗xf6 and if 6...♗xf6 then 7 ♕xh7+! mates).

Black was forced into more positional concessions, **5...e5 6 ♘c3 ♗d8 7 ♘d5 h6** and after **8 ♗c1! ♘xd5 9 exd5 ♗f6 10 ♖e4 ♕f8 11 ♖eg4** he resigned before the capture on h6.

229
Short term plans pay best.

Tarrasch devoutly believed in long-term strategy. In one of his games he claimed his opponent made a decisive error on move seven by creating a pawn structure that inevitably led to a mating attack 20 moves later.

But David Bronstein said Tarrasch was spreading a myth that plans could be carried out "like a theorem in geometry." "I do not think there are such games between opponents of the same strength," Bronstein said. "And the annotator who gives that impression is often the winner of the game, who makes out that what happened is what he wanted to happen."

In other words, GMs sometime lie about their plans. Longterm plans, like elaborate military strategies, rarely survive contact with the enemy.

When Cecil Purdy wrote #229 he added, "The average player will do best to rely on plans that are as short range as possible." That works for great players as well. Anatoly Karpov created masterpieces out of a series of two- and three-move plans. So did Mikhail Tal in his last great game:

Tal – Hjartarson
Reykjavik 1986

White to play

White's book knowledge ended here. On his first real move of the game he chose **1 ♘c2**, based on two short-term plans:

He can attack the only vulnerable target, at b5, with ♕e2, ♖a5 and ♘a3. Or he can make better use of e3 with ♗e3/♕d2. After **1...♘h5** he chose the second plan, **2 ♗e3 ♖a8 3 ♕d2**.

Having completed it, he looked for another plan and found **3...♖xa1 4 ♘xa1!**. He wanted to get the knight to a5 where it plugs up the file and watches c6. That took three moves, **4...f5 5 ♗h6 ♘g7 6 ♘b3 f4 7 ♘a5**.

Following **7...♕b6** White was again in need of a plan. He decided to mine the c-file. That took four moves, **8 ♖c1 ♖a8 9 ♕c2 ♘ce8 10 ♕b3 ♗f6 11 ♘c6**.

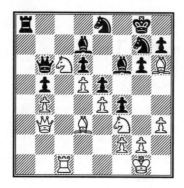

Black to play

Another plan has been completed and that meant White looked for yet another. One stood out: Trading his bad bishop by means of ♗e2-g4. But **11...♘h5 12 ♕b2 ♗g7** alerted him to opportunities on the kingside.

Instead of planning, he was able to calculate from here on, **13 ♗xg7 ♔xg7 14 ♖c5!** so that 14...dxc5 15 ♘fxe5 is a winning attack, or **14...♕a6 15 ♖xb5** and wins as the game went.

In retrospect he was following a rule of thumb in the main lines of the Ruy Lopez – White should attack the queenside until he sees a weakness on the kingside. But even Tarrasch wouldn't have dared claim White had planned that all along. "A plan is made for a few moves only," Reuben Fine wrote, "not for the whole game."

Notice how each of the mini-plans carried out by Tal could be characterized as improving the placement of a piece or two. That's the basic component of most good plans, not the 20-move grand designs that Tarrasch claimed. The priority of piece placement leads to the next maxim:

230

There are no good or bad pieces in the middlegame.

Mihai Suba argued with these words, in *Dynamic Chess Strategy*, that there are only misplaced pieces and they are a temporary problem. If one player can steadily improve the placement of his pieces, while his opponent cannot or can do so only minimally, the first player eventually will get the upper hand even if his position is structurally inferior.

This is significant because we often exaggerate the value of pawn structure. Because of structure we used to automatically rate the next position, a French Defense middlegame, as a plus-over-minus edge for White.

Black to play

He has the better pawns, the better pieces and the better of the tactics (1...♕f7 2 ♗xh7+! ♔xh7?? 3 ♘g5+).

But only the pawn structure is lasting. After 1...g6! Black makes his bishop a bit worse but sets in motion a plan to improve almost all his pieces, with ...♕g7, ...♗d7, ...♖f7, ...♖af8 and so on.

In response, White needs his own plan, such as 2 ♘a4 and ♘c5. In Marjanovic-Timman, Sarajevo 1986 he lost any claim to advantage after 2 ♗b1 ♕g7 3 ♔h1 ♗d7 4 ♖e1 ♖f7 5 ♘e2 ♔h8 6 a3 ♖af8. Black later carried out a remarkable new plan, ...h6, ♗e8-f7-g8 and ...g5!, that helped him win.

231
Worst piece first.

The piece to improve first is the one that stands worst, according to Tarrasch. Since he believed that a single badly-placed piece made a position bad (#85), it followed that getting that piece to a better square must improve the position as a whole.

We know Tarrasch overstated the case of the one bad piece. But his worst-first maxim is perhaps the most useful guideline to follow when there's "nothing to do."

Iordachescu – Tiviakov
Vlissingen 2003

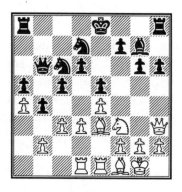

White to play

White has just completed his development with ♖ad1 but sees that the natural continuation, 1 d4, is at best unclear after 1...cxd4 2 cxd4 exd4.

That indicates he should reposition his pieces before changing the pawn structure. He started with his two worst minor pieces, 1 ♘d2! ♕c7 2 ♗e2!.

Black began to improve his own bad pieces with 2...♘b6 and both players made progress, 3 ♖a1 ♕d7 4 ♗g4 ♕e7 5 ♗d1! ♕e6 6 ♕g3 h5 7 h3 ♗h6!.

However, 8 ♗b3 ♕f6 9 ♘c4 ♘xc4 10 ♗xc4 revealed that White had done a better job. His bishop is now the best minor piece on the board and he was able to turn his attention to a new plan, opening the f-file, and that won the game.

The Russians credit Vladimir Makogonov, a second-tier Soviet master, with a version of the Tarrasch maxim: "If you encounter difficulty in choosing a plan, determine which piece is most poorly placed and try to transfer it to a stronger position."

232
A bad plan is better than no plan at all.

Chessplayers embrace this maxim as if they owned it. "Better to carry out a wrong plan logically than to play with no plan at all," Viktor Korchnoi wrote in *Learn from the Grandmasters*. But other versions of it have been attributed to non-players, such as Charles de Gaulle, Jan Paderewski, and various anonymous soldiers who tried to justify following a strategy that seemed stupid to them.

Of course, a really bad chess plan can be just as fatal, in the long run, as a blunder is in the short run. But players like to place their trust in a plan, even a slightly misguided one. By giving them direction, a plan prevents floundering about. It also helps avoid time pressure, said Nikolai Krogius. Amateurs without a plan may move a knight randomly toward the queenside on this turn, and then move another piece randomly toward the kingside on the next move. Or they'll move the knight back to the square it just left. Planning tends to force players to coordinate their pieces better.

The perils of planlessness are illustrated best by the world-class players who are incapable of planning, the computers. We saw that in the examples that illustrated #93 and #157.

233

A weak point is a *square* – not necessarily occupied – which can be attacked by heavy pieces.

Steinitz gave us the term "hole" to identify a particular kind of positional Achilles' heal. Lasker went further in *Common Sense in Chess* with #233, a broader definition of any weak point. He added that your opponent's weak points are your strong points, and they are targets for occupation.

Kramnik – Carlsen
Dortmund 2007

White to play

White's strong point at b4 is under attack and 1 bxa5 c5 is not the solution. He got his priorities straight with 1 ♘b3! axb4 2 ♘a5 and then 2...♗a8 3 ♘ac6.

This showed that c6 was a second strong point. He maintained his occupation after 3...♗xc6 4 ♘xc6 ♕d7 by means of 5 ♗xd5 exd5 6 axb4.

This allowed him to pound at b5 and c7, 6...♖fe8 7 ♖a5 ♗f8 8 ♘e5. Black shortened the game when he mistakenly thought he could liquidate the queenside, 8...♕e6 9 ♖xb5 ♖b8 10 ♖xb8 ♖xb8 11 ♕xc7 ♗d6 12 ♕a5 ♗xb4? 13 ♖b1! ♕d6 14 ♕a4 **Resigns** in view of 15 ♘c6, winning material.

234

Don't drive away an advanced piece which is not hurting you. It will probably retire unassisted.

The maxims collected by English author C.D. Locock often seem quaint and naive today. But there's also a lot of truth in some of them, like #234.

Tarrasch advised driving back an enemy piece because it usually means you gain space and that was a Tarrasch priority. However, if the piece isn't doing you any harm you may be reminding your opponent to find a better square for it – and wasting a tempo to remind him.

Stanec – Belyavsky
Graz 1996

White to play

Black has just recaptured on c6 with a pawn, not a rook, because he wanted to retain winning chances against a weaker opponent and that meant stopping d4-d5. He reasoned that the d4-pawn can be

attacked more easily than the c6-pawn.

The right response for White was 1 ♖ac1 and then 1...♖d7 2 ♘e2. Instead, he played **1 ♘e4 ♖d7 2 a5?**.

This forced Black to find a new home for the knight. The obvious one is d5 but there it would obstruct his attack on the d-pawn. A better square is f5 and it headed there with **2...♘c8 3 ♕a4 ♘e7 4 ♘g5 ♖d5 5 ♘f3 ♕d6**.

White's queenside was weakened due to 2 a5? and after **6 h3 ♖b8 7 ♖d2 ♕b4! 8 ♕xb4 ♖xb4** Black had strong pressure that won the ending, **9 ♖c2 f6 10 a6 ♔f7 11 ♖e1 h5 12 h4 ♖d6 13 g3 ♘f5** and so on.

235
Strategically important points should be overprotected.

Aron Nimzovich summed up one of his most important principles in these words. His credo was: First, try to identify the square that is most valuable to you. Second, reinforce it before it is threatened.

He argued in *Chess Praxis* that overprotection not only benefits the point being protected but also the pieces doing the protecting. They will "be posted favorably in every respect" and their task "covers them with glamour."

Today this sounds like typical Nimzovich hyperbole. But it makes sense in certain positions. Just don't try to overprotect every day.

Kasparov – Bareev
Cannes 2001

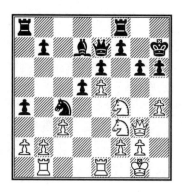

Black to play

In another "nothing-to-do" position, Black was content to shift his rooks, **1...♖g8**, and wait for an opportunity to break out with ...f6.

White didn't have an obvious plan either so he decided to overprotect e5 with **2 ♖e2! ♖af8 3 ♖be1**. That drove ...f6 off the table because it would allow exf6! followed by ♘xd5 or ♘xe6.

After Black passed with **3...♖c8**, White tried to add "glamour" to his knight by getting it to f6 – **4 ♘h2!**, with the idea of 4...♗b5 5 ♘g4 ♖gd8 6 ♘h5! gxh5 7 ♘f6+ and ♕d3-h7.

Black fought back with **4...g5! 5 ♘h5 gxh4**. But White's position was strategically more solid thanks to **6 ♕h3! ♖g5 7 ♘f6+ ♔g7 8 f4!**. Control of the strong points at e5 and f6 led White to victory after **8...♖g6 9 ♘hg4 ♖h8 10 ♘h5+ ♔f8 11 ♘gf6 ♗c6 12 ♕xh4**.

236
To get squares, ya gotta give squares.

Bobby Fischer's insight, expressed in typical Bobby-talk, flows from Tarrasch's maxim about every move having a drawback. Each move relinquishes control of certain squares. Players often agonize about making such concessions. But they are being short-sighted, Fischer said. What matters is whether the new squares you attack are better than the ones you gave up.

Larsen – Fischer
Candidates match 1971

Black to play

The pawn structure indicates – Tarrasch would say "demands" – that Black attack the kingside, specifically g2. The auto-pilot moves are ...♔h8 and the doubling of rooks on the g-file.

Yet Black chose **1...f4!**, the kind of move that horrifies many a King's Indian player. If the knight is headed to h4 via f5, why not get there via g6? Why give up e4?

The answers are two. A White knight on e4 looks nice but wouldn't defend the kingside as well as it would on g3. Also, 1...f4 opens up light squares to Black's bishop, and that weighs more than what it does for White's bishop.

Black was vindicated by **2 ♗e4 ♘f5 3 ♖c6 ♕g7 4 ♖b1 ♘h4** and he won soon after **5 ♕d3 ♗f5! 6 ♔h1 f3! 7 ♘g3 fxg2+ 8 ♔g1 ♗xe4 9 ♕xe4 ♘f3+**.

Note that White enjoyed plenty of space and mobility on the queenside. But these assets are temporary. They matter little if White can't put them to work, as the next saying emphasizes:

237

An advantage in mobility means nothing unless it can be converted into something tangible.

This could be said about all non-material advantages, including the initiative, a lead in development and superior pawn structure. But Neil McDonald, in *Chess Secrets: The Giants of Strategy*, was emphasizing the ephemeral nature of having more mobile pieces or operating room. They are another use-it-or-lose-it asset.

Lautier – Kramnik
Tilburg 1997

Black to play

Black is the first to cross the fourth rank no-man's land and his pieces have more range. But if he doesn't act quickly "the 'Botvinnik bishop' at b2 would have his say," he commented.

He meant that White would eventually play f2-f3 and e3-e4 and liberate his two bishops as Botvinnik had in his most famous game. If Black restrains the pawns with 1...f5? then 2 f3 ♘d6 3 a4 and a White edge will slowly emerge.

Black had to use his mobility quickly and he turned it into something tangible with **1...g5!** **2 ♘g2 g4!** and then **3 f3 ♘g5!** **4 fxg4 ♘h3+ 5 ♔f1 ♕g5**.

White defended with **6 ♘f4** **♗xg4 7 ♕d2 ♗f5 8 ♕g2** but **8...♘xf4 9 gxf4 ♕xg2+ 10 ♔xg2** **♗xc2 11 ♖xc2 f5!** got Black to a very favorable, eventually winning endgame.

238

Before making a pawn break, make sure your pieces are on their best squares.

You can't take back a pawn push. But you can usually control the timing of the push. It makes sense to get your army on the best squares before taking such an irrevocable step. Violating #238 cost White this game, he said afterwards.

Pelletier – Shredder
Match 2002

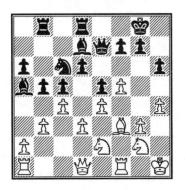

White to play

His most natural plan is to push the f- or g-pawns or both. But before a push he should rearrange his pieces so that they don't get in each other's way. For example, ♘e3-d5 and ♗g2-h3 are good preparations. To go further he needs to get his QR and Q involved.

But White was looking mainly at f5-f6 and became concerned that 1 ♘e3 f6 would leave the g3-g4-g5 plan too difficult.

So he played **1 f6? ♛xf6! 2 ♗h5 ♛e7** and found that his pieces were in no position to make much of a capture on f7. For example, 3 ♖xf7 ♛e6.

As the game went, **3 ♗xf7+ ♔h8**, he realized 4 ♘e3 ♗h3! would be bad. He lost faster with **4 h5? ♛g5 5 ♘h4 ♗g4 6 ♖f5 ♛e3 White resigns**.

239

It is more important to frustrate your opponent's strategy than to be obsessed with your own sly designs.

This is how Larry Evans characterized the anti-strategy that had been known since Philidor's day and was given the name "prophylaxis" by Nimzovich. Prophylactic moves seem mysterious because they're designed to anticipate an enemy idea that is not yet a threat or even a hint of a threat.

To carry this anti-strategy out requires "constantly asking yourself what your opponent wants, what he would do if it was his move, not yours," said Mark Dvoretsky.

Petrosian – Dvoretsky
Moscow 1965

Black to play

Black knew that once the dark-squared bishops had been traded, the routine strategy is to put his pawns on dark squares (...e5/...f6) as per #158. But for perhaps "the first time in my life" he employed prophylactic thinking, he recalled.

He reasoned that White wanted to repair the backwardness of his c-pawn with c2-c4. So he played **1...b5!** and realized he had guessed White's thinking when there followed **2 c4?! bxc4 3 ♕xc4.**

Then came **3...e5 4 f4 ♗e6 5 ♕b4 ♖c8 6 ♘f2 ♘c6 7 ♕d2.** Black again tried to figure out what White wanted to do. The answer: to rid himself of the bishop with ♗g4.

Black discouraged that with **7...exf4! 8 ♕xf4 ♘e5** (in view of 9 ♗g4 ♖c2!). His position improved Petrosian-like, **9 ♖fc1 ♕b6 10 ♕d2 ♖xc1+ 11 ♕xc1 ♖c8 12 ♕d2 ♖c5 13 ♗d1 ♖b5!.**

White resigned after **14 b3 ♖c5 15 ♖c1? ♖xc1 16 ♕xc1 ♕a5! 17 ♔f1 ♕xa2 18 b4? ♕xf2+.**

240
There is no such thing
as an absolute freeing move.

Another sweeping generalization from Nimzovich. By freeing move he meant one that significantly relieves a cramped position. A pawn break that gains space and frees your pieces is a typical example. One reason why it is not absolutely freeing is that opening the position will also benefit your opponent because when you are cramped, he's the one who usually has better placed pieces.

Another explanation is that the squares that are freed for occupation by such a break may fall into enemy hands. Nimzovich revived the 1 e4 e6 2 d4 d5 3 e5 variation by showing how the natural freeing moves, ...c5 and ...f6, can be exploited by White if he occupies e5 and d4 following dxc5 and exf6. A modern case is:

Leko – Anand
Bastia 2001

Black to play

In this Caro-Kann position Black is reluctant to exchange knights – 1...♘xe5 2 ♗xe5 eases his congestion but it gives White a dominating square for the bishop.

Another freeing move is **1...c5**, to dissolve the support for the e5 outpost. Often this idea works well but here the opening of the center favors White's better developed pieces – **2 ♘e4! cxd4 3 ♕xd4** and now 3...♘xe5 4 ♕xe5 ♕b6 5 ♗xh6!.

In this game Black preferred **3...♘b6**. But **4 ♘xf6+ ♗xf6 5 ♕e4 ♕e7 6 ♘g4** and ♘xf6+ was excellent for White.

For these reasons, Black usually delays his freeing ideas in favor of moves such as 1...♕a5 and ...♖ad8.

241

When you don't know what to do, wait for your opponent to get an idea. It's sure to be bad.

Tarrasch's acerbic comment applies to static positions in which maneuver is the order of the day. Maneuvering not only has objective benefits but a psychological one. It may convince your opponent to try for something more concrete, something that isn't justified. An example of that occurred in a position similar to the one we saw at the beginning of this chapter:

Grischuk – Zhang Zhong
Shanghai 2001

Black to play

Again the thematic plan for White would be maneuvering a knight to b4 and d5. But that fails because ♘1a2 drops the a-pawn and ♘d3 allows ...d5!.

On the other hand, the most natural way for Black to improve his pieces is ...♘c5. But by blocking the c-file, this allows the positionally desirable ♘d5! without fear of ...♕xc2.

This means neither player can accomplish much quickly. White even suggested that Black's best was 1...♗f8. And if 2 ♖d1, then 2...♗e7!?.

But Black decided that doing something was better than passing. He played **1...h4 2 ♖d1 ♘c5?**.

Then **3 ♘d5! ♗xd5 4 exd5** favored White because his pawns steadily expand (4...♘h5 5 b4! ♘d7 6 c4 f5 7 c5! and he won). Sometimes when you reach an inferior "nothing to do" position, the best policy is to do nothing.

CHAPTER FOURTEEN: **STUDYING**

242
He who analyzes blitz games is stupid.

There is general agreement that the best way to improve is by studying master games and playing your own. But not all master games are instructive. Speed games, which are often filled with blunders, don't teach much. Seeking the truth from them is a waste of time, as Rashid Nezhmetdinov, a brilliant blitz player, indicated with #242 (cited in *Kramnik – My Life and Games*).

But there are exceptions. Masters defend so well today that their slow games are not very instructive either. You rarely see the kind of textbook masterpieces in which a Capablanca could mercilessly exploit a minor error. But you might see this in speed games:

Lautier – Karpov
Cap d'Agde 2002

Black to play

White's play in this rapid game had been a model of positional precision and he won the ending when Black made two instructive errors. Black violated Tarrasch's rule by not getting his rook to a2 and he wrongly played actively on the kingside – **1...♖d5? 2 a4 h5? 3 gxh5 ♖xh5** – where he should be passive.

There followed **4 ♔g3 ♖c5 5 a5 ♔g6 6 ♖a8 ♔g7 7 a6 ♖a5 8 ♔f3 ♖a4 9 h5! f5 10 a7 e5 11 h6+!** so that 11...♔xh6 12 ♖h8+ allows him to queen.

Black played **11...♔h7** but his pieces were paralyzed and he lost after **12 ♔e2 ♖a3 13 f4! exf4 14 exf4 f6 15 ♔d2** and ♔d3-d4-d5-e6 etc.

243

Until you are 1800,
your first name is tactics,
your second name is tactics
and your last name is tactics.

Jose Capablanca heads the list of authorities who claimed that the road to mastery begins with endings. "To improve your game you must study the endgame before anything else," he wrote. Other great players emphasized mastering pawn play or middlegame planning, and so on.

But these skills become significant higher up the food chain, according to Ken Smith, FIDE master and chess book publisher/author. With #243 he meant that most games played by non-masters are decided by tactics and therefore the easiest way to improve is to develop a better handling of them.

Simple tactics decide fewer and fewer games as you go above 1800 but they are always a latent factor. If you saw a game begin **1 d4 ♘f6 2 ♗g5 d5 3 e3 c6 4 ♗d3 ♗g4 5 ♘e2 ♘bd7**:

White to play

...and **6 c4?? dxc4 7 ♗xc4 ♕a5+** and **...♕xg5**, you might conclude White was rated below 1800. In fact, in one 2006 game White was a grandmaster. In 2007 the blunder was made by a world-class player, although in a rapid game.

Masters exaggerate the value of studying endings – then spend their own study time on openings. You might say that once you are over 2200 your first name is theory, your second name is theory and your last name is theory. As Sophia Polgar put it:

244

The stronger you are, the more important opening preparation becomes.

The good news here is this also means that lower-rated players can achieve excellent results with a fairly limited knowledge of openings.

When Reuben Fine was an up-and-coming player he won games with moves like 1 h3?! or 1 f3?!. His goal was to get out of book as soon as possible. One of his early games went **1 f3?! d5 2 e4 e5**.

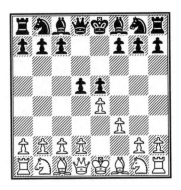

White to play

This looks like a drunken Caro-Kann, reversed. White was already worse after **3 ♘c3 c6 4 d4 dxe4 5 dxe5 ♛xd1+ 6 ♘xd1 exf3 7 gxf3**.

But it was Fine's opponent who quickly went astray and lost after **7...♗e6 8 ♗h3 ♗d5 9 ♘e3 ♗c5 10 c4 ♗xe3? 11 cxd5 ♗xc1 12 ♖xc1 ♘d7 13 f4 cxd5 14 ♖c7!**.

As Fine got stronger he spent more and more time on openings. By the time he was a world-class player he was beating theoreticians with his own prepared variations.

Lev Polugayevsky, an opening fanatic, said the best way for non-masters to budget their study time is: 50 percent on the middlegame, 30 percent on endings and only 20 percent on openings.

245

When a player decides to change his openings, it's a sign that he's growing up.

With these words Viktor Korchnoi expressed his conviction that replacing one favorite opening with a new one was a maturing process. The variations you once scored well with may hold you back later on.

This proved true for King's Gambiteers, like Paul Keres and Alexander Morozevich, when they switched to the more solid Ruy Lopez. "Previously I would periodically blunder a pawn," Morozevich said of 1 e4 e5 2 f4. "But now I have grown up."

Those who change openings not only grow up, they typically have better results, according to Adrian Mikhalchishin in *64* (July 2005). He cited the example of Lajos Portisch. At the relatively late age of 34, positional stylist Portisch adopted the super-sharp Najdorf Variation of the Sicilian Defense and his performance level rose.

Tal – Portisch
Varese 1976

White to play

Portisch tried various defenses to 1 e4 in his six previous games as

Black against Mikhail Tal and managed only one draw. Here in a variation that would seem to suit his opponent more, he outplayed him: **1 f5?! ♘e5! 2 fxe6 fxe6 3 ♗h5+ ♔d8!** to get his king to safety on the queenside.

Rather than face a Black initiative after 4 ♖xf6 ♖c8 and ...♕b4, White tried **4 ♖ab1 ♖c8 5 ♘e2**. Black emerged with the upper hand after **5...♗e7 6 ♘f4 ♔c7 7 ♗e2 ♔b8 8 ♘a5? b5** and he eventually won after **9 ♘b3 ♗d8! 10 ♔h1 ♗b6**.

246

One can see more over the board than in the quiet of one's study.

Nikolai Krogius observed that the intensity of a game situation had a way of focusing a player's mind better than when he prepares openings in relaxing surroundings. He recalled, in *Psychology in Chess*, that "very often" he tried to follow his home preparation in a tournament game, only to discover holes in his analysis when he played it over the board. You see more when choosing a move really counts, he explained.

Anand – Lautier
Biel 1997

Black to play

In a book position of the Center Counter Defense, Black tried **1...♗g2**. He thought his bishop would end up on d5 in any event and he would benefit, after 2 ♖g3

♗d5, by the extra tempo he'll gain from ...♗d6.

White had seen all this at home, where he concluded 2 ♖g3 would favor him. But when he checked his analysis over the board he realized that **2 ♖e3!** was better. The bishop is still threatened, by f2-f3 and ♔f2, and the rook is far more useful on e3.

After **2...♘b6 3 ♗d3 ♘d5 4 f3!** White had a major edge in view of 4...♘xe3 5 ♗xe3 and 6 ♔f2. "A fresh look at a position during a game can often turn up better moves than those found during home preparation!" he wrote in his game collection.

247
One mind is good, two are better.

This was Grigory Levenfish's way of urging students to test their home analysis in over-the-board play. He suggested 15 to 20 practice games, played at shorter-than-normal time controls, was a good trial for an opening you want to adopt.

He recalled how 3 e5 in the French Defense had fallen far out of favor until Aron Nimzovich began testing it against the best Riga players. After two years of this, Nimzovich was ready to try 3 e5 on the big stage and had a spectacular success with it at Karlsbad 1911. At about the same time Emanuel Lasker played hundreds of practice games with the Exchange Variation of the Ruy Lopez and discovered what he thought was every mistake White or Black could make in the opening.

Among those who followed #247 was Mikhail Botvinnik. In 1936, before heading to his biggest international test at Nottingham, Botvinnik played a series of training games with his friend Vyacheslav Ragozin.

One game went **1 e4 e6 2 d4 d5 3 ♘c3 ♝b4 4 a3!?** and now **4...♝xc3+ 5 bxc3 dxe4 6 ♕g4 ♘f6 7 ♕xg7 ♖g8 8 ♕h6 c5 9 ♘e2**

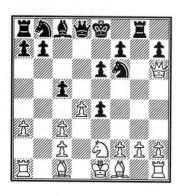

Black to play

White's last move was considered so strong at the time that 4 a3 seemed to threaten the health of the Winawer Variation. Botvinnik tested his new idea, **9...♘c6**, and obtained the better of **10 ♝b2? ♝d7 11 ♖d1 ♖g6 12 ♕e3 ♕a5!**.

Then **13 dxc5 0-0-0 14 ♘g3 ♘g4 15 ♕xe4 ♕xc5** led White to a lost position by move 25. Thanks to this test, Botvinnik felt confident enough about 9...♘c6 – and about 3...♝b4 – to play the line in games that counted. Another maxim from the "Patriarch":

248
Don't play against your own weapons.

Botvinnik said a player should devise an opening repertoire so that he doesn't have to face the same variations with White that he is prepared to defend as Black, and vice versa. In this way he avoids the psychological limbo of trying to beat his own ideas.

Botvinnik followed his own advice. After adopting the Winawer Variation as Black, he almost always played 3 ♘d2 as White when facing the French. And when he devised his own line of the QGD for Black (1 d4 d5 2 c4 c6 3 ♘c3 e6 4 ♘f3 ♘f6 5 ♗g5 dxc4!?) he took care that when he was White he played 4 e3 or the Exchange Variation and never had to face the Botvinnik Variation.

"Players who are devoted to certain opening systems know how unpleasant it can be to play against oneself in the purely psychological sense," Yefim Geller wrote. David Bronstein, a King's Indian player, felt at a disadvantage when playing against it because "I did not want to reveal the strongest way to play against it...and as a consequence I often ended up in inferior positions."

Garry Kasparov used this approach against Anatoly Karpov when he was trailing badly in the 1984-5 World Championship match. He adopted his opponent's favorite Queen's Indian Defense line and played the Petroff Defense for the first time in his life.

249

The best time to repair a damaged opening is right after the game in which it was damaged.

This sound recommendation from Paul Keres relies on a basic incentive of opening preparation: You are motivated the most when there is an emotional reason – "I don't want this to happen again!" – rather than a theoretical one – "How would I respond if this ever occurred to me?"

Peter Leko recalled how a last-round loss in a Nimzo-Indian Defense in 2006 forced him to find the improvement. "I was very upset and could not calm down until me and my team found solutions that satisfied us," he wrote in *New In Chess*. The next year he won a Candidates match game with the improvement.

By finding a way to play your damaged line you bolster your confidence:

Ivanchuk – Karpov
Monaco 1996

Black to play

This arose out of a Caro-Kann line that Anatoly Karpov liked as Black. But when this position occurred in a second-round game in this tournament he couldn't figure out how to meet ♗d4 followed by ♘c4.

He was lost after **1...♖hd8?! 2 ♗d4 ♕c7 3 ♘c4 ♗c5 4 ♗e5!**. The variation suddenly looked so bad that Karpov considered abandoning his beloved Caro-Kann for the rest of the tournament.

But he allowed this position again, two rounds later, because he had prepared an improvement, 1...♗d5 followed by ...♖fc8 ...♔f8. By repairing the opening immediately after the first game he felt confident enough to play it again.

250

Time trouble is almost always curable.

Botvinnik made this comment in several interviews late in his career. In *Grandmasters in Profile*, he said:

"My advice is extremely simple. In training it is necessary to play games paying no attention to their quality but only to the clock. One should play in this manner until one has become quite used to dealing with time."

"Ninety percent of those players who fail when time is at stake can be cured by this method," he said. "The others are incurable."

Botvinnik followed his own advice by periodically reacquainting himself with the dangers of time trouble in training games. He played more than 150 training games over a 25-year period, a remarkable number considering he played fewer than 300 tournament games during that time.

Botvinnik said that if you learn to handle the clock prudently you will always leave yourself with five minutes for the last move of a time control. He felt that time was needed because an exceptional number of blunders were committed on the "control move."

His star pupil, Anatoly Karpov, was almost never in time trouble until his mid-30s. Karpov's most famous time control collapse came in the final game of the 1987 World Championship when he made a series of slips just before the 40th move that allowed Garry Kasparov to win a difficult endgame and retain his title. If Karpov had saved just a little of his time earlier it would have made a decisive difference. "Imagine," Karpov told *Noviy Izvestia* in May 2006, "for 20 seconds I lost the world championship title. And if you're talking about money, 600,000 dollars."

251

Book knowledge is more useful in rook endings than in any other department of chess.

The arcane and unique nature of rook and pawn theory supports Cecil Purdy's claim. Rook endings set themselves apart because they occur much more often than other basic endings and because there are many more "book draws" and "book wins" to know, beginning with the winning Lucena position and Philidor drawing method. Logical moves turn out to be blunders more often in them than in other endings.

Khairullin – Inarkiev
Moscow 2006

White to play

Common sense says 1 ♔g2 must be right because the king stays near the pawn and prevents Black's king from penetrating to h3.

In reality, **1 ♔g2??** lost because after **1...f4! 2 gxf4+ ♔xf4** Black's king elbows White's king on the other wing – **3 ♔f2 ♖b2+ 4 ♔e1 ♔e3 5 ♔d1 ♔d3 6 ♔c1 ♔c3 7 ♖h6 ♔b3** and Black reaches Lucena (**8 ♖h3+ ♔a2 9 ♖h4 ♖b1+ 10 ♔d2 b3**).

Yet the illogical-looking **1 ♔e2!** draws because White's king gets to the queenside first following **1...f4 2 gxf4+ ♔xf4**. He also draws after 1...♔g4 2 ♖g6+ ♔h3 3 ♔f2 ♖b2+ 4 ♔f3 ♔h2 5 g4!.

But few players have the patience to master endgame "book." "Being told to study the endgame is like being told not to smoke," Boris Spassky said. "Sure it's good advice. But following it is the hard part."

252

You only know you are improving when your opponents seem to be playing badly more often than before.

Maturing players often go through periods in which they don't realize they are getting better. They rely on their rating as a gauge but it can be misleading. Even when they are maturing and understanding more, their Elo may be stagnant or oscillate with rises and falls, always arriving back at the same plateau.

But what is noticeable to the improving player is how often a worthy opponent makes a mistake, as Loek van Wely pointed out with #252 in *New in Chess*. He experienced this phenomenon in his rise up the grandmaster ranks.

van Wely – Salov
Amsterdam 1995

Black to play

White was facing a former world championship Candidate when he was surprised by **1...b5**. He

recognized quickly that it was bad and why it was bad. It hands White a powerful plan of b2-b4, ♖a1 and a2-a4.

He obtained a big edge with routine moves, **2 b4 ♔e7 3 ♖d2 ♖hb8 4 ♖a1 g5 5 a4 ♔d7 6 ♕d1 ♗d8 7 ♖da2 bxa4 9 ♖xa4**, and won without much effort (9...a5 10 bxa5 ♖b2 11 a6 ♗f6 12 ♖1a2 ♖bb8 13 a7 ♖c8 14 ♖a6 and so on).

In retrospect van Wely had improved in the period before this game. But he didn't realize it until opponents seemed to allow him to play at the higher level he had reached.

253

You will have to lose hundreds of games before becoming a good player.

This was Jose Capablanca's phrasing, in *Primer of Chess*, of a much older observation. Howard Staunton's version was: "Think of how many thousands of games Philidor must have lost before he attained his highest excellence."

The message here is conciliatory: Don't despair when you lose. After all, you should lose if you are lucky enough to play strong opponents. Garry Kasparov underwent a huge leap in strength during his miserable first match with Anatoly Karpov. He became champion a year later with what he learned. "Figuratively speaking, Kasparov of 1985 can give pawn and move to Kasparov of 1984," Vladimir Kramnik said on *e3e5.com*.

The message of #253 is also hopeful: You will improve by examining your losses because then you won't make the same mistakes again. "Won games are meant for bragging," Alex Yermolinsky said in *The Road to Chess Improvement*. "Lost games are meant for studying."

Capablanca – Corzo
Match 1901

White to play

Capablanca didn't say how many games he lost before he became a master. Only a few have been preserved. In this one, the first of a match, he commits the kind of positional horror he would never make again, **1 g4?**.

He was quickly punished, **1...♗c8! 2 ♕h5 ♕xh5 3 gxh5 ♗g4 4 ♖c1 e4 5 ♗f1 d4** and resigned soon after **6 h6 g6 7 ♖g1 ♗h5 8 ♔c2 ♖f8 9 ♖g2 ♖f5 10 ♖e1 ♖af8 11 ♖xe4 ♗f3**.

Capablanca's opponent, Juan Corzo, was a respected master, just the right strength to benefit him. "It's necessary to play in competition where the opponents are only slightly stronger than you," Mikhail Botvinnik advised. Stronger opponents can lead to very bad results and "psychological trauma," he said. But Capablanca suffered no trauma. He went on to win the Corzo match.

254

A vast majority of chess games are won and lost because you can't play two moves in a row.

A major difference between chess and war is that a general can make two moves in a row but a chessplayer can't. And because he can't, Cecil Purdy cited #254 in *His Life, His Games and His Writings*. The most common way to win a game is to create two simultaneous threats. If the player facing the threats can't meet both with one move, he loses.

Therein lies the power of tactics. The basic tactical themes involve attacking two things at once, such as in a knight fork, or two things in a row, such as in a pin or skewer. If you can threaten more than two things at once, the defender is all the more helpless:

Ioseliani – Hort
Prague 1995

Black to play

White threatens ♖xg6. But Black thought he had a tactical defense in **1...♗e4**, exploiting a pin (2 fxe4 ♖xh3) and threatening either of two killing captures on f3.

White shot back **2 ♘g5!!**. Black is faced with a threat to his king (3 ♘f7 mate), to his queen (3 ♕xc8+) and to his bishop (3 ♘xe4).

If Black could play two moves in a row he would win. But he resigned in view of **2...♗xf3+ 3 ♕xf3! ♖xf3 4 ♘f7 mate**.

255

A knowledge of combination is the foundation of position play.

Richard Reti's opening line from *Masters of the Chess Board* is supported by studies of how games are decided. In one review of 8,000 games, conducted before the database era, Hans Muller found that 82 percent were won by combinations.

What both Reti and Muller meant by combination was what we normally call tactics and threat-making. "The scheme of a game is played on positional lines, the decision of it is, as a rule, effected by combinations," Reti wrote. He indicated that all positional games reach a point where a tactical shot creates a decisive advantage.

The tactics may not actually occur on the board but lurk in the background as threats:

Serper – Lutz
Dortmund 1993

White to play

Black would stand well if he could organize his pieces with ...♘c4, ...♗f6 and perhaps ...♗d7-c6. But White seizes the upper hand with 1 ♘e5!.

This stops two of the Black ideas and is based on a tactical answer to the third, 1...♗f6 2 ♖ad1!. Then 2...♗xe5 3 ♖xd5 is a triple fork that regains the piece at a pawn profit.

Instead, play went **1...♗e6 2 ♖ad1 ♗f6 3 ♘d3!**. White is using another tactical idea, 3...♗xc3? 4 ♘f4 and ♘xd5, which would favor his better pieces.

His positional advantage grew further after **3...♘c4 4 ♗d4 b6 5 ♕b3 ♗xd4 6 cxd4 ♖c8 7 ♘f4**. With new threats, like e2-e4, he made Black's bad bishop worse, **7...♕d6 8 ♖fe1 a6 9 ♕f3! ♖fd8 10 ♕h5 f5**.

But he lost his way, and then the game, when he missed a favorable tactic later on.

256
You can't play what you can't see.

Dan Heisman's comment, in *Everyone's 2nd Chess Book*, emphasizes the importance of developing tactical sight. This is the ability to quickly spot the tactical components in any position, such as checks and captures.

"The main thing in chess is the process of 'vision,'" is the way Grigory Levenfish put it in *Shakhmaty v SSSR* in 1940. "At first it's necessary to learn to see everything that is under attack by you and your opponent," he added. Then you train yourself to look for double attacks and eventually learn "the harmonious coordination of your and your opponent's pieces which leads to a combination."

When a good tactician allows a tactical shot it's usually because a potential check or capture is heavily masked:

Kasparov – Anand
Wijk aan Zee 2001

White to play

White can't play bxa5 because of ...♘c5. If he anticipates that fork with 1 ♕d5 Black can reply 1...♖xc3! 2 ♖xc3 ♕xc3 3 ♕xb7 ♕xd2 4 bxa5 ♕xe3+.

So White decided to secure his king from checks with **1 ♔h2?**. But

Black quickly saw what White didn't. The king is now lined up with Black's queen.

Even though there are two pawns on that diagonal, Black found a way to exploit it, **1...d5!** so that 2 exd5?? e4+ (or 2 ♕xd5?? ♖d8).

White got the worst of it with a second mistake, **2 ♕b5?**, overlooking that the diagonal could still be opened by **2...d4!** (3 exd4 exd4+). But he managed to draw after **3 bxa5 dxc3**.

There is a division of labor here. Strategy tasks the brain. Tactics task the eyes. As Max Euwe wrote in *Strategy and Tactics in Chess*, "Strategy requires thought. Tactics requires observation." Another Euwe comment on the subject should comfort beginners:

257

Learning tactics is for the greater part a matter of practice and routine.

Euwe and Evgeny Znosko-Borovsky were among the first to point out how pattern recognition is the basis of spotting tactics. Themes ranging from a last-rank mate to the two-bishop sacrifice can be mastered by learning to recognize them in different guises.

This is the simplest of chess' learning curves. Levenfish said naturally talented players can acquire "the vision" in two to three months. Others take years. But with good training the process can be speeded up, he said. It's a matter of practice.

Lee – Zhang
Kuala Lumpur 2002

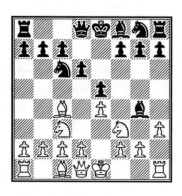

Black to play

Black retreated the bishop, **1...♗h5**, and White recognized the conditions were present for one of the oldest combinations. It dates back to at least 1750 and is called Legall's mate. After **2 ♘xe5!** Black cannot play 2...♗xd1 in view of 3 ♗xf7+ ♚e7 4 ♘d5 mate and limped away with **2...♘xe5 3 ♕xh5** to a lost endgame (3...♘xc4 4 ♕b5+ and 5 ♕xc4 keeps the extra pawn).

Databases reveal dozens of games with 1...♗h5? including several that Black won. In those cases White didn't play 2 ♘xe5! because he failed to recognize the pattern.

258
Loose pieces drop off.

John Nunn's tactical motto, shortened to LPDO, is a handy way of remembering the dangers of leaving a piece unprotected. The reason they drop off the board is that "unguarded pieces are always vulnerable to double attack," as Andrew Kinsman said in *Improve your Middlegame Play.*

This is illustrated by the next diagram. It could be a Sam Loyd puzzle, said *ChessPro.com.* Which piece will Black lose in four moves?

V. Georgiev – Kozul
Heraklion 2007

Black to play

The answer came after **1...e5** created a flight square to meet the threat of 2 ♕xh7+ ♔f8 3 ♗h6.

White won with **2 dxe6 ♘xe6 3 ♖xc8+** and **4 ♕xa5!**. The answer to the puzzle should be obvious

once you ask a second question: Which is the only unprotected Black piece in the diagram?

Note that LPDO has less application as the endgame nears. This is because you don't need to protect all your pieces when there are fewer enemy pieces to threaten them. In fact, being "loose" can be good. In some basic endings, such as Q-vs.-R, the defender's best policy may be to keep the rook at a distance from his king so that it can freely deliver checks. Amateurs typically keep their rook as close to their king as possible in that ending to avoid a tactical surprise. They end up losing faster than if they had kept it "loose."

In the middlegame, unguarded aren't always vulnerable as Kinsman said but they are usually a "tactical weakness." Euwe used this broader definition:

259

Any piece or pawn that is attacked as often as it is defended is a tactical weakness.

A piece or pawn is in no danger if there are fewer pieces attacking it than protecting it. But if the tally is equal, then the addition of one more attacker makes the target vulnerable.

This is one of those rules that few players consciously employ when choosing a move. Good tacticians develop an intuitive sense of when there are too many attackers or too few defenders.

Topalov – Nisipeanu
Sofia 2007

White to play

Let's count: White's knight is attacked once and defended once. So is his e3-bishop and c-pawn as well as Black's d5-knight. They are tactical weaknesses because one

more attack on any of those pieces or pawns puts them at risk.

But tactics aren't based solely on arithmetic. White played **1 ♕d3**, which defends the knight and threatens 2 ♗xe6 fxe6 3 ♕xg6+. But this allowed the remarkable **1...♗d4!!**.

It's a move that can be easily overlooked because the bishop is attacked three times on d4 and defended only once. But this shot works because 2 ♗xd4 or 2 ♘xd4 allows a knight fork on f4. White resigned after **2 ♗xe6 ♘xe3+ 3 ♔h2 ♕f2+ 4 ♔h3 ♕f3+ 5 ♘g3 ♕g2+.**

260
Your best tactical clue is your opponent's last move.

This is a tactical application of Tarrasch's rule about every move making some weakness. When it becomes your turn to move, your eyes should look for the captures, checks, forks and so on that were not possible before but are possible as a result of opponent's last move.

We saw that in the example of #256, when 1 ♔h2? made the unlikely 1...d5 possible. We saw that in the last example when 1 ♕d3 set up the knight fork on f4. And here:

Piket – Topalov
Groningen 1997

Black to play

After putting his queen on h6 White began to think about combinations involving ♕g7, ♘f5+, ♘xe6 and ♗h5xf7. Right now, they don't work, and if it were White's move, he would consider a quieter idea, such as f2-f4-f5xe6, instead.

But once he saw **1...♗c6?** the situation changed. Some players would look only at what it threatens (2...♗xe4). But White saw what it allows, **2 ♘xe6!**.

The variations are not long: 2...fxe6 3 ♕g7+ loses outright and 2...♔xe6 allows 3 ♗g4+ or 3 e5 ♕xe5 4 ♗g4+ ♔e7 5 ♖fe1. Black found nothing better than **2...♕e5** and resigned soon after **3 ♘d4** and **4 f4**.

In practice, there's one typical case when you have a tactical shot that wasn't made possible by your opponent's last move. It happens when you made a threat with your previous move and he failed to meet it.

261

If you don't spot a winning shot in the first moments you look at a position, you're not going to find it.

This is the Law of Diminishing Tactical Sight. As Tigran Petrosian put it, "Personally, I am of the view that if a strong master does not see such a threat at once he will not notice it even if he analyzes the position for 20 or 30 minutes."

He was explaining why he overlooked an opponent's simple threat even though he had plenty of time (vs. Korchnoi, Moscow 1963). This law also applies to one's own tactical opportunities:

Levenfish – Riumin
Moscow 1936

White to play

The knee-jerk reaction to Black's last move, ...♕e2, is a retreat of the attacked knight that threatens the queen. But White's tactical antennae told him he might have a forced win and he focused on two ideas, ♕e7 and ♘xg7.

He saw that 1 ♕e7 would prepare 2 ♕g5 but also threaten 2 ♖d8!, with an immediate mate. He spent a lot of time on 1 ♕e7 h6! but the trail runs dry after 2 ♘xg7 ♔xg7 3 ♖d8 ♖xd8 4 ♕f6+ ♔g8 5 ♕xd8+ ♔h7 6 ♕f6 ♕h5. White also investigated 1 ♘xg7 but it, too, led nowhere.

He ended up playing 1 ♘g3?. Afterward he commented it was "a blunder, the more strange in that I looked for a decisive combination for more than 15 minutes." It never occurred to him that **1 ♘f6+! gxf6 2 exf6** wins outright because both **3 ♕g3+** and **3 ♕xf8+!** lead to mate.

The longer he examined the position in the diagram, the more he was looking much further into the future than three moves. He wasn't going to find 1 ♘f6+! that way.

262

In every position look at all checks and captures – and jump-mates, jump-checks and jump-captures.

Cecil Purdy used these words to describe moves that would be possible if an obstructing piece were removed. In the #256 example, 1...d5 was a jump-check because only the Black e-pawn lay between the Black queen and White king.

A jump-check, like a jump-mate and jump-capture, isn't useful in itself. But it can be part of a combination, as Black showed in that case. Here's another:

Topalov – Morozevich
Cannes 2003

Black to play

White's last move, ♖b5, defended a pinned piece. But it also created a jump-capture: ♖xb8+ would be possible if the bishop moved. There was a second jump-capture in the air, ♖xe7, once the bishop moves.

This became pertinent when Black blundered with **1...♘d3?**. Then **2 ♗e4!** threatened the knight and turned the jump-captures into real threats. Black resigned in view of **2...♖xb5 3 ♖a8+** and mates.

263

The defensive power of a pinned piece is only imaginary.

My System is not a system but a collection of Aron Nimzovich's observations, many of them idiosyncratic and mostly about positional chess. But he included a few perceptive comments about tactics. For example, the power of a double check "lies in the fact that of the three defenses...two are nugatory." The only defense is "flight."

With #263, Nimzovich alluded once more to tactical vision. A player who recognizes a pin will spot the three actors, the pinning piece, the pinned piece and the piece behind it. But his eyes can play tricks on him when it comes to the second actor. Not only its defensive power but also its attacking power can be a mirage:

Shirov – Adams
Candidates match 2007

White to play

Black's extra Exchange is temporary because of the pin of Black's f7-rook. White doesn't want

to release the pin with 1 ♗xf7+ ♔xf7 2 ♖xd8 ♗xd8 because Black has a superior king and a passed pawn (3 ♔e2 ♔e6 4 ♔d3 ♔d5).

White might have an easier task after 2 ♖c1 ♗d4 3 ♔e2 and 4 ♗e3. But easier still, he felt, was the immediate 1 ♗e3 and then 1...♗d4 2 ♗xf7+ ♔xf7 3 ♗xd4.

He overlooked that his bishop was both pinning and pinned and that weakness was revealed by **1 ♗e3?? ♔h8!**. After **2 ♗xf7 ♖xd1+** (or 2 ♗xc5 ♖fd7!) Black won.

And finally:

264
Tactics have the final say.

Rules and maxims serve as signposts to heed on the road to finding the best move. When they contradict one another – as they inevitably do – a player has to determine which principle takes precedence. But when a rule comes into conflict with tactics, the rule must give way.

**Zhao Xue/Short
– Xie Jun/Bareev**
Yong Chuan 2003

Black to play

The two players on each team alternated moves. When Xie Jun chose **1...♗xg3**, she realized that her Chinese opponent both feared

and expected it. But the two male grandmasters, who were more steeped in positional play, took an instinctive dislike to 1...♗xg3!.

Nigel Short explained later that he would have to think at least half an hour over 1...♗xg3 because it violates general principles by giving up a strong bishop for such a knight.

But thanks to tactics, the rules are suspended. White was quite lost after **2 hxg3 ♕b5! 3 b3 ♖e2+ 4 ♔b1 ♖xf2!** and so on.

"General principles are important," said Lev Alburt in *Chess Rules of Thumb*. "But tactics have the final say."

CHAPTER SIXTEEN: **TECHNIQUE**

265

The hardest game to win is a won game.

This cliché dates back to at least the 1890s when a version was attributed to Wilhelm Steinitz. It's also one of the exaggerations that is rarely challenged. There is general agreement that good technique is extraordinarily hard to master. Converting an advantage often seems like an entirely separate game, with unique rules.

Adding to the impression of difficulty is that mistakes are more easily detected in the "just a matter of technique" stage of a game. Earlier an error by the stronger side may sharply reduce his advantage but we can't be sure by how much. Not so in cases like:

Kasparov – Ye Jiangchuan
Bled 2002

White to play

The term "won" game is a tad misleading. More accurate is "winning." It's still a process, not a completed action, in positions like

this when White, two pawns up, threw victory away with **1 c4??**.

It appears he will queen first (1...f3 2 c5 f2 3 ♖f4+! and b2-b4-b5 etc.). But after **1...♚e6! 2 c5 ♚d5** Black threatens not only ...♚xc5 but to queen after ...f3-f2.

Even after the best try, 3 ♖a6! ♚xc5 (not 3...♚e5?? as played in the game) 4 ♖xg6 Black can hold with 4...f3! 5 ♖f6 ♚d4 6 a4 ♚e3 7 a5 ♖h1 followed by ...♖xh4 and ...♖a4+ or ...♖f4.

Better was **1 b4!** and **1...♚e6 2 b5 f3 3 ♖f4**. That's still not "won" but further along the "winning" road.

266

When you win material you lose interest.

"What hinders winning a game when you have sufficient material advantage to do so is, in the large majority of cases, of a non-chess nature," Pyotr Romanovsky wrote in *Shakhmaty v SSSR* in 1955. This maxim is a paraphrase of what he said in describing how a player relaxes because he thinks his extra material will win the game for him.

"You say to yourself, 'Now I've achieved the goal.' While your opponent is thinking about a move, you don't sit at the board but get up and look at other boards, get distracted by incidental conversations," he wrote.

A case can be made that players maintain their focus better when they have a non-material edge because they don't get hypnotized by an extra pawn. "Contrary to the general notion, a positional advantage–that is, a better disposition of pieces – is always easier to exploit than an equivalent advantage in material, even for the weaker player." Cecil Purdy wrote.

For non-masters it's best to keep in mind the distinction made in the discussion of #154: A material advantage of two pawns or more should be sufficient to win without exceptional effort. But anything less than that will require work to make it decisive.

When Mikhail Botvinnik ran his celebrated school for talented Soviet youngsters, he would occasionally have fun with the students who were in awe of him. According to *64* (December 2007) Botvinnik would sternly pose a question to members of his class, "How did Capablanca realize an extra pawn?" After the frightened silence that followed, with no one daring to venture a reply, Botvinnik answered his own question: "He waited until his opponent hung a second pawn!" Botvinnik was making the point that Capa understood that winning a pawn didn't win the game.

267

The simplest and shortest way of winning is best.

This comes from the chess pioneer with the longest name, Tassilo von Heydebrand und der Lasa, and is important for two reasons. First, it rejects the notion that there is only one way to win a favorable position. Usually there is a choice, and that's where von der Lasa's second point comes in.

He recommended simplicity. A player who has profited from complexity in the middlegame, to gain an advantage, doesn't need any more of it to cash in. James Mason put it in a similar way: "When winning is possible it is best to win in the simplest possible way."

Karpov – Shirov
Prague 2002

White to play

White saw he had at least two reasonable winning methods. He can maintain his pressure on the d-file and queenside in hopes of a knockout. Or he can win a pawn through trades of minor pieces.

White looked first for the knockout. But when he didn't find 1 ♕a5 or 1 ♕xa6 convincing he settled for **1 ♘xc7 ♕xc7 2 ♗xd7 ♖e7 3 ♗xe6 ♖xe6**, which was sufficient to win.

This approach may take a lot longer than if there had been a knockout. But, as John Nunn said in *Secrets of Grandmaster Play*, "You don't get extra marks for winning quickly." White was following another morsel of Mason wisdom:

268

First, exhaust the enemy so that *he* may not win the game.

Ideally the simple way to win is also the shortest way. But the two are often in conflict. And when they are, Mason recommended the Neanderthal policy of taking more and more enemy pieces off the board. This "is not chivalry," he said. "But to lose where one should win is stupidity – or worse."

In other words, the first order of business is to reduce the number of possible outcomes of the game from three to two: you win or you draw. By exhausting the enemy forces, which includes trading queens, you eliminate the third possibility, a loss.

Topalov – Grischuk
Wijk aan Zee 2005

White to play

Two pawns up, White might be expected to push his passers. But Black has real chances involving checks on the h2-b8 diagonal and ...♖d2.

White hurried to trade queens even at the cost of his extra material, **1 ♖f5 ♖d2 2 ♕b5 ♗d4 3 ♖f3 ♗xf2 4 ♕f5+** and then **4...♕xf5 5 ♖xf5 ♗d4 6 ♘b5 ♗xb2.**

He could regain a material edge with **7 ♖xf7?**. But **7...♗e5+ 8 ♔g1 ♖a2 9 ♖a7 ♗g3!** offers virtually no winning chances, and some losing chances.

White's "two outcome" strategy led to an Exchange-up ending that he might have won against normal defense, **7 a5! f6 8 a6 ♗e5+ 9 ♔g1 ♖a2 10 a7**. But Black found **10...♖xa7 11 ♘xa7 ♗d4+ 12 ♔f1 ♗xa7** and drew by giving back a pawn to create an air-tight fortress.

Mason's maxim is consistent with a more modern saying:

269

If you can deliver mate or "eat" the queen, take the queen.

Another version of this that masters quote is "A winning pawn ending is much better than a mate in four." But how can either be true?

The answer is that the mate you think you see may be a mirage. Your calculation may be wrong. But if you grab the queen or reach a winning pawn ending, in the vast majority of cases that will be a sure win. Evgeny Bareev attributed #269 to his "first chess teachers" in his *64* notes to the following:

Bareev – Ki. Georgiev
Pardubice 1994

White to play

White wanted to play 1 ♖f7 with the idea of a quick Arabian mate,

e.g. 1...♘ec6 2 ♘h5 ♘e5 3 ♖e7 ♘xd3 4 ♘f6! and ♖h7 mate.

However, 3...♘dc6! is not at all clear. That's why White preferred 1 ♖f6!, winning at least a pawn.

While that's hardly the equivalent of an extra queen, it soon ended the game: **1...♘ec6 2 ♖xh6+ ♔g8 3 ♘f5 ♖e8 4 ♖g6+ ♔f8 5 ♖f6+ ♔g8 6 ♘xd4 ♘xd4 7 ♖d6 ♖e3 8 ♗a6! Resigns** in view of ♗b7xd5+, e.g. 8...♖e5 9 ♖xd5 ♖xd5 10 ♗c4.

270

Good technique is good tactics.

Great tacticians, going back to Mikhail Tchigorin, Frank Marshall and Rudolf Spielmann, have been great endgame players. A mastery of tactics may, in fact, reward you more in the endgame than in the middlegame. You can be surer of two- and three-move tactics in an ending because there are fewer pieces to make things fuzzy.

The wisdom of Yasser Seirawan's aphorism, from his *Inside Chess* magazine, is illustrated by examples such as this:

Svidler – Ivanchuk
Monaco 2007

White to play

After the simple pin **1 ♖h2!** Black can resign. His king can't stop the White pawns and his own pawns run into his frozen pieces.

Instead, White played **1 e6? ♘c4 2 e7?**, which allowed the freed Black pieces to make their own tactics, **2...♘e3+ 3 ♔g1 ♖g2+! 4 ♔h1 ♖e2!**.

Since queening would allow 5...♖xe1+ 6 ♔h2 ♘f1+ and 7...♖xe8, White struggled on with **5 ♗g3 ♘f5** but eventually drew.

271

Never look for other possibilities when you have one satisfactory winning line.

Paul Keres, writing in *Chess Life* (July 1972), cited this pragmatic guideline. If you spot what appears to be a cold win, it pays to spend clock time to make certain. But once you're certain, it doesn't pay to look at other candidates. You only have to win a chess game once.

The only risk you run by following Keres' rule is that you'll overlook something faster or prettier.

Piket – Gulko
Groningen 1990

White to play

White played **1 ♗xc6**, based on 1...♕xc6 2 ♘e5, threatening ♕xf7+ and ♘xc6. He correctly concluded that the endgame after 2...♕e6 3 ♕xe6 and 4 ♗e7 would be winning.

The key question then is what would happen after **1...bxc6**. White analyzed 2 ♗d6 ♕xd7 3 ♘e5 and felt 3...♕b7 4 ♘xc6 ♖e8 5 ♕b5 or 3...♕e6 4 ♕xe6 would be overwhelming. White had found his "satisfactory winning line," played 1 ♗xc6 and won quickly.

But he missed the faster – and spectacular – **1 ♕xf7+!! ♔xf7 2 ♘g5+ ♔g8 3 ♗c4+ ♔h8 4 ♘f7+ ♔g8 5 ♘xd8+**.

Because of Keres' rule, Vladimir Kramnik overlooked how he could have mated Garry Kasparov in four moves in one of their first games. Kramnik had found a crushing win of material and didn't look further. He didn't need to win the game twice.

272

The whole process of technique aims at converting the less durable into the more durable advantage.

Larry Evans elaborated on these words of his when he likened the laws of technique to the principle of conservation in physics. Matter cannot be lost. But it can be converted into energy and vice versa. In the same vein, an acquired advantage cannot be lost as long as you play the best move, he wrote in *New Ideas in Chess*. The object is to convert it to a harder currency.

This commonly means transforming an initiative into an extra pawn. But if the principle of conservation is working, a pawn can be converted into another advantage, one that may be more immediately useful. This is a common theme of the Benko Gambit. It is rare for White to win through the single-minded policy of advancing his extra, outside a-pawn. Instead:

Kramnik – Topalov
Wijk aan Zee 2003

White to play

White would like to defend the d-pawn with 1 e4. But that invites ...c4/...♘c5-d3 trouble. Instead he played **1 b3!** so he could meet 1...♗b7 with 2 e4!.

Black had nothing better than regaining his pawn, **1...♗xc3 2 ♗xc3 ♘xd5**. But White got the two bishops in return, as well as a strong follow-up, **3 ♘e5!**.

Black couldn't play 3...♘xc3? because 4 ♘xd7 ♛b4 5 ♖bc1 costs material. He had to allow another conversion – the two bishops were transformed into a superior pawn structure after **3...♘xe5 4 ♗xd5 ♗b7 5 ♗xb7 ♖xb7 6 ♗xe5! dxe5**.

A case can be made that his advantage is now more "durable" than the extra pawn. He built up pressure against the isolated c-pawn until he either captures it or pushes the a-pawn, **7 ♖ec1 f6**

8 ♕e4 ♔g7 9 ♖c3. When the time was right he swapped one weak pawn for the other, **9...♖ab8 10 ♕c2 ♕e6 11 a5 ♔f7 12 ♖a1!**.

There followed **12...♖xb3 13 ♖xb3 ♕xb3 14 ♕xc5 ♕b2 15 ♕c4+ ♔g7 16 ♕a2 ♕xa2 17 ♖xa2**.

The a-pawn is much stronger than it was in the previous diagram and White won after one more conversion – a trade of the a-pawn for kingside pawns. Black resigned when he saw White's g-pawn about to queen.

In retrospect, we saw White turning an extra pawn into the two bishops, then into a better pawn structure, and finally into an outside passed pawn. What makes this aspect of technique difficult is that White had to appreciate that his advantage is not decreasing at any point along the way but is being preserved, as in the principle of conservation cited by Evans. Computers don't believe this. Some programs think White had a big edge in the first diagram but it declined a bit by the time he played 3 ♘e5 and declined still further after 7 ♖ec1. Only well into the rook ending do they feel White stood as well as he did in the first diagram.

In a way, going from the first diagram to the second was just a process of stripping away what was extraneous, as per:

273

Remove all unnecessary pieces
from the board.

Boris Gelfand called this the "Rubinstein maneuver" in his book on the great Polish player. The superior side trades off material that he doesn't need to win, as Akiba Rubinstein seemed to do with great regularity.

The trick here is figuring out which pieces are "unnecessary." Experienced players have learned how to recognize them by knowing what a simplified, winnable position looks like:

Carlsen – Aronian
Candidates match 2007

Black to play

Black, with the superior minor piece, might have consolidated with

1...♛xe4 and then 2 ♘xb5 ♝f4 and ...d5.

But the first move he looked at was **1...♝xd4!** because he liked the looks of the Q+R ending (2 ♛xd4 ♜a8). He saw that either the a- or e-pawn must fall and, more important, knew the result would be a winning position. He didn't have to examine the alternatives, a la #271.

He was proven correct after **3 ♜a1 c3 4 ♛b4 ♛c5! 5 ♛b3+ ♚h8 6 ♜a2 ♜a4 7 ♜e2 ♜xa3 8 ♛d1 ♜a8 White resigns**.

274
Technique is most of all limiting counterplay.

This was how Adrian Mikhalchishin expressed another Soviet school credo. The good technician isn't concerned with increasing his advantage, which often means stirring things up. Rather, he wants to calm things down. If play continues without any excitement, the extra material or other edge he possesses will tell. Excitement comes in the unwelcome form of counterplay.

Taimanov – Aronin
Moscow 1949

White to play

Add two queens and this becomes a middlegame in which 1 ♖ed1 makes excellent sense. But in an endgame that move would allow Black to penetrate on the a-file. For example, 1...♖xd6 2 ♖xd6 ♖a4! and then 3 ♖d7+ ♔e6 4 ♖xb7 ♖a2!, when the prospect of a last-rank mate creates messy complications (5 ♗c3 ♖c2 6 ♗e1 e4 and ...♘e5).

They are not only messy but needless. White can play 1 ♖dd1! instead. Then after 1...♖xd1 2 ♖xd1 ♖a4 he keeps control of the situation with 3 ♗c3 ♖a3 4 ♖c1. Once calm prevails he can turn his attention to activating his king.

Black had more chance of roiling the waters with 2...♖a2. But thanks to his rook, White slowly pacified the position with 3 ♖d2 e4 4 f3 exf3 5 ♖f2! ♘h4 6 g3 ♘f5 7 e4 and 8 ♖xf3+ eventually won.

275

The good technician knows where he ought to be going.

Amateurs often believe that good technique means knowing many winning endgame positions, of the R+P-vs.-R kind. Yes, there is a voluminous amount of "book" positions that masters have mastered. But much more useful is knowing what to do 10 or 15 moves earlier – when there are more pieces and more decisions to be made about which one belongs where.

As C. H. O'D. Alexander said in his book on the first Fischer-Spassky match: "The grandmaster's advantage in technique consists in his being able to identify far more favorable and unfavorable points than his opponent, i.e. he knows where he ought to be going."

Shirov – Short
Groningen 1996

White to play

On paper White has a winning material advantage. Deciding where to put his queen and knight are the first questions he faces, and a likely answer is 1 ♕c2 followed by ♘b3-c5.

But after 30 minutes he found a superior idea, **1 ♘c2! ♗e7 2 ♘e3 ♖d8 3 ♕c2!**, and that saved him a lot of work.

Black cannot defend the c-pawn easily (3...♘b4 4 ♕e4 ♗f8 5 ♕e6+ ♔h8 6 ♘f5 is lost). The main question is whether **3...♘xe3+ 4 fxe3 ♖d6** was too.

White had foreseen that it would because of **5 ♕e4! ♗f8 6 g4! g6 7 ♕e8 ♔g7 8 h4** with ideas of ♔f3-f4 and h4-h5.

Play continued **8...c5 9 dxc5 ♖d2+ 10 ♔f3 ♗xc5 11 g5 ♖d5** and Black played out **12 gxf6+ ♔xf6 13 ♕c6+ ♔e5 14 e4! ♖d3+ 15 ♔e2 ♖e3+ 16 ♔d2 ♔d4 17 ♕d5 mate.**

276

The more you are winning, the more you should think defense.

This contradicts what inexperienced players fervently believe. They ride a tide of rising expectations as they get closer to victory. But when Dan Heisman wrote #276 in *Everyone's 2nd Chess Book*, he was saying a player's level of caution should grow with the magnitude of his advantage. "When you are winning easily, you should make sure you will not lose," he added.

Timofeev – Zhang Zhong
Taiyuan 2006

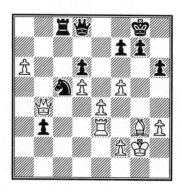

White to play

With an extra pawn and a good B-vs.-N matchup White had ample reason to expect to win. But as he examined a natural candidate, 1 a7, he was amazed at how easily Black could get strong winning chances after 1...♖a8!, e.g. 2 e5 ♖xa7 3 e6 ♖b7 4 ♕e1 b2!.

That's why he played **1 ♖xb3!** ♘xb3 2 ♕xb3. White has virtually no losing chances since he can eliminate the d-pawn, in worst case scenarios, by indirectly trading it for the a-pawn, e.g. 2...♕e7 3 ♕b4 ♖d8? 4 e5.

Black played **2...♕c7?!** instead and the best he could obtain was a perpetual check. He lost when White was able to trade queens, **3 ♕b4 ♖a8 4 ♗xd6 ♕a7 5 ♗e7 ♕xa6 6 ♕d4 ♕b5 7 d6 ♖a4? 8 ♕d5! ♕xd5 9 exd5.**

277

If you can't force a win, let your opponent try to force a draw.

Jacob Aagaard, in *Excelling at Technical Chess*, said that when your advantage isn't large enough to make it count by direct means, you should maneuver a bit. This follows the "Don't hurry" rule (#55) and often provides your opponent enough rope to hang himself.

This is particularly good advice to follow when facing an opponent who prefers active to passive defense:

Piket – Kasparov
KasparovChess GP 2000

Black to play

This kind of endgame often appears in primers to explain when an extra pawn isn't enough to force a win. If White trades two or three pairs of pawns, Black's king should be able to stop any resulting passer.

White does have winning chances. If he can get his king to f6

or his rook to the seventh rank he might be able to win a second pawn or create a pair of connected passed pawns.

Those are only "chances" because Black can draw if he keeps White's king and rook out, say by putting his own king at h6 and passing with his rook on his second rank.

Instead, Black decided to use his rook actively and force a draw. He played **1...罝d3?! 2 含h3 罝e3?** to rule out e5-e6.

Both sides missed chances in the next stage, **3 含h4 含g7 4 含g5 罝e1 5 罝c7 罝e2** but **6 罝e7!** created the decisive threat of e5-e6 that won the game. It ended with **6...罝a2 7 f5!** (not 7 e6? 罝a5+) **gxf5 8 e6 h4 9 罝xf7+ 含g8 10 含f6 Resigns**.

278

A game is not over until the clocks are stopped.

Mikhail Tal cited this adage to emphasize that won games don't win themselves. One of the earlier versions came from Salo Flohr – "A game is considered won only when the opponent announces his resignation."

I.Sokolov – Sakaev
Neum 2000

White to play

After White sacrificed the Exchange to pin the rook, Black delivered a "spite" check. White saw that 1 ♔g1 and then 1...♕c1+ 2 ♕f1! is an easy win after 2...♕xf1+ 3 ♔xf1 or 2...♕c7 3 ♕f6+.

He went ahead with **1 ♔g1??** and realized after **1...♔g8!** that the win was gone. Perpetual check or worse will follow 2 ♕xe5 ♕c1+ or 2 ♗xe5 ♕c1+ 3 ♕f1 ♕xe3+.

The win would have been preserved by **1 ♔h2!** since then **1...♔g8 2 ♗xe5** allows no perpetual. Then it really is "just a matter of technique."

279
Prolong!

This was one of Mikhail Botvinnik's mottoes. He reminded himself of it in notes to himself before tournament games. The longer that tension could be maintained, the more likely that his opponent would face difficult decisions and make a mistake, he believed.

Many amateurs feel strong pressure is better than long pressure. They think if they can sharpen the position as much as possible, their winning chances are greater than in a prolonged battle. But GMs know that when you create an explosive position by move 20 there's a risk that your opponent will only have to find two or three critical moves and the position may be lifeless and drawish by move 30.

The best policy in a must-win position is long pressure, as Artur Yusupov showed in the final game of a 1991 Candidates match, Garry Kasparov used to save his title in the final game of the 1987 World Championship match and a computer demonstrated in this:

Deep Fritz – Kramnik
Match 2002

Black to play

After a conservative opening White kept up the pressure until he won a pawn. Black could now trade into a queen ending (1...♕xa7 2 ♕xe5 ♕xa2 3 ♕b8+ ♔h7 4 ♕xb6) which is drawish because all the pawns are on the kingside.

But the extended tension got to Black. He didn't want to defend the queen ending for hours. "I just had a blackout" he said of **1...♕xa2!? 2 ♘c8 ♕c4??**, which lost immediately to **3 ♘e7+** and **4 ♕xe5**.

"You see this very often," a member of Deep Fritz team said. "If the computer keeps the pressure for a long time then this kind of blunder occurs."

280

Drink your coffee when it's your opponent's move.

With these words, Mikhail Tal warned against allowing anything to interfere with your normal thought process at the board. His normal process, after his opponent had moved, was to recheck the variations he previously calculated. However he cited a cautionary tale:

Tal – Fischer
Candidates tournament 1959

Black to play

Well before this position occurred, Tal concluded that it would be good for him because a quiet move such as **1...♗e5** would allow **2 h3! ♕g5 3 ♕e6**.

That chases the rook off c8, e.g. **3...♖b8 4 ♘xc7 ♖b2 5 ♕e8+** when 5...♔g7? loses to 6 ♘e6+ and 5...♖f8 to 6 ♕xf8+! and ♘e6+.

But before the diagrammed position actually occurred he spotted a possible hole in his calculations. If Black plays 5...♔h7 he might escape after 6 ♕xf7+ ♔h8 because of the threat of ...♕xg2 mate.

So when 1...♗e5 was played he needed to take a deep breath and recheck 2 h3. (He would have seen that **5...♔h7??** loses to **6 ♕xf7+ ♔h8** and queen checks at e8 and d7 and then ♕g4.)

But at that moment "somebody brought me a cup of coffee," he recalled in his memoirs. He chose another move, **2 ♖cf1?**, and turned his attention to his cup. His advantage disappeared and he had to win the game all over again. But at least he had coffee to console himself.

281
Knowing how to manage time should be intuitive.

Botvinnik meant that a player should develop an instinct that tells him when he is moving too slowly or too quickly. At the start of the game, he might follow a rule of thumb, such as Botvinnik's personal formula ("To avoid time trouble you must train yourself to play the first 15 moves in half an hour."). But by the second hour, each player has to rely on an internal sense of when it is worth investing big minutes, Botvinnik felt.

Even experienced players can lose their sense of proportion:

Kuzmin – Uhlmann
Leningrad 1973

White to play

Black had just innovated (...♕b6 in place of ...♖fe8). White replied **1 ♗xe7** and Black inexplicably sank into thought.

There wasn't much to look at because after 1...♗xe7? 2 ♕xd5 ♖ad8 3 ♕c4 his compensation for a lost pawn would be scant.

Nevertheless, Black spent 80 minutes (!) before making the obvious recapture **1...♘xe7**. He was soon in time trouble in the **2 ♕d4 ♕xd4** endgame and lost.

Yes, some moves are worth a lot of minutes. But as John Nunn said, "There is no point thinking half an hour about a possible advantage or disadvantage of what a computer calls '0.1' of a pawn."

282

In every game there arises a critical moment. The two players go up the mountain and meet at the top. The one who makes the right decision remains on top.

"So it is in life," Boris Spassky added to his comment in *64* (June 2004). The critical moments are the times when finding the best move really matters, he said. James Mason said such moments "will be distinguished without difficulty by the experienced player."

Actually, it's often hard to identify those times. But you budget clock time for them. Often a critical moment comes when you have to choose a plan:

Timofeev – Kasparov
Moscow 2004

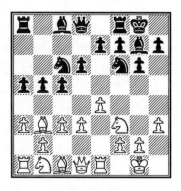

Black to play

Black went into a very long think because it was time to figure out how to play the middlegame. He decided to keep the center closed and to pressure the queenside. He worked out how to build the pressure – by pushing ...a4 and putting his knights at a5 and b6.

Play went **1...♘d7! 2 ♗e3 a4 3 ♗c2 ♘b6 4 ♘bd2 e5** and Black had both a slight edge and a good plan of ...b4, thanks to the wise decision to invest time at the diagram.

But there's a caveat that comes with spending time on critical moments:

283
Big thinks rarely lead to good moves.

Jonathan Rowson's observation, in *British Chess Magazine* (January 2004), is confirmed every time a player spends more than 15 minutes on a move that turns out to be second best. Or worse than second best. For many years the record for longest expenditure of time on a single move was the two hours that Yefim Bogolyubov invested on what turned out to be a blunder.

What's truly embarrassing is when a player spends big minutes on a bad move and then can't explain what he was thinking about:

Fischer – Petrosian
Candidates match 1971

Black to play

White was reeling after falling into a prepared variation. Black thought more than 30 minutes but rejected the move he had analyzed beforehand, **1...♖xg2!**, even though he knew it would favor him significantly.

After the game he couldn't explain why he chose **1...♗f5?** instead – or why following **2 ♗d3** he thought another 17 minutes and rejected **2...e4!** in favor of **2...♗xd3?**. White survived the crisis and went on to win.

284
Don't begin decisive action before a time control.

This warning of Botvinnik's was cited in *64* (March 1995), which recalled how the former world champion delayed changing the pawn structure during time pressure in one of his last games. Instead, Botvinnik made five "pass" moves just before move 40 and waited until he had ample time, at move 42, to make sure the critical move would decide the game strategically.

Changing the pawn structure is risky when short of time because you need a clear head to consider all the nuances of the change:

Leko – Khalifman
Istanbul 2000

White to play

The pieces are lined up on the left but White will need a breakthrough on the right to win. Since there were three moves to go before the time control, he more or less repeated the position, **1 ♔b3 ♖c7 2 ♖3a2 ♔b7 3 ♔b4 ♔a6**, until he could think without worrying about the clock.

Only then did he make the break, **4 f5! exf5 5 gxf5**, and won with his kingside pawns. "I was following the old rule that says: never change the pawn structure in time trouble," White recalled.

285
Time pressure has its own laws.

The normal rules don't apply at moments of great tension or tiredness because of the greater likelihood of a blunder. Instead, there are other laws:

"The importance of luft grows in (reverse) proportion to the time control," is one offered by GM Andrei Devitakin. Other rules of thumb concern knights. "The shorter the time, the stronger are some pieces," wrote Mihai Suba, speaking of queen and knight. Jonathan Speelman went further with the claim that in five-minute games, a knight is stronger than a rook.

Time scrambles also tend to scramble a player's move selection practices. Someone who relies on calculation won't have time to count out tree branches. Garry Kasparov's intuition was often faulty, according to Alxander Belyavsky and Adrian Mikhalchishin, and he was on thin ice when he didn't have enough time to double-check the first move he liked. It showed in games like this:

Yusupov – Kasparov
Barcelona 1989

Black to play

Black had less than four minutes to reach the time control ten moves away. He "suddenly lost orientation and the ability to calculate variations" and began to play "on general principles," his trainer Alexander Nikitin wrote in *64*.

If he had time to calculate he would surely found the win after 1...♘xf4 2 ♕xf4 ♗e5 3 ♕e3 f4! or after 2 gxf4 ♕g6! (3 ♘e3 ♗xe3 4 fxe3 ♕g3+).

Instead, play went **1...♘e5? 2 f3 ♘d3? 3 ♘e3 ♘xf4 4 gxf4 ♗b6?**. (He missed another win, 4...♕h4 5 ♕xd4 ♖g3!.)

The game ended with **5 ♕f2 ♕g6? 6 ♖e2 ♗c5? 7 fxe4 fxe4? 8 f5 ♕h5 9 ♖d2 ♖g5 10 ♕f4 ♕e8 11 ♘g4** and now that time control was reached, **Black resigned**.

One of the most useful rules for *zeitnot* comes from Botvinnik:

286

In time pressure your pieces must protect one another.

His reasoning was that unprotected pieces are the chief source of tactical mistakes (LPDO) when short of time. Only a computer – or a human with sufficient time – can afford to leave pieces unprotected.

Kasparov – Karpov
World Championship 1986

Black to play

In this battle of Botvinnik students, Black was a victim of the teacher's rule. He played **1...♕xb2**

so that all of his pieces are defended.

But it turned out to be the losing move. White was able to break the chain of protection with **2 ♔h1 ♔h8 3 ♘d4!**.

Then Black's knight is hanging and 3...♘d7 4 ♖xf7 or 3...♖e8 4 ♖xf7! ♘xf7 5 ♕f6+ lose. He played **3...♖xd4 4 ♕xe5!** and forfeited on time for the first time in his career.

Note the ingenuity of 2 ♔h1. It frees White's queen to move without fear of ...♖xg2+ and follows another tenet of the Soviet school:

287

In your opponent's time pressure, make non-forcing moves.

This makes no sense to many non-masters. If your opponent is short of time, why not make threats, they ask? After all, forcing moves often win outright against weaker players because they overlook the threat.

True, but stronger opponents will spot the threats and have an easier time when all they have to do is find "only" replies. More subtle is the technique, perfected by Tigran Petrosian and Anatoly Karpov, of making quiet moves that improve your position:

Petrosian – Spassky
World Championship 1969

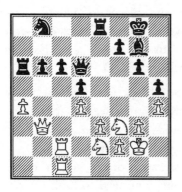

White to play

As both players headed into time pressure White strengthened his position in the most microscopic

manner, 1 ♘f4 ♖d8 2 ♘d3! ♗f8 3 ♘fe5 ♖c8 4 ♖c3!.

His last move stopped the bid for an endgame, 4...♕a3, and left Black without a good idea.

Play went 4...♗e7 5 ♘f4 ♗f6.

It looks like nothing has happened since the diagram but in reality Black has been completely outplayed. White didn't even need to cash in with 6 ♘xd5 because he knew a pawn would fall after 6 ♘5d3!, e.g. 6...♘d7 7 ♘b4.

Non-forcing moves shortened the game, which ended after 6...♖a5 7 ♕xb6 ♖xa4 8 ♖c5! with a threat of ♖xd5.

288

If your opponent offers you a draw, try to work out why he thinks he's worse off.

There is more than sarcasm in Nigel Short's advice. The most common reason players offer draws is lack of confidence in their position. If an opponent offers a draw, it pays to look at the board from his point of view and wonder what worries him.

It may be something you aren't giving sufficient attention to. Petrosian wasn't the only world-class player who offered draws after he realized he had blundered:

Reshevsky – Mastichiadis
Dubrovnik 1950

White to play

White played **1 ♘d2** and offered a draw. This should have set off alarm bells. White was much the stronger player and would seem to have a traditional plus-over-equals advantage of an Exchange Variation QGD.

But Black accepted the draw – only to discover that **1...♘xf2!** would have been crushing. As Miguel Najdorf said, "If Reshevsky offers you a draw, it means you need to look for a way to mate him in two moves."

INDEX OF QUOTED PLAYERS
by # number